The Problem of Evil for Atheists

The Problem of Evil for Atheists

YUJIN NAGASAWA

Great Clarendon Street, Oxford, OX2 6DP,
United Kingdom

Oxford University Press is a department of the University of Oxford.
It furthers the University's objective of excellence in research, scholarship,
and education by publishing worldwide. Oxford is a registered trade mark of
Oxford University Press in the UK and in certain other countries

© Yujin Nagasawa 2024

The moral rights of the author have been asserted

Some rights reserved. No part of this publication may be reproduced, stored in
a retrieval system, or transmitted, in any form or by any means, for commercial purposes,
without the prior permission in writing of Oxford University Press, or as expressly
permitted by law, by licence or under terms agreed with the appropriate
reprographics rights organization.

This is an open access publication, available online and distributed under the terms of a
Creative Commons Attribution – Non Commercial – No Derivatives 4.0
International licence (CC BY-NC-ND 4.0), a copy of which is available at
http://creativecommons.org/licenses/by-nc-nd/4.0/.

Enquiries concerning reproduction outside the scope of this licence
should be sent to the Rights Department, Oxford University Press, at the address above

Published in the United States of America by Oxford University Press
198 Madison Avenue, New York, NY 10016, United States of America

British Library Cataloguing in Publication Data

Data available

Library of Congress Control Number: 2023952571

ISBN 978–0–19–890188–4

DOI: 10.1093/oso/9780198901884.001.0001

Printed and bound in the UK by
Clays Ltd, Elcograf S.p.A.

Links to third party websites are provided by Oxford in good faith and
for information only. Oxford disclaims any responsibility for the materials
contained in any third party website referenced in this work.

In memory of my grandparents

Acknowledgements

I have read parts of the present book at various stages of development at conferences, workshops, seminars, and colloquia that have taken place at many institutions worldwide, including: Auburn University, Chulalongkorn University, De La Salle University, the Ludwig Maximillian University of Munich, Manchester Metropolitan University, the National University of Singapore, Toronto Metropolitan University, the University of Birmingham, the University of Campinas, the University of Hertfordshire, the University of Innsbruck, the University of Leeds, the University of Liverpool, the University of Macau, the University of Maribor, the University of Oklahoma, the University of Oxford, the University of St Andrews, the University of Uppsala, the University of Verona, UWC Red Cross Nordic, and Waseda University. I would like to thank the audiences for helpful discussions. For detailed feedback on this work, I am particularly indebted to Andrew Bailey, Jc Beall, John Blechl, Ben Blumson, Andrei Buckareff, Beverley Clack, Stephen R. L. Clark, Paul Draper, Andrew Gleeson, Francesca Greco, Adam Green, Francis Jonbäck, Jeremiah Joven Joaquin, Guy Kahane, Robert Lawrence Kuhn, Klaas Kraay, Thaddeus Metz, Masahiro Morioka, Josh Spears, Erik Steinhart, Jack Symes, Terrence Tilley, Nick Trakakis, Oliver Wiertz, Mark Wynn, and anonymous referees for Oxford University Press. I would also like to thank students at the University of Oklahoma who took a graduate seminar to discuss the manuscript of this book. I would also like to extend my gratitude to Samuel Jonathan for his diligent efforts in indexing this work.

The publication of the present book was made possible through the support of a grant from the John Templeton Foundation for the Global Philosophy of Religion Project, an international initiative that I led from 2020 to 2023 at the University of Birmingham. I am especially thankful to Alex Arnold at the foundation for his guidance and motivation throughout the project. The opinions expressed in this publication are my own and do not necessarily reflect the views of the John Templeton Foundation. I am deeply thankful to my colleagues at both the University of Birmingham and the University of Oklahoma for their support and encouragement. Additionally, I would like to extend my appreciation to Tom Perridge,

viii ACKNOWLEDGEMENTS

Aimee Wright, and their dedicated team at Oxford University Press for their exemplary editorial assistance.

Some parts of the present book build upon my previously published material: 'Modal Panentheism', in Andrei Buckareff and Yujin Nagasawa (eds.) (2016), *Alternative Concepts of God*, Oxford: Oxford University Press, pp. 91–105; 'The Problem of Evil for Atheists', in Nick Trakakis (ed.) (2018), *The Problem of Evil: Eight Views*, Oxford: Oxford University Press, pp. 151–163; 'Personal Theism vs. A-personal Axiarchism', in Georg Gasser and Simon Kittle (eds.) (2021), *The Divine Nature: Personal and A-Personal Perspectives*, London: Routledge, pp. 23–41; 'Evil and Impermanence in Medieval Japanese Philosophy', *European Journal for Philosophy of Religion* 14 (2022), pp. 195–226. I would like to thank the publishers for allowing me to use the material here. My gratitude also goes to Thomas McAuley and Jack Stoneman for generously allowing the use of their translations of Japanese waka poems in Part III of this book.

Finally, I wish to express my deepest appreciation to my family and friends for their invaluable love and unwavering support, with a special note of thanks to my wife, Sylwia, for her unyielding encouragement and understanding.

Contents

List of Figures	xiii
Introduction	1

PART I: THE PROBLEM OF EVIL FOR TRADITIONAL THEISTS

1. The Problem of Evil: Its Structure and Important Variations	7
1.1 Introduction	7
1.2 Terminology	8
1.3 Three Variables That Constitute the Problem of Evil	9
1.4 Variable (iii): Allegedly Conflicting Relationships between God and Evil	11
1.5 Variable (ii): Evil	19
1.6 Conclusion	34
2. The Problem of Evil as a Problem of Axiological Expectation Mismatch	35
2.1 Introduction	35
2.2 Being a Traditional Theist Is Neither Necessary nor Sufficient for Being a Target of the Problem of Evil	36
2.3 The Problem of Axiological Expectation Mismatch	40
2.4 Existing Responses to the Problem of Evil as Attempts to Reconcile the Mismatch	46
2.5 Conclusion	51

PART II: THE PROBLEM OF EVIL FOR PANTHEISTS AND AXIARCHISTS

3. The Problem of Evil for Pantheists	55
3.1 Introduction	55
3.2 Traditional Theism and Its Alternatives	56
3.3 Why I Set Panentheism Aside	60
3.4 Pantheism and the Problem of Evil	62
3.5 The Divinity Problem of Evil for Pantheists	64
3.6 The Experiential Response to the Divinity Problem of Evil	67

x CONTENTS

3.7	Difficulties with Pantheists' Experiential Response to the Divinity Problem of Evil	68
3.8	Pantheists' Non-Experiential Approach	70
3.9	The Advantage of Traditional Theism Over Pantheism	73
3.10	Multiverse Pantheism	75
3.11	How Multiverse Pantheists Avoid the Shortcoming of Standard Pantheism	77
3.12	How Multiverse Pantheism Responds to the General Problem of Evil	81
3.13	The Problem of Evil for Multiverse Pantheists	83
3.14	Possible Responses to the Divinity Problem of Evil for Multiverse Pantheism	85
3.15	Conclusion	89

4. The Problem of Evil for Axiarchists		91
4.1	Introduction	91
4.2	The Problem of Actual Evil and the Problem of Non-Actual Evil for Traditional Theists	92
4.3	Axiarchism as an Alternative to Traditional Theism	93
4.4	The Problem of Actual Evil and the Problem of Non-Actual Evil for Axiarchists	95
4.5	Response 1: The Actual World *Is* the Best Possible World	96
4.6	Response 2: All Possible Worlds, Including the Actual World, Exist	99
4.7	Responses 3: The Actual World Is One of the Overall Good Possible Worlds	101
4.8	Response 4: All Overall Good Possible Worlds/Universes, Including the Actual World/Universe, Exist	106
4.9	An Axiarchic Rebuttal	109
4.10	Conclusion	113

PART III: THE PROBLEM OF EVIL FOR ATHEISTS/NON-THEISTS

5. The Problem of Systemic Evil		117
5.1	Introduction	117
5.2	Pain and Suffering in Nature	118
5.3	The Nature of Systemic Evil	121
5.4	The Allegedly Conflicting Relationship between God and Systemic Evil	127
5.5	Systemic Evil as a Challenge	129
5.6	Conclusion	131

CONTENTS xi

6. Optimism		133
	6.1 Introduction	133
	6.2 The Origin of Optimism	134
	6.3 Optimism and Axiology	134
	6.4 Leibnizian Optimism and Modest Optimism	135
	6.5 The Scope of Modest Optimism II	140
	6.6 Why We Should Think That Atheists/Non-Theists Would Accept Modest Optimism	142
	6.7 Conclusion	153
7. The Problem of Systemic Evil for Atheists/Non-Theists		154
	7.1 Introduction	154
	7.2 The Problem of Systemic Evil for Modest Optimists	155
	7.3 The Emotive Element of the Problem of Systemic Evil	159
	7.4 The Apology Paradox and the Hope Thesis	164
	7.5 Conclusion	169
8. The Advantages that Traditional Theists Enjoy		170
	8.1 Introduction	170
	8.2 The Painting Analogy	171
	8.3 Comparing Traditional Theism with Atheism/Non-Theism: Which One Wins?	173
	8.4 Responding to Objections	175
	8.5 Conclusion	191

PART IV: THE PROBLEM OF EVIL FOR EASTERN ATHEISTS/NON-THEISTS

9. The Problem of Impermanence		195
	9.1 Introduction	195
	9.2 *Hōjōki* and the Problem of Evil	196
	9.3 The Problem of Impermanence	200
	9.4 The Problem of Impermanence as a Version of the Problem of Systemic Evil	208
	9.5 Conclusion	209
10. Responses to the Problem of Impermanence		211
	10.1 Introduction	211
	10.2 Responses to the Problem of Impermanence	212
	10.3 Assessing the Responses	221
	10.4 Conclusion	229
	Conclusion	231

References	233
Index	249

List of Figures

3.1 Traditional theism	57
3.2 Pantheism	57
3.3 Panentheism	57
3.4 Merotheism	58
3.5 Axiarchism	58
3.6 Atheism	58
3.7 Acosmism	59

Introduction

The eighteenth-century philosopher George Berkeley faced criticisms from contemporaries who argued that his metaphysical system, that is, idealism, lacked a compelling solution to the problem of evil. In response, Berkeley did not propose a solution to the problem of evil. Instead, he pointed out that his system was not unique in failing to solve the problem; every alternative system had also encountered the same difficulty. He therefore remarked, 'The problem of evil is everyone's problem, and everyone's problem is no one's problem!' I heard this anecdote from Daniel Stoljar, who heard it from David Armstrong in his undergraduate philosophy class at the University of Sydney in the 1980s. The anecdote is most likely based on Armstrong's heavily paraphrased version of Berkeley's view about philosophical disagreement.[1] Yet, this anecdote is my inspiration for writing the present book.

The problem of evil poses a challenge for traditional theists by asking how they could rationally believe in the existence of an omnipotent and wholly good God given that the world is filled with evil manifested in such events as wars, crimes, and natural disasters. This is widely considered one of the most significant challenges to belief in God and has evoked many responses from traditional theists. However, it is not my aim in this book to propose another

---

[1] Stephen Clark and John Blechl have pointed out in personal communication where Armstrong's reference to Berkeley may have originated. Clark says that the likeliest passages he has found are the following two: (1) a sermon on religious zeal: 'In our nonage while our minds are empty and unoccupied many notions easily find admittance, and as they grow with us and become familiar to our understandings we continue a fondness for them . . . But we would do well to consider that other men have imbibed early notions, that they as well as we have a country, friends, and persons whom they esteem. These are pleas which may be made for any opinion, and are consequently good pleas for none' (Berkeley 1955/1709–12, p. 20); (2) the second dialogue of the *Three Dialogues Between Hylas and Philonous*: 'But to arm you against all future objections, do but consider, that which bears equally hard on two contradictory opinions, can be proof against neither' (Berkeley 1979/1713, p. 91). Passage (1) suggests that an argument for anyone is an argument for no one in particular and passage (2) suggests that an argument against all is an argument against no one in particular. Blechl says that Armstrong's reference is probably a paraphrase of Berkeley's thesis, which he states in a number of places: an objection which weighs equally on both sides of an issue cannot be used to discredit either one. I am grateful to Clark and Blechl for this information.

The Problem of Evil for Atheists. Yujin Nagasawa, Oxford University Press. © Yujin Nagasawa 2024.
DOI: 10.1093/oso/9780198901884.003.0001

response to the problem or to evaluate the effectiveness of existing responses at length. I deliberately refrain from such endeavours. Instead, I take a step back from the ongoing debate surrounding the problem and adopt a unique perspective which transcends the familiar perennial debate between traditional theists and atheists.

When Berkeley claimed that the problem of evil was a problem not only for his view but also for its alternatives, he probably had in mind other early modern metaphysical systems that are also based on the traditional theistic worldview. Hence, what Berkeley meant was that the problem of evil is a problem for all types of traditional theists, not just traditional theists who subscribe to idealism, and, hence, it is not a problem unique to those in the idealist camp. My central thesis in this book is much more radical than Berkeley's: the problem of evil is a problem the scope of which ranges *beyond traditional theism*; the problem arises not only for traditional theists but also for most people, including those who reject traditional theism. I have chosen *The Problem of Evil for Atheists* for the title of the present book to underscore the most radical assertion I put forth—namely, that the problem of evil constitutes a substantial obstacle even for atheists. As I elaborate extensively in my discourse, however, my reasoning extends to various categories of 'non-theists', encompassing not only atheists but also pantheists, axiarchists, and even adherents of Eastern religious and cultural traditions.

The thesis that the problem of evil is a problem beyond traditional theism is radical enough. Yet, I argue for an even more radical thesis in this book: supernaturalist theists enjoy advantages that naturalist atheists/non-theists lack when responding to the problem of evil because there is greater hope that the problem can be solved when supernaturalist resources are in place. This thesis, I argue, entails an additional interesting thesis: the problem of evil is a more significant challenge for atheists/non-theists than for traditional theists. This conclusion should surprise many because the problem of evil is often presented as an argument *for* atheism/non-theism as well as an argument *against* traditional theism.

This book is a contribution to my ongoing aspiration to advance the philosophy of religion as a global field of inquiry.[2] When we approach the problem of evil within the confines of the traditional Western monotheistic context, it looks as if the problem is a challenge uniquely and specifically to traditional theists. Yet, scrutinizing it from a broader, global perspective

---

[2] For my global approach to the philosophy of religion, see Buckareff and Nagasawa (2016), Nagasawa (2018a), and Nagasawa and Zarepour (forthcoming).

raises a much deeper problem that is relevant to people representing diverse religious and philosophical backgrounds.

Again, Berkeley said that the problem of evil is everyone's problem and that everyone's problem is no one's problem. In the present book, I intend instead to establish the following two theses. First, the problem of evil is (nearly) everyone's problem, so everyone has to take it seriously. Second, the problem may well be a more formidable obstacle for naturalist atheists/ non-theists than for supernaturalist theists.

PART I

THE PROBLEM OF EVIL FOR TRADITIONAL THEISTS

1
The Problem of Evil
Its Structure and Important Variations

1.1 Introduction

It is hardly an exaggeration to state that the problem of evil stands as one of the most extensively debated subjects in philosophy and theology. Barry L. Whitney's comprehensive 650-page annotated bibliography, which encompasses discourse on the problem of evil from 1960 through 1990, provides compelling evidence of the pervasive presence of the topic in academic literature (Whitney 1993). This bibliography suggests that at least 4,237 books, papers, or dissertations on the problem were produced within that thirty-one-year period alone. Whitney writes, 'If there is a more pressing and contentious issue faced by contemporary theologians [than the problem of evil], I am uncertain what it could be' (Whitney 1993, p. 3). J. P. Moreland and William Lane Craig also write, 'Undoubtedly the greatest intellectual obstacle to belief in God is the so-called problem of evil' (Moreland and Craig 2003, p. 536). The enormous size of the literature and these remarks show how seriously the problem of evil has been taken by scholars.

Philosophers and theologians—both theistic and atheistic—tend to approach the problem of evil through a narrow framework centred on the age-old dispute between traditional theists and atheists. Consequently, despite the attention drawn to the problem of evil, profound reflections on its scope, structure, and diversity are infrequently encountered in the literature. The present chapter addresses this gap by offering a detailed, comprehensive, and systematic analysis of the problem of evil. I argue that the general scheme of the problem of evil consists of three essential 'variables' and that we can obtain numerous versions of the problem by assigning them distinct values. As we will see in the following chapters, this is an important step towards developing versions of the problem of evil that range beyond the traditional theistic framework.

This chapter has the following structure. In Section 1.2, I briefly discuss terminological issues for stage-setting purposes. In Section 1.3, I argue that

The Problem of Evil for Atheists. Yujin Nagasawa, Oxford University Press. © Yujin Nagasawa 2024.
DOI: 10.1093/oso/9780198901884.003.0002

8   THE PROBLEM OF EVIL FOR ATHEISTS

the general scheme of the problem of evil consists of the following variables: (i) God, (ii) evil, and (iii) an allegedly conflicting relationship between (i) and (ii). In Section 1.4, I explain how we can obtain distinct versions of the problem of evil by assigning distinct values to variable (iii). In Section 1.5, I explain how we can obtain distinct versions of the problem of evil by assigning distinct values to variable (ii). Section 1.6 concludes.

1.2 Terminology

Before beginning our discussion, I wish to make some preliminary terminological remarks. First, throughout the present book I use the term 'traditional theism' to refer to the following view that is widely accepted in the Judeo-Christian monotheistic tradition: there is God, who is the greatest possible being or an omnipotent and wholly good being, and this being is also a personal being who created the actual world and interacts with human affairs. Accordingly, I use the term 'traditional theists' to refer to proponents of such a view. (The exception is found in Chapter 2, where I briefly discuss some philosophers who have considered themselves to be traditional theists yet reject God's being omnipotent or wholly good). When the meaning is evident from the context, however, I also use simpler terms such as 'theism' and 'theists' to refer to traditional theism and traditional theists, respectively. With the term 'non-theists' I refer to people who reject traditional theism. This class includes not only atheists but also pantheists, panentheists, axiarchists, and so on. As I explain in subsequent chapters, though, I focus primarily on non-theists who adopt a naturalistic, rather than supernaturalistic, ontology. I set aside, for instance, pantheists and panentheists who endorse supernaturalism.

I use, in most cases, the term 'wholly good' rather than 'omnibenevolent' or 'all-loving' to describe God's goodness according to traditional theism because, as we will see below, I begin my discussion with J. L. Mackie's formulation of the problem of evil, which adopts this term. This term is also helpful in highlighting the contrast between the *goodness* of God according to traditional theism and the presence of *evil* in the world. However, my argument in the present book does not depend on this specific terminology. Also, for the sake of simplicity, I often use the terms 'God' and 'an omnipotent and wholly good God' interchangeably. When I discuss the concept of God according to alternatives to traditional theism, I use specific terms, such as the 'pantheistic God' and the 'panentheistic God', unless the meaning is

THE PROBLEM OF EVIL   9

evident from the context. Also, the terms 'problem of evil' and 'argument from evil' are commonly used in the literature, often interchangeably. I mainly use the term 'problem of evil' because, in the present book, I consider the problem to be a *challenge* for proponents of traditional theism and its alternatives, not necessarily an attempted refutation of these views. Perhaps this is analogous to the problem of consciousness in the philosophy of mind. Physicalists acknowledge that the problem challenges their view substantially, but it is not always presented as an attempted refutation of physicalism. It is rather a puzzle or 'mystery' that physicalists need to resolve to defend their view. I explain this point in detail in Chapters 2, 5, and 7, especially in the fourth and fifth sections of Chapter 5.

1.3 Three Variables That Constitute the Problem of Evil

It is common to begin any discussion of the problem of evil by referring to Mackie's 1955 paper 'Evil and Omnipotence'. This is because that paper presents a clear formulation of the problem, which has defined the shape of the contemporary dispute between traditional theists and atheists ever since. Before providing the formulation, Mackie describes the nature of the problem of evil as follows:

> The problem of evil, in the sense in which I shall be using the phrase, is a problem only for someone who believes that there is a God who is both omnipotent and wholly good. And it is a logical problem, the problem of clarifying and reconciling a number of beliefs: it is not a scientific problem that might be solved by further observations, or a practical problem that might be solved by a decision or an action. These points are obvious; I mention them only because they are sometimes ignored by theologians, who sometimes parry a statement of the problem with such remarks as 'Well, can you solve the problem yourself?' or 'This is a mystery which may be revealed to us later' or 'Evil is something to be faced and overcome, not to be merely discussed'. (Mackie 1955, p. 200)

The first key point here is that Mackie specifically targets traditional theists who believe that there is an omnipotent and wholly good God. The other key point is that Mackie considers the problem of evil to be a *logical* problem; it is not an empirical, practical, or personal problem. That is why Mackie's version of the problem is commonly referred to as the 'logical problem of

10   THE PROBLEM OF EVIL FOR ATHEISTS

evil'. According to him, the problem cannot be resolved by appealing to empirical investigations, practical considerations, or personal taste. Mackie then offers the following succinct formulation of the problem:

> In its simplest form the problem is this: God is omnipotent; God is wholly good; and yet evil exists. There seems to be some contradiction between these three propositions, so that if any two of them were true the third would be false. But at the same time all three are essential parts of most theological positions: the theologian, it seems, at once *must* adhere and *cannot consistently* adhere to all three. (Mackie 1955, p. 200)

In the above passage, Mackie suggests that the following apparently inconsistent set of three propositions constitutes the logical problem of evil:

(1) God is omnipotent.
(2) God is wholly good.
(3) Evil exists.

Mackie's atheistic stance shows that he does not endorse propositions (1) and (2). Additionally, it is essential to highlight that he is not committed to proposition (3) either. As an error theorist, he has no ontological commitment to any kind of evil. His purpose in introducing the logical problem of evil is to point out that traditional theists (or 'theologians' as he calls them), who are committed to (1), (2), and (3), are in trouble because the three propositions form an inconsistent set. (As I explain later, throughout the present book I focus mainly on views that recognize the existence of evil and set aside perspectives like the error theory, which denies the existence of evil.) It is helpful to amend this set of propositions to make the core of the problem of evil even more explicit. First, (1) and (2) can be combined because they form a pair of propositions that constitutes the concept of God according to traditional theism. (Exactly what being omnipotent or wholly good means is a contentious topic that we need not address here.) Second, the thesis that God *exists* has to be explicitly stated and incorporated into the combination of (1) and (2) because the logical problem as Mackie conceives it does not arise for those who do not believe that God exists. One can consistently hold that while God is correctly understood as an omnipotent and wholly good being, He just does not exist, in the same way that one can consistently hold, for example, that while a unicorn is correctly understood as a horse with a spiralling horn, it just does not exist. Third, in relation to what I address in Section 1.5 below, it is helpful to make it explicit that Mackie focuses on the existence of God and the existence of evil *in the actual world*, not in a merely possible world. Fourth, it is also helpful to make it explicit that Mackie tries to reveal a *logical* inconsistency between God and evil; this is in fact the most salient feature of his formulation of the problem of evil. Taking these points into account, Mackie's version of the problem of evil can be revised as follows:

The Logical Problem of Evil

(1L) An omnipotent and wholly good God exists in the actual world.
(2L) Evil exists in the actual world.
(3L) Propositions (1L) and (2L) are logically inconsistent.

The above revised formulation shows that Mackie's version consists of three propositions—(1L), (2L), and (3L)—which correspond to the following three elements:

(i) God.
(ii) Evil.
(iii) An allegedly conflicting relationship between (i) and (ii).

As I explain below, Mackie's logical problem of evil is not a popular formulation of the problem of evil today, even among atheists. Yet the above formulation is instructive because nearly all versions of the problem of evil consist of three parallel elements. We can call these elements *variables* because there is a variety of values that we can assign to them. In the rest of this chapter, I introduce and discuss many formulations of the problem of evil for traditional theists which we can obtain by assigning distinct values to variables (ii) and (iii). In Chapter 2, I move on to variable (i), which has been neglected in the literature. I argue that by assigning distinct values to (i) we can obtain distinct versions of the problem of evil that range beyond the traditional theistic framework.

1.4 Variable (iii): Allegedly Conflicting Relationships between God and Evil

We have seen in the previous section that Mackie's logical problem of evil consists of three variables: (i) God, (ii) evil, and (iii) an allegedly conflicting

12   THE PROBLEM OF EVIL FOR ATHEISTS

relationship between (i) and (ii). Mackie is specific about variable (i). By God he means an omnipotent and wholly good being. Mackie is not, however, clear about variable (ii). He does not spell out exactly what he means by evil. Yet it is charitable to assume that by evil he means, at a minimum, states of affairs in the actual world that are widely considered evil, such as events in which innocent people are severely harmed. Mackie is specific about variable (iii). He claims that the conflicting relationship between God and evil that he intends to reveal is a *logical* inconsistency. There are, however, many interpretations of logical inconsistency and many alternative values that we can assign to variable (iii). In this section, I focus on this variable. I fix variables (i) and (ii) in the way they are typically understood and see how we can obtain distinct formulations of the problem of evil for traditional theists by assigning distinct values to variable (iii).

Again, the most salient feature of Mackie's logical problem is that, as its name suggests, he assigns a value to variable (iii) by saying that there is a *logical* conflict between God and evil. Logical inconsistency is the strongest type of inconsistency, and indeed it seems too strong. As Alvin Plantinga says, the set of propositions that God exists and that evil exists is not *explicitly contradictory* because neither of the propositions alone entails the negation of the other proposition (Plantinga 1974a, p. 12). That is, the set in question is not comparable to logically inconsistent sets consisting of such propositions as that P and that *not-P*. Neither is it *formally contradictory* because one of the propositions cannot be shown to entail the negation of the other proposition by the laws of logic alone. Furthermore, it appears unlikely that it is *implicitly contradictory* either, because there does not seem to be a necessarily true proposition a supplement of which shows that either of the propositions entails the negation of the other proposition.

To show that the set of propositions is indeed implicitly *consistent*, Plantinga introduces the 'free will defence', according to which the non-existence of God cannot be deduced from the existence of evil because there is a logically possible scenario in which an omnipotent and wholly good God and evil coexist (Plantinga 1967, 1974a, 1974b; see also Chapter 2 of the present book). The scenario that Plantinga has in mind can be summarized roughly as follows: an omnipotent and wholly good God chooses to create a world in which there are humans who have freedom in a libertarian and morally significant sense because such freedom is intrinsically valuable. Humans sometimes however abuse their freedom and, hence, there is evil in the world despite the omnipotence and goodness of God. If such a scenario is logically possible, even if it is not actual, Mackie's logical problem

THE PROBLEM OF EVIL   13

collapses; it is not the case that, as a matter of logic alone, God and evil cannot coexist or that we cannot but reject the existence of God logically once we accept the existence of evil. Many philosophers consider the free will defence a successful response to the logical problem of evil.[1] William L. Rowe (1979), despite his atheistic commitment, acknowledges the strength of the free will defence by stating that, 'granted incompatibilism, there is a fairly compelling argument for the view that the existence of evil is logically consistent with the existence of the theistic God' (Rowe 1979, p. 335, ft 1).

Interestingly enough, Mackie appears to be aware of the above point. He states that to derive a contradiction from the existence of God and the existence of evil we have to add some extra assumptions or 'quasi-logical rules' such as that good is the opposite of evil (and hence a wholly good being always eliminates evil as much as it can) or that there is no relevant limit to what an omnipotent being can do (Mackie 1955, pp. 200–1; Plantinga 1974a, pp. 12–24). This suggests that, after all, even Mackie himself does not think that the 'logical problem of evil' is a purely logical problem.

One might suggest at this point replacing logical inconsistency with a weaker relationship such as nomological inconsistency. However, nomo-logical inconsistency is too weak. Proponents of the problem of evil do not claim that it is merely a matter of the contingent laws of nature that God and evil cannot coexist; the conflict between God and evil is deeper than that. This means that we should formulate the problem of evil in terms of metaphysical inconsistency, which is stronger than nomological inconsist-ency but weaker than logical inconsistency. Such a move is compatible with Mackie's introduction of quasi-logical rules which purport to link 'good', 'evil', and 'omnipotence'; how they are related should be a matter of pri-marily metaphysics rather than logic or the laws of nature. Insofar as it seems clear that the allegedly conflicting relationship between God and evil, if there is any, is not purely logical or nomological, I assume throughout this book that the problem of evil should be formulated in terms of a metaphys-ical relationship.

Why does Mackie call his version of the problem of evil the 'logical problem' if he states explicitly that we need quasi-logical rules, that is, rules that operate outside of logic in a strict sense, to show the inconsistency between God and evil? Perhaps that is because he thinks that the problem

---

[1] This does not mean that no one defends the logical problem of evil today. For recent defences of the logical problem of evil, see Toby Betenson (2021), John Bishop and Ken Perszyk (2011, 2016), J. L. Schellenberg (2013), and James Sterba (2019).

14   THE PROBLEM OF EVIL FOR ATHEISTS

that he presents implies a *deductive* argument against the existence of God. That is, Mackie may think that if we present his version of the problem of evil as an argument against traditional theism, we cannot but accept the conclusion (that an omnipotent and wholly good God does not exist in the actual world) given the premise (that evil exists in the actual world) and relevant quasi-logical rules. If this interpretation is correct, it appears more appropriate to call Mackie's problem the 'deductive problem of evil' rather than the 'logical problem of evil'. I explain below, however, that calling Mackie's problem '*the* deductive problem of evil' is problematic because there is a deductive version of the problem of evil that is distinct from Mackie's.

Many atheists today defend the so-called evidential problem of evil, which is more modest than the logical problem of evil. There are many distinct formulations of the evidential problem. Still, the thrust of the problem is that while it may not be possible to deduce the non-existence of God from the existence of evil purely logically, the existence of evil still constitutes strong *evidence* against the existence of God. In principle, the logical problem can be considered an extreme version of the evidential problem. Proponents of the logical problem could argue that the existence of evil is evidence against the existence of God *because* the existence of evil logically contradicts the existence of God. However, the term the 'evidential problem of evil' is normally used to refer to the view which denies the logical inconsistency between God and evil yet affirms a sufficiently significant evidential value of evil against the existence of God. Hence, when I use the term 'evidential problem of evil', I assume that the alleged evidence is not solely logical.

The evidential problem can be presented as follows:

The Evidential Problem of Evil
(1E) An omnipotent and wholly good God exists in the actual world.
(2E) Evil exists in the actual world.
(3E) The truth of proposition (2E) is strong evidence against the truth of proposition (1E).

As the above formulation shows, we obtain the evidential problem of evil by replacing proposition (3L) in the logical problem of evil with (3E). Put differently, we obtain the evidential problem by assigning a value to variable (iii) in our scheme—a variable concerning an allegedly conflicting relationship between God and evil—by referring to evidence instead of logical

THE PROBLEM OF EVIL 15

inconsistency. If the *logical* problem is presented as an argument against the existence of God, then the conclusion would be that God does not exist. If, however, the *evidential* problem of evil is presented as an argument against the existence of God, then the conclusion would be more modest: it is more likely than not that God does not exist, or it is reasonable to believe that God does not exist. The evidential problem undercuts the free will defence because it does not exclude the logical possibility that God and evil coexist.

The evidential problem is sometimes called the 'inductive problem of evil'. This term is misleading because there are versions of the evidential problem that are not inductive. In what follows, I offer a brief overview of three versions—inductive, deductive, and abductive versions—of the evidential problem of evil by relying on Michael Tooley's taxonomy (Tooley 2019a). Each version can be considered an attempt to elaborate proposition (3E) by specifying in various ways how the truth of proposition (2E) should be construed as evidence strong enough to undermine belief in the truth of proposition (1E).

Consider, first, the *inductive* version of the evidential problem. This version is based on a relatively straightforward inductive inference: no state of affairs with property p that we know of has property q; therefore, no state of affairs with property p has property q. William L. Rowe (1991) defends this version by appealing to the following proposition:

> P. No good state of affairs *we know of* is such that an omnipotent, omniscient being's obtaining it would morally justify that being's permitting E1 or E2. (Rowe 1988, p. 120; 1991, p. 72; emphasis added[2])

'E1' and 'E2' refer to instances that most, if not all, of us would regard as evil, such as states of affairs in which a fawn dies in a slow and painful process during a bushfire or an innocent person is brutally assaulted. From the above premise P, Rowe derives the following proposition inductively:

> Q. No good state of affairs is such that an omnipotent, omniscient being's obtaining it would morally justify that being's permitting E1 or E2. (Rowe 1988, p. 121; 1991, p. 72)

---

[2] For a slightly amended version, see Rowe (1996, p. 263). Rowe suggests in that version we have to attribute the property of being wholly good as well as the properties of being omniscient and omnipotent to the being described in propositions P and Q.

16 THE PROBLEM OF EVIL FOR ATHEISTS

Hence, Rowe claims that *E1* and *E2* are strong evidence against the existence of God. From *Q* and the existence of *E1* and *E2* in the actual world, Rowe deductively infers that there is no omnipotent, omniscient (and wholly good) being. This version of the problem of evil is considered inductive because any inference that is at least partly inductive is considered inductive. The inference from proposition *P* to proposition *Q* is inductive even though the inference from proposition *Q* to the conclusion that God does not exist is deductive. The inductive version of the evidential problem of evil can be understood as a way to assign a value to variable (iii) concerning an allegedly conflicting relationship between God and evil by claiming as follows: there is a conflict between God and evil, such that the existence of evil can be used to show inductively that God does not exist.

Consider now the deductive version of the evidential problem of evil, which appeals to the following application of Bayes's Theorem (Tooley 2019a, p. 41):

$$\Pr(God\ exists|evil\ exists) = \frac{\Pr(evil\ exists|God\ exists) \times \Pr(God\ exists)}{\Pr(evil\ exists)}$$

Rowe (1996) presents a more complex and sophisticated version involving background information on which we rely in forming judgements about the likelihood of relevant propositions, but the above simple version is sufficient for our purposes here. This version suggests that once we assign appropriate values to the probabilities that relevant propositions obtain, the probability that God exists given that evil exists, that is, $\Pr(God\ exists\mid evil\ exists)$, is shown to be sufficiently low. The key feature of this version is that while it appeals to probabilistic reasoning, it is still a deductive argument because the conclusion itself is a probabilistic claim. Once we assign values to each proposition, it is a matter of deduction that the conclusion follows. The fact that there is a deductive version of the evidential problem of evil suggests that it is not appropriate to call the evidential problem of evil the '*inductive* problem of evil' or to call Mackie's logical problem of evil '*the* deductive problem of evil'. The deductive version of the evidential problem of evil can be understood as a way to assign a value to variable (iii) concerning an allegedly conflicting relationship between God and evil by claiming as follows: there is a conflict between God and evil, such that the existence of evil can be used to show probabilistically and deductively that God does not exist.

Consider, finally, the abductive version of the evidential problem of evil. This version relies on abductive reasoning, which is also commonly known as 'inference to the best explanation'. As we saw above, the deductive version is concerned only with the probability that God exists (given that evil exists).

THE PROBLEM OF EVIL   17

The abductive version, on the other hand, treats traditional theism as a hypothesis and compares the probability of its truth with the probability of the truth of its competing hypothesis. Paul Draper (1989), who introduced this version, postulates the following view as a hypothesis that competes with traditional theism:

> The hypothesis of indifference (*HI*): Neither the nature nor the condition of sentient beings on earth is the result of benevolent or malevolent actions performed by non-human persons [for example, God].
>
> (Draper 1989, p. 332)

The hypothesis of indifference subsumes a variety of alternatives to traditional theism. Let '*O*' stand for 'a statement reporting both the observations one has made of humans and animals experiencing pain or pleasure and the testimony one has encountered concerning the observations others have made of sentient beings experiencing pain or pleasure' (Draper 1989, p. 322). Draper tries to establish, through abductive inference and an appeal to biological considerations of pain and pleasure, that the following is true:

$$\Pr(O \,|\, HI) > \Pr(O \,|\, theism)$$

This proposition suggests, roughly speaking, that the existence of evil is less surprising if we accept the hypothesis of indifference as an alternative to traditional theism. Draper makes a further claim that O itself is much more likely to be true provided that the hypothesis of indifference is true than provided that traditional theism is true and, hence, that '[o]ther evidence held equal, traditional theism is very probably false' (Draper 2009, p. 343). The abductive version of the evidential problem of evil is similar to the deductive version of the evidential problem in the sense that it appeals to probabilistic reasoning. However, it utilizes abductive, rather than deductive, inference; it is concerned with which view—traditional theism or the hypothesis of indifference—better explains the existence of evil. The abductive version is also distinct from the inductive version of the evidential problem of evil in the sense that it does not appeal to our past observations to determine regularity in the world.

The abductive version of the evidential problem of evil can be understood as a way to assign a value to variable (iii) concerning an allegedly conflicting relationship between God and evil by claiming as follows: there is a conflict between God and evil, such that the existence of evil can be used to show probabilistically and abductively that God does not exist.

18   THE PROBLEM OF EVIL FOR ATHEISTS

We have seen four versions of the problem of evil. Following the convention, I have classified them into two broad categories: logical and evidential. I have then classified three versions of the evidential problem. My classification can therefore be presented as follows:

- The Logical Problem of Evil (Mackie 1955)
- The Evidential Problem of Evil
  - The Inductive Version (Rowe 1988, 1991)
  - The Deductive Version (Rowe 1996)
  - The Abductive Version (Draper 1989)

Our discussion thus far shows, however, that this classification is potentially problematic because Mackie's logical problem of evil is not a solely logical problem. Also, the deductive version of the evidential problem of evil is not the only deductive version of the problem of evil. There are non-probabilistic and probabilistic versions of the deductive problem. Mackie's logical problem corresponds to the former and the deductive version of the evidential problem corresponds to the latter. One might contend, therefore, that the following classification makes more sense:

- The Deductive Problem of Evil
  - The Non-Probabilistic Version (Mackie 1955)
  - The Probabilistic Version (Rowe 1996)
- The Non-Deductive Problem of Evil:
  - The Inductive Version (Rowe 1988, 1991)
  - The Abductive Version (Draper 1989)

Alternatively, we can classify them as follows:

- Non-Probabilistic Problem of Evil:
  - Non-evidential Version (Mackie 1955)
  - Evidential Version (Rowe 1988, 1991)
- Probabilistic Problem of Evil
  - Deductive Version (Rowe 1996)
  - Abductive Version (Draper 1989)

In any case, the critical point for us here is that we can obtain at least four formulations of the problem of evil in our scheme by assigning distinct values to variable (iii), a variable concerning an allegedly conflicting relationship between God and evil.

1.5 Variable (ii): Evil

Again, the problem of evil consists of three variables: (i) God, (ii) evil, and (iii) an allegedly conflicting relationship between (i) and (ii). We have seen that we can obtain distinct versions of the problem of evil by assigning distinct conflicting relationships to variable (iii). Let us now focus on variable (ii). As I noted above, Mackie (1955) does not specify precisely what he means by evil when he presents his logical problem of evil. In the above, therefore, I assume that by evil he means states of affairs in the actual world that are widely considered evil, such as events in which innocent people are severely harmed. However, this assumption is not sufficiently specific. In what follows, I explain how we can obtain numerous versions of the problem of evil by assigning specific manifestations of evil to variable (ii). The following list summarizes distinct aspects of evil that we discuss in this section in relation to variable (ii).

Quality

- Nature of Evil
  - Axiological Evil vs Deontological Evil
  - Unspecific Evil vs Specific Evil
- Causes of Evil
  - Moral Evil vs Natural Evil
  - Individual Moral Evil vs Collective Moral Evil
- Victims of Evil
  - Humans vs Non-Human Sentient Animals
- Kinds of Evil
  - Gratuitous Evil vs Non-Gratuitous Evil
  - Varieties of Pain and Suffering

Quantity

- Intensity of Evil
- Extensity of Evil
  - Individual Victims vs Group Victims
  - Space
  - Time
  - Modality

As the above list shows, aspects of evil that are relevant to variable (ii) are broadly classified into two categories: quality and quantity. Let us consider quality first.

20 THE PROBLEM OF EVIL FOR ATHEISTS

1.5.1 Nature of Evil: Axiological Evil vs Deontological Evil

The most basic question that we can raise concerning evil is, 'What is evil?' This is a simple yet profound philosophical question which cannot be easily answered. If, however, we limit ourselves to the concept of evil in relation to the problem of evil, we can answer the question by pursuing either of the following two options: the axiological approach or the deontological approach (Tooley 2019a, 2019b).

The axiological approach focuses on the existence of things in the actual world that are considered good, desirable, or valuable, on the one hand, and bad, undesirable, and disvaluable, on the other hand. Pleasure is a plausible candidate for the former and pain is a plausible candidate for the latter. According to the axiological approach, evil is understood in terms of the undesirability of pain, which is deemed intrinsically bad (as well as the desirability of pleasure, which is deemed intrinsically good). Atheists who adopt this approach argue that, roughly speaking, the suboptimal axiological value of a particular state of affairs in the actual world or the overall suboptimal axiological value of the actual world represent evil, implying that there is no omnipotent and wholly good God. A version of the problem of evil based on this approach can be called the 'problem of axiological evil'.

According to the deontological approach, on the other hand, evil is understood in terms of the moral status of actions, such as whether one ought to do x or one ought not to do x. Atheists who adopt this approach argue that, roughly speaking, the deontological assessment shows that there are states of affairs in the actual world such that an omnipotent and wholly good God ought not to bring them about or ought not to let them happen. A version of the problem of evil based on this approach can be called the 'problem of deontological evil'.

Tooley, who introduces the above distinction between the two approaches, rejects the axiological approach (2019a, p. 4). He thinks that there is a gap in the problem of axiological evil because it is not clear how the suboptimal value of a particular state of affairs or the suboptimal value of the world as a whole implies the non-existence of God unless we presuppose such a contentious thesis as that an omnipotent and wholly good being would create the best of all possible worlds. One might try to fill such a gap in the axiological problem by appealing to consequentialism. As Tooley points out, though, such an appeal would weaken the dialectical strength of the problem of evil because traditional theists typically reject

THE PROBLEM OF EVIL   21

consequentialism on an independent ground.[3] Tooley, therefore, adopts the deontological approach and argues that certain states of affairs in the actual world, which are deemed evil, are such that an omnipotent and wholly good God ought not to bring them about or ought not to let them happen.

I am inclined to agree with Tooley that the problem of deontological evil can be more vexing than the problem of axiological evil when it is presented as a challenge for traditional theists. The problem of axiological evil, however, cannot be dismissed because, as I argue in Parts II and III of the present book, it can raise a great challenge for some alternatives to traditional theism, alternatives which do not postulate the existence of God or of a being comparable to God that is morally significantly free.

1.5.2 Nature of Evil: Unspecific Evil vs Specific Evil

We can also assign a value to variable (ii) of the problem of evil by referring to either the existence of an *unspecific* type or instance of evil or the existence of a *specific* type or instance of evil.[4] The first option corresponds to what we may call the 'problem of unspecific evil', which poses a challenge for traditional theists by referring to the existence of evil in general. According to this problem, the existence of any type or instance of evil in the actual world undermines belief in the existence of an omnipotent and wholly good God. As long as traditional theists agree that evil in one form or another exists in the actual world, the problem of unspecific evil arises for them. They do not need to identify the types or instances of evil on which they should focus. The second option corresponds to what we may call the 'problem of specific evil'. According to this problem, the existence of a specific type of evil (for example, wars, genocide, natural disasters) or specific instance of evil (for example, World War II, the Holocaust, the Boxing Day Tsunami) in the actual world undermines belief in the existence of an omnipotent and wholly good God. Some atheists may argue that only some specific instances or types of evil undermine belief in the existence of God. That is, only certain versions of the problem of specific evil succeed. However, the problem of unspecific evil and the problem of specific evil are

[3] For issues concerning normative assumptions in the problem of evil, see Toby Betenson (2014).

[4] Michael Tooley draws similar distinctions: an 'abstract formulation of the argument from evil' vs a 'concrete formulation of the argument from evil', and 'highly general propositions about evils' vs 'much more specific propositions about evils' (Tooley 2019a, p. 5; 2019b).

22 THE PROBLEM OF EVIL FOR ATHEISTS

not mutually exclusive. In fact, the problem of unspecific evil entails the problem of specific evil.

The problem of unspecific evil does not depend on a consensus regarding how evil should be defined or which instances or types of states of affairs should be deemed evil, and therein lies its strength. As long as traditional theists agree with atheists that there is some evil in the actual world, whatever it may be, the problem of unspecific evil arises. In response to such a claim, traditional theists could appeal to, for example, the greater-good theodicy by contending that it is not true that any type or instance of evil undermines theistic belief because there are at least some instances or types of evil (for example, minor pain) that are necessary for realizing a greater good (for example, the avoidance of significant bodily damage).

It is relatively uncontroversial that at least some instances or types of evil can be explained away by the greater-good theodicy, but it is highly controversial that all instances or types of evil can be explained away by the greater-good theodicy. Therein lies the strength of the problem of specific evil. For example, if an atheist were to focus on a specific state of affairs which involves so-called gratuitous evil (see below), such as an event in which a fawn dies alone in a bushfire without instantiating any greater good, the greater-good theodicy is ineffective. It is important to note, however, that not all versions of the problem of specific evil are compelling. For the problem of specific evil to be compelling it has to focus on a specific *and* appropriate type or instance of evil. Otherwise, like the problem of unspecific evil, the problem of specific evil will be immediately jeopardized by a theodicy.

1.5.3 Causes of Evil: Moral Evil vs Natural Evil

We have seen that we can assign a value to variable (ii) of the problem of evil by referring to either the existence of general, unspecific evil or the existence of a specific type or specific instance of evil. We have concluded that the problem is more pressing when we refer to a specific (and appropriate) type or instance of evil. This conclusion, however, raises the following question: to which specific type or specific instance of evil should we refer? One way of answering this question is to examine the *causes of evil* and, accordingly, distinguish evil into two specific types: moral evil and natural evil.

Moral evil is a type of evil that is caused by the intention or negligence of a morally significantly free agent. Examples of moral evil include hatred, theft,

THE PROBLEM OF EVIL   23

abuse, assault, and murder. Natural evil is a type of evil that is not caused by the intention or negligence of a morally significantly free agent; it arises in natural processes. Examples of natural evil include earthquakes, tornados, tsunamis, diseases, and flooding. Depending on the type of evil on which we focus, we can present either the 'problem of moral evil' or the 'problem of natural evil'. (According to some religious traditions, events that are commonly considered instances of natural evil, such as earthquakes and tornados, are caused by powerful supernatural agents, such as demons and devils. If this is true and it applies to all similar events, and if these supernatural agents are morally significantly free, natural evil may collapse into moral evil; ultimately, there may be no such thing as natural evil.[5] To sidestep this issue, one may prefer defining moral evil in terms of morally significantly free *human* agents.[6] However, this approach creates a third type of evil— namely, evil caused by a supernatural agent—which is neither natural evil nor moral evil. I set this point aside in our discussion here.)

Moral evil and natural evil are not always distinct. As I explain in detail in Chapter 9, moral evil sometimes amplifies natural evil, and vice versa. For instance, we can imagine a situation in which a morally significantly free individual sets fire to property and the fire damage is intensified by a strong wind that arises naturally. Also, natural evil can entail moral evil, and vice versa. For instance, we can imagine a situation in which a famine causes poverty, which results in a surge of crimes caused by morally significantly free individuals.

It is interesting to note that philosophers have paid more attention to the problem of moral evil than to the problem of natural evil. It seems that this is not because the problem of moral evil is considered more pressing than the problem of natural evil. The reason seems to be rather that philosophers find the problem of moral evil more philosophically intriguing than the problem of natural evil because assessing it requires an analysis of free will and moral responsibility, which is the subject of a perennial philosophical debate. Another reason is perhaps that moral evil is relevant to sin, which is an important concept, particularly in the Judeo-Christian tradition. Conversely, this could mean that the problem of natural evil, which is discussed less frequently, is more pressing than the problem of moral evil because it allows

---

[5] In relation to the free will defence Plantinga discusses the possibility (not the actuality) of apparently natural evil caused by Satan and his cohort. See Plantinga (1974a, p. 58). I address a related point in Chapter 9 of the present book.

[6] Thanks to an anonymous referee on this point.

24 THE PROBLEM OF EVIL FOR ATHEISTS

us to set aside contentious philosophical issues concerning free will and moral responsibility and complex theological issues concerning sin.

1.5.4 Causes of Evil: Individual Moral Evil vs Collective Moral Evil

We have seen that the problem of evil can be classified into either of the following two types: the problem of unspecific evil and the problem of specific evil. We have also seen that if we adopt the problem of specific evil we can present two versions of it, the problem of moral evil and the problem of natural evil, depending on what causes evil. Set aside the problem of natural evil for now and focus on the problem of moral evil. We can then draw the following additional distinction by referring to the number of agents who cause moral evil in particular cases: individual moral evil and collective moral evil.

What we may call the 'problem of individual moral evil' arises when evil is caused by the intention or negligence of an individual. In contrast, what we may call the 'problem of collective moral evil' occurs when evil is caused by the intention or negligence of a group of individuals. Collective moral evil can be further classified into three types: (i) a type in which all of the individuals comprising the group in question are individually morally culpable, (ii) a type in which none of the individuals comprising the group in question is individually morally culpable, and (iii) a type in which some but not all of the individuals comprising the group in question are individually morally culpable.

Ted Poston (2014) introduces the 'problem of social evil', which is based on a version of type (ii). According to him, this problem arises when evil results from game-theoretic interaction involving multiple rational, moral individuals who are well intentioned but collectively and unintentionally bring about undesirable social outcomes. Poston claims that social evil is distinct from ordinary moral evil because none of the individuals is morally culpable. He also contends that social evil is distinct from natural evil because it is a consequence of an act of morally significantly free agents rather than a consequence of a natural process. An example of such a case that is somewhat comparable to social evil but involves individual moral evil, rather than collective moral evil, is that of a morally significantly free agent rescuing one of two drowning children but not both. Obviously, the agent is not morally culpable if she rescues one of the children, which may result in the death of the other child, because, given the 'ought implies can' principle, it is not the case that she ought to rescue both children, which is impossible. I categorize cases like this and cases of social evil as examples of moral evil because choices made by involved morally significantly free agents determine which instances of evil are realized (even though none of the agents may be morally culpable individually).

If we adopt the deontological approach to the problem of evil, perhaps all appropriate instances of evil that constitute the problem of evil should be considered instances of individual moral evil because they are states of affairs such that God, as a morally significantly free agent who is omnipotent, ought not to bring them about or ought to prevent them. This could mean that, ultimately, there is no such thing as natural evil or collective moral evil.

1.5.5 Victims of Evil: Humans vs Non-Human Sentient Animals

We have thus far classified distinct types of evil by referring to their causes. We first distinguished moral evil from natural evil. Moral evil is caused by morally significantly free agents while natural evil is caused by natural processes. We then focused on moral evil and distinguished it into two types: individual moral evil and collective moral evil. Let us now shift our focus from the causes of evil to the victims of evil. We can then see that there are additional types of the problem of evil.

The most commonly discussed forms of evil are instances in which humans, who are morally significantly free, are victims. Call the problem of evil based on these instances of evil the 'problem of evil involving humans as victims'. On the other hand, there are also instances of evil in which non-human sentient animals, who are not morally significantly free, are victims. Call the problem of evil based on these instances of evil the 'problem of evil involving sentient non-human animals as victims'.[7] One might think that the distinction between these two problems corresponds to the distinction between the problem of moral evil and the problem of natural evil. However, that is not correct. Sentient non-human animals can be victims of moral evil, such as animal abuse and environmental degradation, and humans can be

---

[7] For critical discussions of the problem of evil for sentient non-human animals, see Michael A. Corey (2000), Nicola Hoggard Creegan (2013), Trent Dougherty (2014a), Kyle B. Keltz (2020), Michael J. Murray (2008), Ronald E. Osborn (2014), Holmes Rolston, III (1994), John R. Schneider (2020), and Christopher Southgate (2008).

victims of natural evil, such as earthquakes and bushfires. This yields the following four combinations of causes and victims of evil:

Natural cause—sentient non-human victims
Natural cause—human victims
Human cause—sentient non-human victims
Human cause—human victims

The above classification can be expanded if we consider cases where victims consist of both humans and non-human sentient animals as well as cases where the evil in question has both human and natural causes. I suggested above that focusing on the problem of natural evil, as opposed to the problem of moral evil, may be more desirable because in so doing we can avoid philosophical issues concerning free will and theological issues relating to sin in addressing the causes of evil. Parallel reasoning applies to the consideration of the victims of evil: it may be better to focus on the problem of evil involving sentient non-human animals as victims. This is because there can be situations in which morally significantly free human *victims* are at least partially or indirectly morally responsible for evil. To avoid any complications of this kind, perhaps we should focus on a case which represents the first combination above where the cause of evil is natural and the victims of evil are sentient non-human animals.

The above table could be expanded even further by asking the following question, which tends to be neglected in the literature: can *non-sentient* beings be victims of evil? Lloyd Strickland (2021) argues that theodicies should address evil not only for humans and sentient non-human animals but also for plants because: (i) the failure of their flourishing can be considered evil, (ii) there is a moral obligation to preserve plants, and (iii) plants are considered intrinsically valuable. We may call the problem in question the 'problem of evil involving plants as victims'. If this line of reasoning is cogent, we may be able to extend it to formulate the 'problem of evil involving non-sentient biological organisms as victims', which is concerned not only with plants but many other biological organisms that are not sentient.

1.5.6 Kinds of Evil: Gratuitous Evil vs Non-Gratuitous Evil

By focusing on qualitative kinds of evil, we can also distinguish between gratuitous evil and non-gratuitous evil. Rowe defines gratuitous evil as 'an

THE PROBLEM OF EVIL   27

instance of evil such that an omnipotent being could have prevented it without thereby preventing the occurrence of some greater good' (Rowe 1991, p. 80). The most frequently cited example of gratuitous evil, which I have already mentioned, was originally introduced by Rowe: the suffering of a fawn that is burnt badly in a bushfire (Rowe 1979, p. 337). Gratuitous evil is sometimes called 'pointless evil' or 'unjustified evil'. Non-gratuitous evil is, on the other hand, an instance of evil such that an omnipotent being could not have prevented it without thereby preventing the occurrence or possible occurrence of some greater good.[8] Examples of non-gratuitous evil include the experience of mild pain, which serves the necessary function of helping us avoid more severe bodily damage. Assuming that the distinction between gratuitous evil and non-gratuitous evil is cogent, we can assume that the 'problem of gratuitous evil' is more pressing than the 'problem of non-gratuitous evil'.

Mackie makes a useful point related to gratuitous evil by introducing the distinction between 'first-order evil' and 'second-order evil' (Mackie 1982, p. 154). Call basic instances of pain and suffering examples of 'first-order evil' and basic instances of pleasure and happiness examples of 'first-order good'. Instances of 'second-order good', such as compassion and heroism, can be realized through first-order evil. Similarly, 'second-order evil', such as disinterest and cowardice, can be realized through first-order good. As Mackie points out, cases exist where second-order (or higher-order) good outweighs first-order (or lower-order) evil and where second-order (or higher-order) evil outweighs first-order (or lower-order) good. He calls these cases instances of 'absorbed evil' and 'absorbed good', respectively. Unabsorbed evil corresponds to gratuitous evil. The crucial question in formulating the problem of evil is not merely whether evil *simpliciter* exists, but whether unabsorbed or gratuitous evil exists.

1.5.7 Kinds of Evil: Varieties of Pain and Suffering

Another way of considering the quality of evil is to look at the variety of pain and suffering that victims experience. For example, in medicine it is

---

[8] It is important to include the *possibility* that some greater good will occur here. God may be justified in allowing people to fall into vice because, by giving us morally significant freedom, we could develop good characters on our own. However, of course, it is not guaranteed that if we are granted morally significant freedom we will develop good characters. Here, the *possibility* (not just the *actuality*) of good moral character is relevant. Thanks to an anonymous referee on this point.

28 THE PROBLEM OF EVIL FOR ATHEISTS

common to distinguish several types of pain, such as acute pain, chronic pain, neuropathic pain, nociceptive pain, and radicular pain. Referring to religion rather than medicine, it is believed in Buddhism, for instance, that there are three major types of suffering: the suffering of suffering, the suffering of change, and the suffering of conditioned existence (see Chapter 9 of the present book for a discussion of these types). Depending on the qualitative aspect of pain or suffering on which we focus, we can assign distinct values to variable (ii).

Marilyn McCord Adams (1989, 1999) also addresses evil involving a specific type of suffering, which she calls 'horrendous evil'. She defines horrendous evil as a form of evil 'the participation in which (that is, the doing or suffering of which) constitutes prima facie reason to doubt whether the participant's life could (given their inclusion in it) be a great good to him/her on the whole' (Adams 1999, p. 26). Adams's examples of horrendous evil include 'the rape of a woman and axing off of her arms, psycho-physical torture whose ultimate goal is the disintegration of personality, betrayal of one's deepest loyalties, child abuse of the sort described by Ivan Karamazov, child pornography, parental incest, slow death by starvation, [and] the explosion of nuclear bombs over populated areas' (Adams 1999, p. 26). These are horrific instances of evil that impact victims existentially in a very serious manner. Horrendous evil can be understood as an extreme form of evil that is, using the terminology we addressed above, gratuitous and unabsorbed. Adams thinks that the 'problem of horrendous evil' creates a particularly strong challenge for traditional theists.

1.5.8 Intensity of Evil

We have seen how we can assign distinct values to variable (ii) by considering distinct types of evil in reference to qualitative aspects of evil. Let us now consider a variety of evil related to quantitative aspects.

Consider first the degree or intensity of evil. It seems relatively uncontroversial to say that we can compare degrees of evilness. For example, an act of brutally murdering an innocent person is considered more evil than an act of stealing someone's possession. In this sense, at least certain types or instances of evil are value commensurable. In fact, in criminal justice, the appropriateness of punishments imposed on people found guilty of crimes is determined in part based on a comparative consideration of the degree of

THE PROBLEM OF EVIL   29

harm that distinct types of criminal acts cause. Another possible way of measuring evil quantitatively is to consider the intensity of pain and suffering experienced by victims. It seems reasonable to think that, holding all else equal, a state of affairs is deemed more evil if the victims experience more pain or suffering. We have considered the problem of horrendous evil in relation to the consideration of qualitative aspects of evil, but it can also be considered in relation to quantitative aspects. Here horrendous evil can be construed as a type of evil that involves an extreme degree of pain and suffering.

1.5.9 Extensity of Evil: Individual Victims vs Multiple Victims

The intensity of evil is not the only important factor for a quantitative analysis of evil. We can also measure evil quantitatively in reference to its extensity, that is, the number of victims or the distribution of evil.

Consider first the number of victims. We saw above that evil can be caused by an individual or group of individuals. Similarly, evil can impact an individual or group of individuals. For instance, we can imagine a criminal case where there is only one victim and a war where there are millions of victims. Intuitively, evil that involves many victims seems to create a more significant challenge for theists than evil affecting a small number of victims. It is not always the case, though, that the number of victims translates into the overall degree of evil realized because we also need to consider the intensity of pain and suffering experienced by each victim. An example involving the maximum number of victims might not actually constitute the most compelling instance of the problem of evil. For example, a type of evil affecting all sentient beings would likely prompt a very broad, and perhaps less compelling, question such as, 'Why must sentient beings experience pain?'. The attempt to find an instance of evil which creates the largest number of victims therefore seems to lead us to the problem of unspecific evil, which is, as we have seen, less pressing than the problem of specific evil.

1.5.10 Extensity of Evil: Space

Let us now consider the extensity of evil in terms of the distribution of evil. By distribution I mean how evil is spread in a relevant respect—spatially, temporally, or modally.

30 THE PROBLEM OF EVIL FOR ATHEISTS

Spatial distribution is probably more intuitively comprehensible than temporal or modal distribution. Our consideration here asks where in space evil is realized. For example, if there is a devastating tsunami killing many people, we may say that the location of the evil is where the tsunami takes place. Obviously, there are also instances of evil which harm victims in multiple locations that are spatially dispersed. For example, a volcanic eruption can cause disasters in many distinct locations, even in multiple countries. It is also important to note that the lack of location in physical space does not always mean the absence of evil. For instance, a crime that takes place in cyberspace may harm people without having any specific physical location.

It is obviously important to consider where evil takes place when assigning a value to variable (ii) of our scheme of the problem of evil. Interestingly enough, however, considering where evil (or good) *does not* take place can also be important. Take, for example, a version of what I call the 'problem of inequality evil'. This problem arises in certain cases in which we compare the presence of evil in one place (for example, the presence of an epidemic in a certain region) and the absence of evil in another place (for example, the absence of the epidemic in another region) or in which we compare the presence of good in one place (for example, the presence of wealth in a certain country) and the absence of good in another place (for example, the absence of wealth in another country). The problem in question involves considering how an omnipotent and wholly good God could allow this kind of moral inequality. An unequal spatial distribution of evil is an example of higher-order evil arising from the presence of lower-order evil in one place in conjunction with the absence of lower-order evil in another place, or a higher-order evil arising from the presence of lower-order good in one place in conjunction with the absence of lower-order good in another place.[9] The consideration of 'evil here and no evil there' or 'good here and no good there' may not have to be spatial in a rigid sense. Moti Mizrahi considers a version of the problem of inequal evil which he calls the 'problem of natural inequality'. This problem is based on arbitrary inequality with significant moral implications, such as inequality in gender, ethnicity, social class, and natural talents (Mizrahi 2014, p. 129). The extensity of evil remains relevant

---

[9] Stephen Maitzen (2006) also considers a version of the problem of divine hiddenness, rather than the problem of evil, in reference to the demographic distribution of theistic belief around the world.

THE PROBLEM OF EVIL 31

to the problem of natural inequality, but the occurrence of evil in these cases may not correspond to precise spatial locations.

1.5.11 Extensity of Evil: Time

The extensity of evil based on *temporal* distribution is also important in formulating the problem of evil because it can be relevant to determining the significance of evil. Causes of evil can harm people instantly but they can also harm people at a much later time. How long victims have to endure pain and suffering is also an important consideration related to time. One might argue, for example, that the problem of evil is more pressing when it appeals to a case where victims are forced to suffer for an extended period of time (for example, a fawn dying *slowly* in a bushfire). Also, in a manner similar to that in which a spatial consideration can give rise to a version of the problem of inequality evil, a temporal consideration can give rise to a version of the problem of inequality evil. One might compare, for example, periods when natural resources are abundant with those when they are not, or times when advanced medicine and technology are available with those when they are not.

1.5.12 Extensity of Evil: Modality

We have considered spatial and temporal locations of evil, but considering the 'modal location' of evil can also be relevant to determining the extensity of evil.

The problem of evil typically focuses on instances of evil realized (or conceived to be realized) in the actual world; call it the 'problem of actual evil'. Suppose that traditional theists can successfully respond to the problem of actual evil by offering a theodicy. According to some philosophers, this is not the end of the story because there is also the 'problem of non-actual evil', which is concerned with instances of evil realized (or conceived to be realized) in a possible world that is distinct from the actual world.[10] The problem of actual evil focuses on God's omnipotence and goodness, but the

---

[10] Theodore Guleserian (1983) calls the problem in question the 'modal problem of evil', but I call it the 'problem of non-actual evil' to emphasize that the problem focuses on an instance of evil that is present in a world other than the actual world.

32 THE PROBLEM OF EVIL FOR ATHEISTS

problem of non-actual evil focuses on God's omnipotence, goodness, *and* necessary existence.[11] According to the doctrine of divine necessity, God is a necessary, as opposed to contingent, being; that is, God's existence is a matter of logical or metaphysical necessity rather than contingency. By appealing to possible world semantics, this doctrine can be understood as the thesis that God exists in all possible worlds, including the actual world. This implies that God is related not only to all actual evil, which refers to instances of evil realized in the actual world, but also non-actual evil, which pertains to instances of evil realized in possible but non-actual worlds. The problem of non-actual evil asks how God can coexist with certain instances of evil in non-actual worlds, particularly those that are radically distinct from the actual world.[12] Arguably, the problem of non-actual evil is more pressing than the problem of actual evil because when we formulate the problem of non-actual evil we can refer to a possible but non-actual state of affairs that is worse than any state of affairs that we can find in the actual world (for example, a state of affairs in which billions of innocent people are tortured for billions of years). Even if traditional theists can explain away all instances of evil in the actual world, they are likely to struggle to explain away all instances of evil in all possible worlds. Some may argue, however, that the problem of non-actual evil is problematic because it involves speculating about which worlds are possible. It seems difficult to establish

---

[11] Morris argues for God's necessary existence as follows:

> Why have theists endorsed the necessary existence of God? The reasoning from the side of perfect being theology is simple. We live in a world where many things have a very fragile and tenuous existence. Things come to be, things pass away. Many things that could have been never are, and most things that do exist could have failed ever to appear on the stage of reality. We live in a world of contingent beings. But contingency is not the greatest mode of existence imaginable. We can at least conceive of a being who could not possibly cease to exist, whose existence could not have appeared 'from nothing', and whose anchorage in reality is so great that it is not even possible for the being to have failed to exist. Surely it is only this necessary existence, this firmest possible foothold in reality, which is appropriate for a maximally perfect being. (Morris 1991, p. 108)

For further arguments for God's necessary existence, see Alexander R. Pruss and Joshua L. Rasmussen (2018).

[12] For detailed discussions of the problem of non-actual evil, see Theodore Guleserian (1983), Klaas J. Kraay (2011), Thomas V. Morris (1985), and Chapter 4 of the present book. The problem of non-actual evil can be construed as a version of the 'problem of God's apparent inability to sin'. The problem of God's apparent inability to sin involves the question how an omnipotent God can also be wholly good if an omnipotent being is able to bring about a state of affairs in which, for example, billions of innocent people are tortured for billions of years. Alternatively, it asks how a wholly good God can also be omnipotent if a wholly good being is not able, in any circumstances, to bring about such a state of affairs. For the problem of God's apparent inability to sin, see T. J. Mawson (2002), Wes Morriston (2001a, 2001b, 2002, 2003), and Nelson Pike (1969).

which specific instances of evil are realized in worlds dissimilar to our own. Also, the problem of non-actual evil seems to assume the conceivability principle, according to which the conceivability (of a specific world) entails the metaphysical possibility (of such a world). This principle is highly contentious.[13]

We saw above the problem of inequality evil related to spatial and temporal locations. One might present a parallel problem in terms of modal locations. One might compare, for instance, a possible world in which evil is scarce and a possible world in which evil is abundant and ask how an omnipotent and wholly good God can be compatible with such inequality.[14]

The following list summarizes numerous versions of the problem of evil that we have addressed in this section.

Nature of Evil

- The problem of axiological evil
- The problem of deontological evil
- The problem of unspecific evil
- The problem of specific evil

Causes of Evil

- The problem of moral evil
- The problem of natural evil
- The problem of individual moral evil
- The problem of collective moral evil

Victims of Evil

- The problem of evil involving humans as victims
- The problem of evil involving sentient non-human animals as victims
- The problem of evil involving plants as victims
- The problem of evil involving non-sentient organisms as victims

Kinds of Evil

- The problem of gratuitous evil
- The problem of non-gratuitous evil

---

[13] For the conceivability principle, see David J. Chalmers (2002), Tamar Szabó Gendler and John Hawthorne (2002), and Robert Kirk (2005).

[14] A related problem is discussed in Chapter 3 of the present book. See also Michael J. Almeida (2011).

34 THE PROBLEM OF EVIL FOR ATHEISTS

Intensity of Evil

- The problem of horrendous evil

Extensity of Evil

- The problem of inequality evil
- The problem of actual evil
- The problem of non-actual evil

1.6 Conclusion

Beginning with Mackie's logical problem of evil, I have argued that the problem of evil consists of three variables: (i) God, (ii) evil, and (iii) an allegedly conflicting relationship between (i) and (ii). I then considered many distinct values that we can assign to variable (iii). By specifying the relationship between God and evil we can obtain the logical problem of evil as well as three versions of the evidential problem of evil: the inductive version, the deductive version, and the abductive version. I pointed out that the term 'logical problem' is misleading because Mackie's problem is not based entirely on a logical relationship between God and evil. Next, I considered variable (ii). I have argued that we can obtain numerous versions of the problem of evil by assigning distinct values to this variable in reference to the nature of evil, the causes of evil, the victims of evil, the kinds of evil, and the intensity and extensity of evil.

So far, I have not touched on variable (i) because I have treated the problem of evil as a challenge specifically for traditional theists, who believe in the existence of an omnipotent and wholly good God. In the next chapter, however, I focus on variable (i) and argue that the problem of evil is a version of a much broader problem, the 'problem of axiological expectation mismatch', which can raise a challenge even for those who reject traditional theism.

2
The Problem of Evil as a Problem of Axiological Expectation Mismatch

2.1 Introduction

I argued in Chapter 1 that the problem of evil consists of three elements or variables: (i) God, (ii) evil, and (iii) the allegedly conflicting relationship between (i) and (ii). I also explained that we can obtain numerous versions of the problem of evil by assigning distinct values to variables (ii) and (iii). I first addressed variables (ii) and (iii), which are already widely discussed in the literature. Despite the scant attention it has received, however, variable (i), on which we focus in this chapter, is most crucial for the present book because we can develop numerous versions of the problem of evil beyond the traditional theistic framework by assigning distinct values to this variable.

It is commonly believed that the problem of evil poses a challenge that arises uniquely and specifically for traditional theists who believe in the existence of an omnipotent and wholly good God. That is why the problem of evil is normally presented as an argument against traditional theism and the literature on the problem of evil has been shaped through enduring disputes between traditional theists and their critics over the cogency of the argument. In this chapter, however, I argue that the problem of evil is a much deeper one and is relevant not only to traditional theists but also to proponents of many alternative views. To defend my argument, I try to show that the problem of evil is a specific version of a broader problem which I call the 'problem of axiological expectation mismatch'.

This chapter has the following structure. In Section 2.2, I present a straightforward and relatively shallow way of showing that being a traditional theist is neither a necessary nor a sufficient condition for being a target of the problem of evil. In Section 2.3, I present a more substantial way of showing how the problem of evil poses a challenge for atheists/non-theists as well as theists. In Section 2.4, I argue that existing theistic responses to the

The Problem of Evil for Atheists. Yujin Nagasawa, Oxford University Press. © Yujin Nagasawa 2024.
DOI: 10.1093/oso/9780198901884.003.0003

36 THE PROBLEM OF EVIL FOR ATHEISTS

problem of evil can be understood as attempts to resolve the axiological expectation mismatch which the problem of evil raises. In Section 2.5, I conclude the discussion.

2.2 Being a Traditional Theist Is Neither Necessary nor Sufficient for Being a Target of the Problem of Evil

Many philosophers state explicitly that the problem of evil arises uniquely for traditional theists. As we saw in Chapter 1, Mackie remarks, 'The problem of evil, in the sense in which I shall be using the phrase, is a problem only for someone who believes that there is a God who is both omnipotent and wholly good' (Mackie 1955, p. 200). Another atheist, Michael Martin, writes, '[T]he problem of evil presumably does not show that God does not exist when "God" refers to some being that is either not omnipotent or not completely benevolent' (Martin 1974, p. 232). In addressing pantheism as an alternative to traditional theism, Michael Levine also writes that the problem of evil 'is a uniquely theistic problem and one that the pantheist can shrug off since its formulation entails an essentially [traditional] theistic doctrine of deity' (Levine 1994a, p. 217).[1]

In this section, however, I argue that it is not correct to think that the problem of evil is a problem that arises uniquely and specifically for traditional theists. My argument is based on the following two theses: (1) the scope of the problem of evil does not cover all proponents of traditional theism—that is, being a traditional theist is not a sufficient condition for being a target of the problem of evil; and (2) the scope of the problem of evil covers some opponents of traditional theism, that is, being a traditional theist is not a necessary condition for being a target of the problem of evil. My arguments for (1) and (2) in this section are simple and straightforward but also relatively shallow. In the next section, I will present a more substantial argument for thesis (2).

Consider first thesis (1), according to which the scope of the problem of evil does not cover all proponents of traditional theism. Following Mackie, I have assumed that all traditional theists hold that God is an omnipotent and wholly good being. However, this assumption is disputable. Some philosophers are considered traditional theists yet are willing to reject it or

---

[1] See Chapter 3 of the present book for detailed discussion of Levine's view.

at least take the possibility of rejecting it seriously. Peter Geach, for example, encourages Christian theists to give up God's omnipotence:

> Lying and promise-breaking are logically possible feats that Christians cannot hold to be possible for God. And making a thing which its maker cannot destroy is a logically possible feat, a feat some creatures do perform; but whether we say that God cannot perform this feat or that he can, there turns out to be some logically possible feat which God cannot perform. (Geach 1977, p. vi)

For the above reason, Geach concludes that it is more appropriate to think of God's power as 'almightiness' rather than omnipotence. To take another example, in relation to the problem of God's apparent inability to sin, Wes Morriston considers the idea that God is omnibenevolent but not exactly omnipotent.[2] Morriston writes that perhaps what the problem suggests is that God is '(a) necessarily morally perfect; and (b) as powerful as is logically consistent with (a)'. In this way, Morriston says, a necessarily morally perfect God remains powerful enough to create the world and perform miracles without being omnipotent (Morriston 2001a, p. 158).[3] Furthermore, Scott Hill (2014) explicitly encourages traditional theists to give up God's omnipotence because there are many tasks that God cannot perform and abandoning the doctrine of omnipotence is less costly than it is normally assumed to be. (There is a question whether these philosophers give up God's omnipotence in a way that makes it relevant to the problem of evil. For instance, one may reject God's omnipotence because one believes that God cannot cease to exist. It is unclear if this point impacts the problem of evil as a challenge for traditional theists. I address issues that are relevant to this point below.)

Some traditional theists consider the possibility of rejecting God's goodness (in an ordinary sense). For example, in response to the argument from evil, Brian Davies contends that it is 'wholly inappropriate to think of God as

---

[2] For the problem of God's apparent inability to sin, see footnote 9 in Chapter 1 of the present book.

[3] John Bishop also claims that it is reasonable for theists to think that the existence of evil entails that God is not omnipotent. He writes, '[on the basis of the problem of evil] theists should reject the concept of God as an agent outside the natural order who has an absolutely unlimited power of intervention within nature' (Bishop 1993, p. 13). Bishop is not, however, a traditional theist; he develops with Ken Perszyk a view which he calls a 'euteleological' conception of divinity (Bishop and Perszyk 2016, 2023).

38 THE PROBLEM OF EVIL FOR ATHEISTS

something able to be either moral (well behaved) or immoral (badly behaved)' (Davies 1998, p. 178). He writes:

> To be blunt, I suggest that many contemporary philosophers writing on the problem of evil (both theists and non-theists) have largely been wasting their time...They are like people attacking or defending tennis players because they fail to run a mile in under four minutes. Tennis players are not in the business of running four-minute miles. Similarly, God is not something with respect to which moral evaluation (whether positive or negative) is appropriate. (Davies 1998, p. 178)

Mark Murphy (2017) also holds that God as an Anselmian being is not subject to the moral norms to which we humans are subject and, hence, God is not a morally good agent in the sense in which good humans are. In my previous work (Yujin Nagasawa 2017), I myself considered, in relation to the concept of 'maximal God', the possibility that God is the greatest possible being yet not exactly omnipotent or exactly wholly good.

In sum, some traditional theists are willing or prepared to reject the thesis that God is an omnipotent and wholly good being. Some may dispute whether they should be considered genuine traditional theists, but most, if not all, of those discussed above consider themselves to be traditional theists; in fact, they reject the doctrine of divine omnipotence or goodness as it is usually understood precisely because they think it is incompatible with how the concept of God should be correctly understood within the framework of traditional theism.

Mackie, who introduced the logical problem of evil, notes explicitly that theists can avoid the problem of evil by giving up God's omnipotence or goodness:

> It is plain, therefore, that [the problem of evil] can be easily solved if one gives up at least one of the propositions that constitute it. Someone who holds that there is in some sense a god, but one who is not wholly good, or, though powerful, not quite omnipotent, will not be embarrassed by this difficulty. (Mackie 1982, p. 151)

We have seen a quick and straightforward way of motivating thesis (1): the scope of the problem of evil does not cover all proponents of traditional theism. Some philosophers consider themselves traditional theists yet endorse the view that God is not omnipotent or wholly good. For them,

THE PROBLEM OF EVIL AS A PROBLEM OF AXIOLOGICAL   39

the problem of evil as standardly formulated does not seem to arise. Whether they should be considered traditional theists is a contentious issue, but at least it is not obvious that being a traditional theist is a sufficient condition for being a target of the problem of evil.

We can also establish thesis (2), that is, that the scope of the problem of evil may cover some *opponents* of traditional theism, relatively easily. The problem of evil focuses on the concept of God understood as an omnipotent and wholly good being because it alleges that the combination of omnipotence and unrestricted goodness conflicts with the existence of evil. There can, however, be atheists/non-theists who believe in the existence of an omnipotent and wholly good being. For instance, some may believe in the existence of a demigod who is omnipotent and wholly good but lacks some other properties of God according to traditional theism; the problem of evil still arises for them. At this point, one might appeal to the doctrine of divine simplicity and argue that no other being than God can be both omnipotent and wholly good because God is identical with all the divine properties including omnipotence and unrestricted goodness. While such an argument may succeed, it does not mean that those who believe in the existence of an omnipotent and wholly good demigod can avoid the problem of evil without giving up their belief in the existence of such a being. This shows that being a traditional theist is not a necessary condition for being a target of the problem of evil either. It is important to note that even omnipotence and unrestricted goodness are not essential for the problem of evil. For instance, if we believe that there is a being that is always powerful enough to prevent an earthquake and always benevolent enough to wish to prevent an earthquake, then the problem of evil can arise for us even if we believe that the being in question is not omnipotent or wholly good.

I have briefly shown above that it is not accurate to say that the problem of evil is a problem uniquely and specifically for traditional theists. First, traditional theists who reject the idea that God is omnipotent or wholly good are not targets of the problem of evil. Second, atheists/non-theists who believe in the existence of a being other than God that is omnipotent and wholly good (or powerful enough and benevolent enough in this context) *are* targets of the problem of evil. Hence, we can conclude that it is too hasty and misleading to characterize the problem of evil as a problem uniquely and specifically for traditional theists. We can illustrate this point in reference to variable (i), which focuses on God, in our scheme of the problem of evil. If we understand that God is not omnipotent or wholly good, then the problem of evil does not arise. Also, the problem of evil *can* arise even if we

40 THE PROBLEM OF EVIL FOR ATHEISTS

replace God with some other being as the value of variable (i), given that such a being is omnipotent and wholly good, or powerful enough and good enough in a relevant sense.

2.3 The Problem of Axiological Expectation Mismatch

We have seen in the previous section that not all traditional theists are targets of the problem of evil and not all opponents of traditional theism can avoid the problem of evil. Saying that the problem of evil is a problem beyond traditional theism for the reasons explained above is, however, relatively shallow and insignificant because only a very small number of traditional theists hold that God is not omnipotent or wholly good. Also, only a very small number of atheists and other non-theists believe in the existence of an omnipotent and wholly good being (or a being that is powerful enough and good enough in a relevant sense). A crucial and more pressing question for us is, therefore, the following: Can we show that the problem of evil is a problem beyond traditional theism in the sense that it can target alternative views which have many supporters and differ substantially from traditional theism? My answer to this question is affirmative because I believe that the problem of evil is a profound problem that poses a challenge for such serious, extant alternatives to traditional theism as pantheism, panentheism, axiarchism, and atheism.

Consider, once again, our scheme of the problem of evil, which consists of the following three variables: (i) God, (ii) evil, and (iii) an allegedly conflicting relationship between (i) and (ii). As I mentioned in Chapter 1 of the present book, Mackie says that we cannot derive any conflict between God and evil without introducing additional quasi-logical rules. By quasi-logical rules, Mackie means such theses as that 'good is opposed to evil in such a way that a good thing always eliminates evil as far as it can' and that 'there are no limits to what an omnipotent being can do' (Mackie 1955, p. 201). Mackie's point here suggests that, once the quasi-logical rules are in place, (i) entails the expectation that there is no evil in the actual world, which conflicts with our observation that there *is* evil.[4] This means that the ultimate source of the problem of evil is a conflict between the following two propositions:

---

[4] I use the phrase 'observation' here metaphorically. I do not mean that evil needs to be visually observed or witnessed.

THE PROBLEM OF EVIL AS A PROBLEM OF AXIOLOGICAL   41

(a) It is expected that there is no evil in the actual world.
(b) There is evil in the actual world.

Proposition (a) is normally derived from traditional theists' belief in the existence of an omnipotent and wholly good God while proposition (b) is based on our observation of reality. The crucial point for us here is that the core of the problem of evil is intact even if (a) is derived from a view other than traditional theism. In fact, (a) is only a general claim expressing how the actual world is expected to be. This suggests that the problem of evil is not necessarily a problem concerning God specifically; it is a more general problem concerning the apparent mismatch between our expectation that there is no evil in the actual world and our observation of the reality that there *is* evil. Hence, it is more appropriate to use the term 'problem of evil' for this general problem and to call a version of the problem that is explicitly formulated for traditional theists the 'problem of evil *for traditional theists*'.

Given that the problem of evil is a problem concerning evil for and beyond traditional theism, it makes sense that the problem is known as such rather than as the 'problem of God' or the 'problem of traditional theism'. The emphasis is correctly placed on evil rather than God or theism. It also makes sense that, when the problem is raised in relation to traditional theism, the target of the problem is almost always belief in God rather than the observation that evil exists. Proponents of the problem almost always try to undermine belief in God by appealing to the existence of evil, rather than seeking to undermine the thesis that evil exists by appealing to belief in God. Hence, even though the problem of evil is normally formulated in terms of the apparent inconsistency between two variables, God and evil, the emphasis on these variables differs. Evil is meant to create a challenge for belief in God, while God is not meant to create a challenge for belief in evil.

I submit that the problem of evil is a specific version of what I call the 'problem of axiological expectation mismatch', which is a broad problem concerning the apparent mismatch between our expectation of how the actual world should be and our observation of how it actually is.[5] The expectation here is normally—but not always, as I explain in Part III of the present book—based on a worldview, such as traditional theism, while the observation is normally based on everyday experience or empirical investigation. The problem arises when we believe that the actual world

---

[5] Note that 'should' here is an epistemic rather than normative notion.

42 THE PROBLEM OF EVIL FOR ATHEISTS

has property p while our observation suggests that the actual world does not have p. The problem could, in principle, be construed as an indication that our observation that the actual world has p is mistaken. It is more common, however, to construe it as an indication that our expectation that the actual world has p is mistaken. This is a challenge for our worldview if the expectation is derived from it.[6] The scheme of the problem of axiological expectation mismatch can be presented as follows:

(a') It is expected that the world has property p.
(b') The world does not have property p.

We can see that the problem of evil, which consists of (a) and (b), is a specific version of the problem of axiological expectation mismatch, which consists of (a') and (b').

Construed as a specific version of the problem of axiological expectation mismatch, the problem of evil for traditional theists can be crudely presented as follows. Traditional theism says that the world was created by an omnipotent and wholly good God. Many traditional theists, therefore, naturally (and perhaps naïvely) expect the world to have the property of being free from evil. Their observation suggests, however, that the world does not have such a property. Hence, they face an axiological expectation mismatch: there is a gap between their expectation, based on traditional theism, of how the world should be and their observation of how it actually is.

The problem of evil is not the only version of the problem of axiological expectation mismatch discussed in the philosophy of religion.[7] Take, for

---

[6] If we present the problem of expectation mismatch as an *argument* against a metaphysical view, such as traditional theism, then we can present it as follows: the metaphysical view in question is false because there is a gap between our expectation of the state of the world based on our axiological belief and our observation of the actual state of the world. That is, our commitment to the axiological belief makes the actual state of the world *surprising*. The surprise here corresponds to an epistemic gap, which is understood to indicate a flaw in the axiological belief. This is somewhat analogous to some arguments against physicalism which also derive the falsity of a metaphysical view (that is, physicalism) by appealing to a surprise, which corresponds to a metaphysical gap that the view in question creates. For instance, Frank Jackson's knowledge argument purports to derive the falsity of physicalism by appealing to the thesis that Mary, a physically omniscient scientist who has always lived in a black-and-white environment, is surprised when she sees colour for the first time. See my earlier work (Nagasawa 2008) for a relevant discussion. Thanks to Jeremiah Joven Joaquin for his input regarding this point.

[7] In a previous work (Nagasawa 2008b, 2017), I argued that arguments against the existence of God according to traditional theism can be classified into three types: (i) type-A arguments, which purport to show the internal incoherence of God's properties; (ii) type-B arguments, which purport to show the mutual inconsistency between God's properties; and (iii) type-C

THE PROBLEM OF EVIL AS A PROBLEM OF AXIOLOGICAL   43

example, the problem of divine hiddenness, which can be summarized as follows. If traditional theism is true, then there is an omnipotent and wholly good God. An omnipotent and wholly good God would be open to forming personal relationships with all human persons and would ensure that there would be no human persons who are unaware that God exists despite their willingness to believe in God. There are, however, many people in the actual world who are willing to accept God yet are unaware of God's existence.

The problem of divine hiddenness has been discussed extensively in the philosophy of religion, and the above is only a very rough formulation of one version of the problem.[8] However, it should be sufficient to show that the problem of divine hiddenness is a version of the problem of axiological expectation mismatch. The expectation based on traditional theism here is that, given the nature of God, it is expected that the actual world is such that God's existence is manifest to all human persons who are capable of having a personal relationship with God and do not resist it. In reality, though, the existence of God is not manifest to many of them. Hence, there is a gap between our expectation of the world based on traditional theism and the actual state of the world according to our observation.

To take another example, the so-called problem of no best world can also be considered a version of the problem of axiological expectation mismatch: if traditional theism is true, God is the greatest possible being, an omnipotent and wholly good creator of the world. Given that the world is created by such a being, it is expected that the actual world is the best possible world. However, the actual world is not the best possible world. We can easily conceive of a world that is better than the actual world; for example, a world that is identical with the actual world except that a certain minor mishap that occurs in the actual world is absent from that world.[9] Here, again, there is a gap between our expectation of the world based on traditional theism and the actual state of the world according to our observation.

---

arguments, which purport to show the mutual inconsistency between the set of God's properties and a certain fact about the actual world. Type-C arguments correspond to versions of the problem of expectation mismatch.

[8] For critical discussions of the argument from divine hiddenness, see Adam Green and Eleonore Stump (2016), Daniel Howard-Snyder and Paul K. Moser (2002), Michael Rea (2018), J. L. Schellenberg (1993, 2015), Peter van Inwagen (2002), and Veronika Weidner (2021).

[9] The term 'the problem of no best world' was introduced by William L. Rowe (1994). For critical discussions of the problem of no best world, see Robert Merrihew Adams (1972), Klaas J. Kraay (2008), Bruce Langtry (2008), and William L. Rowe (2004).

44   THE PROBLEM OF EVIL FOR ATHEISTS

Notice that the problem of divine hiddenness and the problem of no best world are distinct from the problem of evil.[10] There can be a world in which the existence of God is manifest to all non-resistant human persons but there is moral or natural evil. In such a world the problem of divine hiddenness does not arise but the problem of evil does. There can also be a world in which the existence of God is not manifest to all non-resistant human persons but there is no moral or natural evil. In such a world the problem of hiddenness arises but the problem of evil does not (unless divine hiddenness is deemed an instance of evil). There can also be a world such that it is not the best possible world but is free from evil. In such a world, the problem of no best world arises but the problem of evil does not. Also, if it is shown that even the best possible world has to contain at least some evil, then there can be a world in which the problem of no best world does not arise but the problem of evil does.[11]

It is worth noting that an axiological expectation mismatch can motivate, rather than challenge, traditional theism. Consider, for instance, the fine-tuning of the universe. Some philosophers and scientists claim that the existence of life is grounded on an extremely delicate balance of initial conditions obtained at the beginning of the universe. Stephen Hawking estimates that if the rate of the universe's expansion one second after the Big Bang had been smaller by even one part in a hundred thousand million million, life could not have existed in the universe (Craig and Sinnott-Armstrong 2004, p. 9). However, life does exist in the universe.[12] If we hold naturalism as opposed to traditional theism, it might seem reasonable to expect that the universe is not sufficiently fine-tuned for such a probabilistically unlikely state because, according to naturalism, the universe is an outcome of merely random, natural processes. However, the universe seems to be fine-tuned. Hence, if we assume naturalism, there is a gap between our expectation and reality. Therefore, theism is more likely than naturalism to be true.[13] I do not mean that this inference is cogent, but it is a helpful

---

[10] For the relationship between the argument from divine hiddenness and the argument from evil, see Yujin Nagasawa (2016), J. L. Schellenberg (2009, 2010, 2017a, 2017b), and Peter van Inwagen (2002).

[11] Gottfried Wilhelm Leibniz indeed believes that the actual world is the best possible world even though it contains evil. See Chapter 6 of the present book.

[12] See also John D. Barrow and Frank J. Tipler (1986), Bernard Carr (2007), and John Leslie (1989).

[13] One might argue that the problem of why there is something rather than nothing is a version of the problem of axiological expectation mismatch that also motivates traditional

illustration of the fact that an axiological expectation mismatch can also be used to motivate, rather than challenge, a certain metaphysical view.

The problem of axiological expectation mismatch could be formally presented in terms of confirmation theory and its probabilistic tools, such as Bayes's theorem.[14] I do not pursue this route in the present book because I wish to avoid any unnecessary technicality. Using the terminology of confirmation theory, however, my point here can be presented as follows. The problem of evil is an example of 'disconfirmation' (or an axiological expectation mismatch) for theists while the fine-tuning of the universe is an example of 'confirmation' (or an axiological expectation match) for them. Another theory that is relevant to the problem of axiological expectation mismatch is expectation confirmation theory, which is discussed in several academic fields, including social psychology, marketing, and information systems research.[15] This theory explains how our pre-existing expectations of an event or an object can influence our perceptions, attitudes, and behaviours. For instance, we often have a certain expectation of a product before purchasing it. After purchasing and using it we acquire new information about the product. If the new information contradicts our expectation there may be negative cognitive or emotional impacts, such as disappointment, which correspond to the gap between our expectation and the new information.

I explain in the following chapters that proponents of pantheism, panentheism, axiarchism, and many other alternatives to traditional theism face similar problems because their expectations of how the world should be also fail to match their observations of how the world actually is in relation to evil. This suggests that there are, in a significant sense, versions of the problem of evil for alternatives to traditional theism. The core of the problem of evil is, therefore, an apparent conflict between people's expectations of how the world should be and the existence of evil in the world,

---

theism as opposed to naturalism. If naturalism is true, then there is no such thing as God as a necessarily existent creator. If so, that the actual world contains something rather than nothing seems surprising. There is hence a gap between our expectation of the world based on naturalism and the actual state of the world according to our observation. For the problem of why there is something rather than nothing, see Tyron Goldschmidt (2013), Jim Holt (2012), John Leslie and Robert Lawrence Kuhn (2013), and Bede Rundle (2004).

[14] Thanks to Adam Green and an anonymous referee for raising this point. For philosophical discussions of confirmation theory and Bayesian inference, see Paul Draper (1989), (1992), (2014) and Richard Swinburne (1973).

[15] For expectation confirmation theory, see Susan A. Brown et al. (2008), Mohammad Alamgir Hossain and Mohammed Quaddus (2011), and Chieh-Peng Lin, Yuan Hui Tsai, and Chou-Kang Chiu (2009).

46 THE PROBLEM OF EVIL FOR ATHEISTS

rather than an apparent conflict between an omnipotent and wholly good God specifically and evil in the world. Hence, ultimately, variable (i) in our scheme should not be about how God is understood, but about how the world is expected to be in relation to evil.

To summarize: The problem of evil is a version of the problem of axiological expectation mismatch, which arises when there is a gap between our expectation of the actual world (or some other possible world in the case of the problem of non-actual evil) often based on a particular worldview and our observation of the actual state of the world. The problem of axiological expectation mismatch is broad because the problem need not refer to traditional theism; it can refer to some other worldview. It is broad also in the sense that it can take many forms, such as the problem of divine hiddenness, the problem of no best world, and the fine-tuning problem, as well as the problem of evil. The version of the problem of evil that is commonly discussed in the philosophy of religion is a specific version of the problem of evil which targets traditional theists. The taxonomy of the problems that we have addressed in this section can be summarized as follows:

The problem of axiological expectation mismatch

- The problem of divine hiddenness
- The problem of no best world
- The fine-tuning problem
- The problem of evil
  - For traditional theists
  - For others

By analysing the problem of evil in this way, we can anticipate how the problem may arise for views that serve as alternatives to traditional theism. As long as these views project a certain expectation of the actual world in relation to evil, and such an expectation fails to match our observation of the actual state of the world, the problem of evil arises for them.

2.4 Existing Responses to the Problem of Evil as Attempts to Reconcile the Mismatch

I have argued that the problem of evil can be construed as a version of the problem of axiological expectation mismatch because it arises from an apparent mismatch between our expectation of how reality should be and the actual state of the world. In this section, I defend this construal further by showing that existing responses to the problem of evil introduced by traditional theists can be construed as attempts to reconcile the apparent mismatch. More specifically, I argue that these responses can be understood as efforts to fill or explain away the gap indicated by the mismatch.

It is important to note that my descriptions of the existing responses to the problem of evil here are brief and simplified because our space is limited. Nevertheless, these descriptions are sufficient for our purpose to enable us to survey common ways of responding to the problem of evil discussed in the literature and confirm that they can be understood as attempts to reconcile the axiological expectation mismatch on which the problem of evil is based. It would be unnecessary and indeed distracting to elaborate a long, detailed discussion of each view because my aim in the present book is not to defend or criticize any specific response to the problem of evil.

2.4.1 Response 1: Amendments to Divine Attributes

Again, the problem of evil is normally presented as a problem concerning the apparent conflict between an omnipotent and wholly good God, on the one hand, and evil in the actual world, on the other. According to what I call the 'amended divine attribute response', which we have already seen above, such a conflict is illusory because, contrary to what many traditional theists believe, God is not exactly omnipotent or wholly good. This response is a 'defensive' response because it undercuts the problem of evil only as it is normally presented as a challenge for belief in the existence of an omnipotent and wholly good God. If proponents of the response hope to make it more than a defence, they have to specify what they believe the levels of God's power and goodness to be and explain, in reference to the quality and quantity of evil, what sorts of states of affairs or worlds on the whole are expected to be actualized based on these levels. If they can successfully show that the quality and quantity of evil found in the actual world fall within the range of expectation according to the specified levels, then they succeed in overcoming the axiological expectation mismatch. This strategy can be construed as saying the following in response to the problem of evil understood as a version of the problem of axiological expectation mismatch: God reaches certain impressive levels of power and goodness, yet God is not exactly omnipotent or wholly good. There is no gap between our expectation

48   THE PROBLEM OF EVIL FOR ATHEISTS

and our observation of reality because the levels of God's power and goodness imply the realization of evil of a certain quality and quantity which matches what we find in the actual world.[16]

2.4.2 Response 2: The Free Will Theodicy

The free will theodicy is based on two assumptions: (i) libertarianism about free will is true and (ii) holding all else being equal, a world in which morally significant freedom is realized is better than a world in which it is not realized. These assumptions imply that God's creation of the actual world, in which there are morally significantly free human agents, is justified and that these human agents, rather than God, are responsible for evil in the actual world. To respond to Mackie's logical problem of evil, as I explained in Chapter 1, we need, arguably, only a logical possibility; that possibility does not have to correspond to actuality. The free will response presented in this way is called the 'free will defence' rather than the 'free will theodicy' (Alvin Plantinga 1974a, p. 28). Yet to respond to other versions of the problem of evil we need the free will theodicy, which holds that what is described here is actual rather than merely possible.

The free will theodicy can be construed as saying the following in response to the problem of evil construed as a version of the problem of axiological expectation mismatch: there is no gap between our expectation and our observation of reality because, first, it is expected that an omnipotent and wholly good God would create a world in which there are morally significantly free agents. Second, the amount of evil realized in the actual world also falls within our expectation because evil outcomes involve human agents' use and abuse of morally significant freedom. Critics can of course dispute whether the above assumptions to which the free will theodicy is committed are true or whether free will can explain away *every* instance of evil realized in the actual world. Again, however, it is not my aim here to evaluate any of these responses to the problem of evil.[17]

---

[16] See Section 2.2 of this chapter for references to authors who defend this type of response to the problem of evil.

[17] For critical discussions of the free will defence and the free will theodicy, see William S. Anglin (1990), David Basinger (1996), Laura W. Ekstrom (2021), William Hunt (2021), and Alvin Plantinga (1967, 1974a, 1974b).

2.4.3 Response 3: The Soul-Making Theodicy

The soul-making theodicy says that evil is necessary for humans to cultivate moral virtues or achieve spiritual growth. By exercising freedom responsibly, people learn to make the right choices and avoid temptations. In a paradise-like world where people can perform only morally right actions (and, hence, are not morally responsible), there can be no room for moral or spiritual improvement. One may argue that the soul-making theodicy fails because people who die very young do not have such opportunities. In response, John Hick (1966, 1976), a proponent of the soul-making theodicy, considers the possibility of rebirth so that our spiritual growth is not limited to people's current lives.

The soul-making theodicy can be presented as saying the following in response to the problem of evil construed as a version of the problem of axiological expectation mismatch: there is no gap between our expectation and our observation of reality because it is expected that an omnipotent and wholly good God would create a world where people are given opportunities for moral and spiritual growth and, hence, there is evil. Conversely, there would have been an axiological expectation mismatch if the world had been paradise-like and free from evil and, consequently, people would have been unable to cultivate their virtues or achieve spiritual growth. Like proponents of the free will theodicy, proponents of the soul-making theodicy have to show that the quality and quantity of evil realized in the actual world falls within the range of expectation given the existence of an omnipotent and wholly good God. More specifically, they have to show that the quality and quantity of evil are appropriate for achieving moral and spiritual growth without undermining God's omnipotence and goodness.[18]

2.4.4 Response 4: Sceptical Theism

Sceptical theism is an increasingly popular response to the problem of evil. According to this response, even if God has good reason to allow evil in the actual world, given our cognitive limitations it is reasonable to think that we may not have complete access to God's justification for allowing evil. We should not expect to be able to comprehend exactly why God allows evil because we do not (and probably cannot) know everything relevant about

---

[18] For critical discussions of the soul-making theodicy, see Paul F. Andrus (1975), Harold Hewitt (1991), John Hick (1966), Robert C. Mesle (1991), and Mark S. M. Scott (2010).

50 THE PROBLEM OF EVIL FOR ATHEISTS

the nature of God and morality. This is analogous to a situation in which, for example, a small child has to have dental surgery without understanding why her parents would force her to undergo such a painful procedure. Here the child is analogous to us and the parents are analogous to God. The child does not and cannot comprehend the justification for allowing such 'evil', but that does not mean that the parents lack justification.

Sceptical theism can be construed as saying the following in response to the problem of evil as a version of the problem of axiological expectation mismatch: there *is* a gap between our expectation of reality and how the world actually is with respect to evil. That is why we are puzzled by the existence of evil. This gap does not however have any significant ontological implications, such as the non-existence of God, because the gap arises purely epistemically as a result of our cognitive limitations.[19]

2.4.5 Response 5: The Felix Culpa Theodicy

A response to the problem of evil does not have to be entirely philosophical. If one wishes to show the compatibility between an omnipotent and wholly good God and the existence of evil *within one's own religious framework*, one can incorporate relevant theological ideas into the response. Plantinga's *Felix Culpa* theodicy is a response to the problem of evil which incorporates Christian doctrines of the Fall, sin, the Incarnation, and Atonement. According to this theodicy, God can realize a great world only through the Incarnation and Atonement. The Incarnation and Atonement, however, require the Fall and sin, which involve evil. Evil therefore has to be realized in the actual world, but it does not undermine the existence of an omnipotent and wholly good God. The *Felix Culpa* theodicy can be construed as saying the following in response to the problem of evil construed as a version of the problem of axiological expectation mismatch: there is no gap between our expectation and reality because, given Christian belief, it is expected that an omnipotent and wholly good God would want to create a great world that realizes the Incarnation and Atonement, which are possible only in a world containing a certain quality and quantity of evil. Conversely, there would have been an axiological expectation mismatch if the world had been free from evil but lacked the Incarnation and Atonement.

---

[19] For critical discussions of sceptical theism, see Michael Bergmann (2001), Trent Dougherty (2014b), Trent Dougherty and Justin P. McBrayer (2014), Justin P. McBrayer (2010), and Stephen Wykstra (1984).

THE PROBLEM OF EVIL AS A PROBLEM OF AXIOLOGICAL   51

2.4.6 Response 6: The Greater-Good Theodicy

The greater-good theodicy says that evil is necessary because without it God cannot realize a greater good. Many forms of the greater good, such as altruism, compassion, and generosity, are believed to require evil. If we hold that free will, soul-making, the Incarnation, and Atonement are also instances of the greater good that require evil, then the free will theodicy, the soul-making theodicy, and the *Felix Culpa* theodicy collapse into the greater-good theodicy. Alternatively, the free will theodicy, the soul-making theodicy, and the *Felix Culpa* theodicy can be construed as specific versions of the greater-good theodicy. Using Mackie's terminology that we discussed in Chapter 1, the crucial question concerning the greater-good theodicy is whether there are unabsorbed instances of evil. If there are, a gap between our expectation and our observation of reality will remain. The greater-good theodicy can be expressed as follows in response to the problem of evil construed as a version of the problem of axiological expectation mismatch: an omnipotent and wholly good God is expected to create a world in such a way that not only first-order good but also higher-order good are realized. The quality and quantity of evil found in the actual world fall within the range of expectation because all actual instances of evil are absorbed by instances of higher-order good.[20]

Again, the above discussion provides only a brief overview of popular theistic responses to the problem of evil. If it occurs to readers that these responses are plausible yet incomplete, then combining some or all of them may be worth considering. For instance, one could simultaneously invoke the free will theodicy, the soul-making theodicy, and the *Felix Culpa* theodicy to narrow the gap in the axiological expectation mismatch and rely on sceptical theism to account for any remaining space in the gap.

2.5 Conclusion

I have argued that the problem of evil is not a problem that arises uniquely and specifically for traditional theists. First, being a traditional theist is not a sufficient condition for being a target of the problem; some traditional

---

[20] For critical discussions of the greater-good theodicy, including Plantinga's *Felix Culpa* theodicy, see Marilyn McCord Adams (2008), Kevin Diller (2008), William Hasker (1992), Bruce Langtry (1998), Alvin Plantinga (2004), and Melville Y. Stewart (1993).

52 THE PROBLEM OF EVIL FOR ATHEISTS

theists who reject God's omnipotence or goodness are not susceptible to the problem of evil. Second, being a traditional theist is not a necessary condition for being a target of the problem; some opponents of traditional theism who believe in the existence of an omnipotent and wholly good being (or a being that is sufficiently powerful and good) other than God are susceptible to the problem of evil. The problem of evil is also a problem that hits targets that lie beyond traditional theism in a more significant sense because it is a version of the problem of axiological expectation mismatch, which arises from any apparent conflict between our expectation based on a metaphysical view and our observation of reality in relation to evil. We have seen that not only the problem of evil itself but also existing responses to the problem of evil can be construed within this framework. More specifically, these responses can be construed as attempts to fill or explain away a gap between our expectation and our observation of reality. Our expectation here does not have to be based on traditional theism; it can be based on any relevant worldview.

What we have seen suggests that variable (i) in our scheme should not be limited to belief in God but should represent a more general view concerning how reality should be understood in relation to evil. Accordingly, variable (iii) should also not be limited to an allegedly conflicting relationship between God specifically and evil but should extend to an allegedly conflicting relationship between a broad worldview and evil. In the following chapters, I consider specific atheistic/non-theistic worldviews and argue that the problem of evil arises for their proponents.

Philonous, a character in Berkeley's *Three Dialogues*, claims, 'But, to arm you against all future objections, do but consider: That which bears equally hard on two contradictory opinions can be proof against neither' (Berkeley 1979/1713, p. 91). This claim suggests the following principle: an argument against all is no argument against one. For example, if there is an argument that undermines physicalism, dualism, and idealism, then physicalists cannot undermine idealism by appealing to it. If I succeed in showing in the present book that the problem of evil arises for atheism/non-theism as well as traditional theism, then atheists/non-theists who reject traditional theism by appealing to the problem of evil violate this principle.[21]

---

[21] Philonous's principle may be too simplistic because it may be the case that, while the problem of evil arises for many metaphysical views, it poses a more significant challenge to a certain view than others. I argue throughout the present book that the problem of evil does not pose a more significant challenge for traditional theism than its alternatives because traditional theism enjoys greater advantages than its alternatives for developing a response to the problem.

PART II

THE PROBLEM OF EVIL FOR PANTHEISTS AND AXIARCHISTS

3
The Problem of Evil for Pantheists

3.1 Introduction

We have seen so far that the scope of the problem of evil is much broader than we commonly assume and that its target is not limited to traditional theism. The problem arises when there is a discrepancy between our expectation about evil in the actual world and our observation that conflicts with that expectation. Such an expectation is typically derived from traditional theism, but it does not have to be; it can be derived from an atheistic or non-theistic view as well.

In this chapter, I focus on pantheism, one of the major alternatives to traditional theism. I introduce a version of the problem of evil, which I call the 'divinity problem of evil', and explain how it applies to both pantheism and traditional theism. I discuss possible pantheistic strategies for responding to the problem but argue that they do not succeed. I try to show that traditional theists enjoy advantages over pantheists in responding to the problem.

This chapter has the following structure. In Section 3.2, I discuss traditional theism and its alternatives, including panentheism, pantheism, axiarchism, and atheism. In Section 3.3, I explain why I set aside pan*en*theism in the present book. After that, I focus on pantheism. In Section 3.4, I discuss Michael Levine's claim that the problem of evil as commonly discussed in the literature does not arise for pantheists because it is a problem that arises uniquely for traditional theists. In Section 3.5, I introduce the divinity problem of evil, which targets pantheists' claim that God, as the world or the all-inclusive unity, is divine. In Section 3.6, I discuss how pantheists can respond to the divinity problem of evil by developing an experiential approach to divinity. In Section 3.7, I argue that this approach does not succeed. In Section 3.8, I consider how pantheists may try to respond to the divinity problem of evil by pursuing a non-experiential approach to divinity but argue that this approach also does not succeed. In Section 3.9, I explain advantages that traditional theists enjoy over pantheists in addressing the divinity problem of evil. In Section 3.10, I introduce what I call multiverse

The Problem of Evil for Atheists. Yujin Nagasawa, Oxford University Press. © Yujin Nagasawa 2024.
DOI: 10.1093/oso/9780198901884.003.0004

56 THE PROBLEM OF EVIL FOR ATHEISTS

pantheism and explain how it enables pantheists to develop a non-experiential approach to divinity in a more plausible way. In Section 3.11, I argue that multiverse pantheism avoids many shortcomings of standard pantheism. In Section 3.12, I argue that multiverse pantheists can offer plausible responses to the general problem of evil and other forms of the problem of axiological expectation mismatch. In Section 3.13, however, I argue that even multiverse pantheists cannot avoid the problem of evil because a specific version of the problem arises for them. This version is, in fact, the most extreme version of the problem of evil. In Section 3.14, I critically discuss possible responses that multiverse pantheists might offer and argue that none of them succeeds. Section 3.15 concludes.

3.2 Traditional Theism and Its Alternatives

The most straightforward method for distinguishing traditional theism from its alternatives entails examining the ontological relationship each posits between God and the world. While some critics may find this classification problematic (Göcke 2013, Mullins 2016), I maintain that it offers a valuable initial framework for our purposes in the present book. Attempting to differentiate all variations of alternative views through this simple classification is neither feasible nor practical. Nevertheless, by relying on this classification we can effectively discern how the problem of evil emerges across a range of perspectives.

Consider first *traditional theism*. This view says that God and the world are ontologically distinct (Figure 3.1). The term 'world' here is vague, but for now we can assume that a world is roughly equivalent to the spatiotemporal universe in which we exist, rather than a world as conceived in possible-world semantics. I address this terminological issue in greater detail in Section 3.10. Traditional theists believe that God is ontologically prior to the world in the sense that God's existence does not depend on the existence of the world.[1] They believe that, as a matter of fact, God existed without the world before creation.

---

[1] Along with traditional theism, deism says that God created the world and that, hence, God and the world are ontologically distinct. Deism is distinct from traditional theism, however, because it does not allow for divine intervention beyond the initial creation of the world. I do not discuss deism in the present book because of limited space. However, many of the claims that I make about traditional theism apply to deism. For a recent defence of deism, see Leland Royce Harper (2020).

THE PROBLEM OF EVIL FOR PANTHEISTS   57

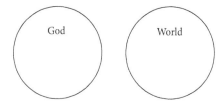

Figure 3.1 Traditional theism

Pantheism says that God and the world are identical (Figure 3.2). It is not that God created the world. God is immanent in the sense that the whole world *is* God. It is important to note that, in the present book, by 'pantheism' I mean naturalistic pantheism, which does not postulate anything supernatural.[2]

Figure 3.2 Pantheism

Panentheism can be seen as a hybrid of traditional theism and pantheism. According to this view, the world exists within God or the world is a proper part of God. However, unlike pantheism, panentheism denies the identity of the world with God. God is therefore immanent in the world, but He also transcends it (Figure 3.3).[3]

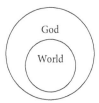

Figure 3.3 Panentheism

A view that reverses the God–world relationship in panentheism is what Paul Draper calls *merotheism* (Draper, forthcoming). According to this

---

[2] For a detailed, critical assessment of naturalistic pantheism, see Brian Leftow (2016).
[3] One may try to formulate panentheism in terms of the constitution relation. Arguably, a statue is not identical to the materials that constitute it because the materials can exist while the statue does not. Similarly, one may argue that the panentheistic God is not identical to the world, but the world constitutes God. Thanks to an anonymous referee for drawing my attention to this formulation. This formulation of panentheism may be susceptible to the problem of evil for pantheism that I discuss in the present chapter.

view, God exists within the world, or He is a proper part of the world (Figure 3.4). Perhaps God has emerged as a product of a natural, evolutionary process in the world.[4]

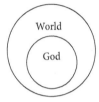

Figure 3.4 Merotheism

Axiarchism, at least the version which I address in this book, says that the world exists not because God created it, but because an abstract 'creatively effective ethical requirement' necessitated its existence (Figure 3.5).

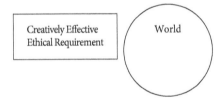

Figure 3.5 Axiarchism

Atheism is the view that the world exists but God does not exist. Atheists can in principle deny the existence of the world as well, but I set aside such a view because very few atheists defend it.(Figure 3.6)

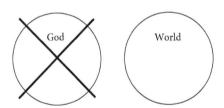

Figure 3.6 Atheism

The view that reverses the God–world relationship in atheism is *acosmism*. According to this view, only God exists and the world does not (or, *ultimately*, only God exists and the world does not) (Figure 3.7).

---

[4] Emily Thomas (2016) argues that Samuel Alexander's view can be construed as merotheism.

THE PROBLEM OF EVIL FOR PANTHEISTS 59

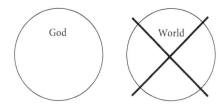

Figure 3.7 Acosmism

The above list does not include *polytheism*. Polytheism is the view that there is more than one god. This means that polytheism negates atheism, according to which the number of gods is exactly zero, and monotheism, according to which the number of gods is exactly one. Polytheism says that the number of gods is two or more. This suggests that there are infinitely many variations of polytheism because the term polytheism covers all views that hold that the number of gods is anything between two and infinity.[5] Polytheism itself does not specify the relationship between gods and the world. Hence, there can be polytheistic counterparts of such views as traditional theism, pantheism, panentheism, merotheism, and acosmism. More unusual versions of polytheism, such as the view that some gods are part of the world and some others are not, or that there is a certain god that is identical with the world and other gods that exist as part of the world, can also be formulated. There is also *henotheism*, which postulates many gods but ascribes supremacy to only one of them. In the present book, to avoid unnecessary complications in our discussion, I do not address any version of polytheism. Many of the claims I make about traditional theism and its monotheistic or atheistic alternatives apply, however, to polytheistic counterparts with appropriate adjustments. I also set aside merotheism and acosmism because they have very few contemporary proponents. This leaves us with five views: traditional theism, panentheism, pantheism, axiarchism, and atheism. I believe that it helps to place these views along the following spectrum that illustrates the resemblances between their accounts of the relationship between the world and God:

Traditional theism → Panentheism → Pantheism → Axiarchism → Atheism

Crudely speaking, on this spectrum a view that falls on the left side is more similar to traditional theism than a view that falls on the right side.

---

[5] According to Shinto, for instance, there are as many as seven million gods or *kami*. It is disputable, however, whether this assertion should be taken literally or whether Shinto truly qualifies as a polytheic religion in the Western sense.

60   THE PROBLEM OF EVIL FOR ATHEISTS

Axiarchism is more similar to traditional theism than atheism in the sense that it explains the existence of the world by appealing to something beyond the material or spatiotemporal universe. Pantheism is more similar to traditional theism than axiarchism in the sense that it affirms the existence of God. Panentheism is more similar to traditional theism than pantheism in the sense that it postulates a God that transcends the world. Throughout the present book, by 'non-theism' I mean any view like pantheism, panentheism, axiarchism, and atheism which rejects traditional theism. By 'non-theists' I mean proponents of any of these views. Non-theism is not, in itself, incompatible with supernaturalism. Throughout the present book, however, by 'non-theism' I mean naturalistic non-theism, which rejects supernaturalism because most non-theists are indeed naturalists.

3.3 Why I Set Panentheism Aside

We have seen in Chapters 1 and 2 many versions of the problem of evil which arise for traditional theists. I do not think that any of them categorically refutes traditional theism, but they raise a significant challenge, which may motivate traditional theists to consider alternative views. In the spectrum above, the view that sits next to traditional theism is panentheism. If we are attracted to traditional theism but find it problematic, panentheism therefore seems to be an obvious choice. However, I do not discuss panentheism in the present book for several reasons.

First, it is difficult to address panentheism as a single view within my space limitations because there are very many distinct versions of it. *Pantheism* is clear about the relationship between God and the world: they are identical with each other. However, the 'en' part of pan*en*theism generates controversy even within the panentheist circle. Panentheists typically advocate the rich presence of God in the world while maintaining the ontological distinction between God and the world. There are, however, numerous formulations in which panentheists understand the relationship between God and the world. Some of these formulations are similar to traditional theism while others are akin to pantheism. There are also distinct formulations that remain vague about the precise relationship between God and the world. Philip Clayton, for instance, lists as many as thirteen distinct versions of panentheism: participatory panentheism, 'divine energies' panentheism, ecclesial or communal panentheism, eschatological panentheism,

THE PROBLEM OF EVIL FOR PANTHEISTS   61

sapiential panentheism, emergentist panentheism, sacramental panentheism, Trinitarian panentheism, pan-sacramental naturalistic panentheism, process or dipolar panentheism, 'Body of God' panentheism, neopanentheism, and pansyntheism (Clayton 2004, p. 250).[6]

Second, related to the above point, there is no consensus among panentheists regarding its precise definition or regarding its necessary and sufficient conditions. R. T. Mullins (2016) writes, 'One of the most notorious difficulties for panentheism is its vagueness. It is incredibly difficult to pin down exactly what panentheism is and how it differs from rival models of God' (Mullins 2016, p. 325). In fact, many recent papers focus on the difficulty of determining what panentheism is rather than assessing whether panentheism is true (Georg Gasser 2019, Raphael Lataster and Purushottama Bilimoria 2018, Mullins 2016, Gregory R. Peterson 2004, Mikael Stenmark 2018). Benedikt Paul Göcke (2015) goes so far as to say that, because there are so many distinct ways of understanding key claims made by panentheists, there is no clear research programme or paradigm of panentheism upon which all panentheists can agree.

Third, most importantly, one of the aims of the present book is to show that the problem of evil arises for proponents of alternatives to traditional theism who do not normally consider the problem to be a challenge for them. Panentheists have however already addressed the problem of evil intensively.[7] Hence, the claim that the problem of evil arises for panentheists is not news to them. Another aim of the present book is to argue that supernaturalists enjoy advantages over naturalists in responding to the problem of evil because they can utilize supernaturalist resources which naturalists lack. This argument does not apply to all versions of panentheism, however, because, like traditional theism, many versions of panentheism are understood as forms of supernaturalism. In this sense, panentheism

---

[6] Clayton also addresses a list of thirteen distinct interpretations of the core thesis of panentheism, according to which the world is 'in' God: (1) The world is God's literal location, (2) God energizes the world, (2) God experiences or 'prehends' the world, (3) God ensouls the world, (5) God plays with the world, (6) God 'enfields' the world, (7) God gives space to the world, (8) God encompasses or contains the world, (9) God binds up the world by giving the divine self to the world, (10) God provides the ground for emergence in, or the emergence of, the world, (11) God befriends the world, (12) All things are contained 'in Christ', and (13) God graces the world (Clayton 2004, p. 253; this list was originally created by Thomas Oord).
[7] For recent discussions of panentheism and the problem of evil, see Robin Attfield (2019), John Bishop (1998), John Bishop and Ken Perszyk (2016), Benedikt Paul Göcke (2019), and Chad Meister (2017).

62   THE PROBLEM OF EVIL FOR ATHEISTS

is largely on a par with traditional theism with respect to my approach to the problem of evil. Throughout the present book, therefore, I focus mainly on the three remaining views: pantheism, axiarchism, and atheism.

3.4 Pantheism and the Problem of Evil

I have explained above that pantheism is the view that God and the world are identical. I have also noted that by pantheism I mean naturalistic pantheism, which does not postulate any supernatural entities in its ontology. This observation is still, however, not informative enough to advance our discussion. I add to the above, therefore, Alasdair MacIntyre's formulation of pantheism: '[E]verything that exists constitutes a unity and... this all-inclusive unity is divine' (MacIntyre 1967, p. 34). This formulation is widely accepted among pantheists, and it is also adopted in Michael Levine's book *Pantheism: A Non-Theistic Concept of Deity*, which is by far the most comprehensive monograph on pantheism in contemporary analytic philosophy of religion (Levine 1994a, p. 25). This formulation can be divided into the following two theses:

The unity thesis: everything that exists constitutes a unity.
The divinity thesis: the all-inclusive unity is divine.

The 'all-inclusive unity' corresponds to the world or the spatiotemporal universe in which we live. Hence, the unity thesis says that the world exists as the all-inclusive unity and the divinity thesis says that this unity is divine (and, hence, that it should be considered God).

The claim that pantheists face a version of the problem of evil is not entirely new. H. P. Owen, for example, writes:

Pantheists are bound to find the fact of evil (and especially moral evil) an enormous embarrassment. It is difficult enough to square this fact with belief in an omnipotent and infinitely loving Creator. It is much more difficult to square it with the view that an evil world is an actual expression of God's perfect nature. (Owen 1971, p. 72)

Levine disagrees with Owen's allegation. He contends that the problem of evil 'is a uniquely theistic problem and one that the pantheist can shrug off since its formulation entails an essentially [traditional] theistic doctrine of deity' (Levine 1994a, p. 217).

THE PROBLEM OF EVIL FOR PANTHEISTS   63

Levine maintains that the problem of evil consists of the following three propositions:

(1) There is God who is omnipotent, omniscient and wholly good.[8]
(2) God would prevent all preventable evil.
(3) The world contains preventable evil.

(Levine 1994a, p. 207)

Levine claims that pantheists accept proposition (3). They acknowledge, like most people, that the world includes pain and suffering that are preventable. He also claims that pantheists accept proposition (2) on the condition that it is construed as a counterfactual thesis: *if* there was an omnipotent, omniscient, and wholly good God, He would prevent all preventable evil. Levine claims, however, that pantheists reject proposition (1). Pantheism is distinct from traditional theism so there is no reason for pantheists to believe that the pantheistic God, that is, the world or the all-inclusive unity, is omnipotent, omniscient, and wholly good. He writes:

> ... since there is no such God why suppose that proposition (3) requires a special explanation or is cause for any conceptual or spiritual malaise on the part of the pantheist—as it is for some theists? For all that has been said thus far, the existence of preventable evil, does not even constitute a *prima facie* reason for rejecting either the probability of the existence of the pantheistic all-inclusive divine Unity, or the coherence of the notion. (3) is not incompatible with anything the pantheist believes to be true. It is not compatible with (1) since the pantheist denies the truth of (1), and it is not incompatible with (2), which is only hypothetically true for the pantheist. The pantheist has no need *either* to explain evil, or to *explain evil away*—at least not in any way resembling theism's need to do so. (Levine 1994b, p. 137, emphasis in the original)

Levine concludes, therefore, that the problem of evil is a problem only for traditional theists who believe that God as an omniscient, omnipotent, and wholly good being exists. Levine's point here is reminiscent of Mackie's

---

[8] To make it explicit that the first proposition concerns the *existence* of God, I have modified Levine's formulation slightly. His original statement is 'God is omnipotent, omniscient and perfectly good'. Additionally, I have replaced Levine's term 'perfectly good' with 'wholly good' to make it consistent with my terminology.

64 THE PROBLEM OF EVIL FOR ATHEISTS

claim which we discussed in Chapters 1 and 2: 'The problem of evil, in the sense in which I shall be using the phrase, is a problem only for someone who believes that there is a God who is both omnipotent and wholly good' (Mackie 1955, p. 200).

In Chapter 2 of the present book, I argued that the problem of evil is a version of the problem of axiological expectation mismatch, which arises when there is a mismatch between our expectation of how the world should be and our observation of how it actually is. Levine thinks that such a mismatch arises only for traditional theists, not for pantheists. Evil is not a surprise for pantheists because they do not believe in the existence of a God who is good or benevolent enough to want to eliminate evil and has the knowledge and power needed to deliver elimination. More generally speaking, pantheists are not committed to any mechanism which would eliminate evil in the world. Levine concludes, therefore, that the problem of evil does not arise for pantheists.

I agree with Levine that the problem of evil *for traditional theists* does not arise for pantheists. However, a crucial question is whether there can be a distinct version of the problem of evil which applies to pantheism. In what follows, I defend what I call the 'divinity problem of evil', a unique version of the problem of evil which does apply to pantheism.

3.5 The Divinity Problem of Evil for Pantheists

The 'divinity problem of evil' challenges pantheists by saying that the following two pantheist theses are in conflict: (i) the world or the all-inclusive unity is divine and (ii) evil of considerable quantity and quality is realized in the world. Claim (i) corresponds to the divinity thesis and claim (ii) is based on our observation of reality. Take the most horrendous instance of evil that has been realized. According to pantheism, such an instance is part of the divine because, by definition, everything actual is part of the all-inclusive unity, which pantheists consider to be divine. Many horrible events take place but, according to pantheists, none of them affects the divinity of the world even though they constitute a portion of the unity. In fact, no *possible* state of affairs can undermine the divinity of the unity; whatever is realized is part of the divine, all-inclusive unity. The divinity problem says that this is a counterintuitive implication of pantheism. Either pantheism relies on a skewed conception of divinity or it does not take evil seriously.

THE PROBLEM OF EVIL FOR PANTHEISTS   65

In Chapter 1 of the present book, I argued that the problem of evil consists of three variables: (i) God, (ii) evil, and (iii) the allegedly conflicting relationship between God and evil. What I have shown is that variable (i) does not have to have an omnipotent and wholly good being as conceived in traditional theism assigned to it; if the pantheistic God, that is, the world or the all-inclusive unity, is assigned to it the divinity problem of evil for pantheists arises. The divinity problem of evil suggests that there is an axiological expectation mismatch for pantheists because evil is not expected to be part of the divine, all-inclusive unity.

Levine anticipates the divinity problem of evil and responds to it as follows:

> In theism it is assumed that what is divine cannot also be (in part) evil. But why assume this is the case with pantheism? Even in Otto's account of the 'holy' the holy has a demonic aspect. There seems little reason to suppose that what is divine cannot also, in part, be evil. At any rate, there is little reason for the pantheist to argue that what is divine can also be evil, since they can deny that evil falls within the purview of the divine Unity. To say that everything that exists constitutes a divine Unity (i.e. pantheism's essential claim) need not be interpreted in such a way that it entails that all parts and every aspect of the Unity is divine or good. There can be a Unity and it can be divine without everything about it always, or even sometimes, being divine. (Levine 1994a, p. 208)

Levine makes mainly two points in the above passage. The first point is that the fact that the all-inclusive unity contains evil does not undermine its divinity or holiness because the divine or holy can have evil aspects.[9] The second point is that the pantheist claim that the all-inclusive unity is divine does not entail that all constituents of the unity and their aspects are divine. I agree with Levine on these two points. Regarding the first point, even traditional theists commonly believe that God can have frightening or terrifying aspects without compromising God's divinity. If traditional theists are right about this there seems no reason that pantheists have to give up the divinity of the world because of its 'demonic' or evil aspects.[10] Regarding the

---

[9] The focus of Otto's work (1917) which Levine quotes is on holiness rather than divinity but, following Levine, I set aside the difference between the two and assume that they are sufficiently similar for our purposes.

[10] Some traditional theists may argue that when they discuss the frightening or terrifying aspects of God, they do not intend to imply that these aspects are bad or evil. They represent God's significance in contrast with our human finitude. On the other hand, pantheists must

66 THE PROBLEM OF EVIL FOR ATHEISTS

second point, critics of pantheism cannot assume that the divinity of the all-inclusive unity entails the divinity of all of its constituents because such an assumption would commit the decomposition fallacy. The inference from the thesis that the all-inclusive unity is divine to the conclusion that every constituent of the unity is also divine is analogous to, for example, the fallacious inference from the fact that an aeroplane can fly to the conclusion that every part of the aeroplane can also fly.

I argue, however, that pantheists do not succeed in responding to the divinity problem of evil by appealing to the above two points. What these points suggest is that the all-inclusive unity can in principle include certain instances of evil as its constituents without undermining its divinity. This does not however entail that no instance of evil can undermine it. In fact, Levine's own claim that the divine can be evil *in part* implies that he thinks that divinity can be undermined by evil even within the pantheistic framework. The all-inclusive unity cannot be divine if it is entirely evil or includes too much evil in quality or quantity. Hence, even though pantheists distance themselves from the theistic concept of God as an omniscient, omnipotent, and wholly good being, they cannot dismiss the problem of evil.

The divinity problem is a version of the problem of axiological expectation mismatch. Pantheism says that the world is divine, yet our observation shows that there is evil of considerable quantity and quality in the world, which seems to be in conflict with divinity. Hence, there is a gap between pantheists' axiological expectation of how the world should be and how it actually is.

It is important to note that while the divinity problem of evil is a challenge for pantheists, it is also a challenge for traditional theists. Traditional theists hold that God is divine and the world was created by God. It is natural to infer then that the world represents God's divinity. However, the world includes evil of considerable quantity and quality. Hence, there exists a gap between the anticipated state of the world as envisioned by traditional theists (as well as pantheists) and the reality they observe. In the following two sections (3.6 and 3.7), I introduce an attempt to defend pantheism from the divinity problem of evil by appealing to experience but argue that it fails. In Sections 3.8 and 3.9, I argue that traditional theists enjoy advantages over pantheists in responding to the divinity problem of evil.

---

affirm that not only the frightening or terrifying aspects but evil itself is part of the world or the all-inclusive unity. In this regard, the problem of evil seems to be more significant for pantheists than traditional theists. Thanks to an anonymous referee on this point.

3.6 The Experiential Response to the Divinity Problem of Evil

How can pantheists respond to the divinity problem of evil? That is, how can pantheists establish that the world or the all-inclusive unity is divine despite the considerable quality and quantity of evil it includes? Levine recommends appealing to experience:

> Why do pantheists ascribe divinity to the Unity? The reason is similar to why theists describe God as holy. They experience it as such. In Otto's experiential account, what is divine is what evokes the numinous experience. This can be a theistic god, but it can also be a pantheistic Unity. (Levine 1994a, p. 48)

Levine accepts Otto's claim that the holy is a sui generis category which is irreducible and primitive (Levine 1994a, p. 48). Levine writes, 'Not all pantheists mean by "divine" what Otto means. However, it is plausible to suppose that, for many, the pantheistic intuition and ground for attributing divinity to the Unity (i.e., the pantheist's intimations of divinity) rests on numinous experience or something like it' (Levine 1994a, p. 58). Levine says that pantheists can defend the thesis that the all-inclusive unity is divine because they experience the world as such, in the same way that traditional theists defend the thesis that God is divine because they experience God as such. Levine thinks that this appeal to experience is a good reason for pantheists to believe that the world is divine (despite the existence of evil), or at least as good as traditional theists' appeal to experience in justifying their belief that an omniscient, omnipotent, and wholly good God is divine (despite the existence of evil).

Levine argues that even though the concept of divinity is often associated with traditional theism, it does not have to be. He writes that while Otto treats the Christian (Lutheran) God as the apotheosis of the holy, the holy includes 'more than God and more than one kind of god' (Levine 1994a, p. 48). Saying that the all-inclusive unity is divine, therefore, does not imply that the world is similar to God according to traditional theism. If experience is considered to be reliable and if pantheists have genuine numinous experience of the world's being divine, then, according to Levine, pantheists are justified in believing that the world is divine; and, hence, the divinity problem of evil disappears.

I argue in the next section, however, that pantheists cannot dismiss the divinity problem of evil merely by appealing to experience.

68   THE PROBLEM OF EVIL FOR ATHEISTS

3.7 Difficulties with Pantheists' Experiential Response to the Divinity Problem of Evil

We have seen the pantheists' attempt to respond to the divinity problem of evil by appealing to their experience of the world or the all-inclusive unity as divine. I do not reject this experiential approach entirely. In this section, however, I explain the limitations of this approach and argue that it is at best incomplete as a response to the divinity problem of evil.

First, it is unclear how the experiential approach can respond directly to the divinity problem of evil. This problem is, again, a version of the problem of axiological expectation mismatch. Here, pantheists need to fill a gap between their expectation of the world based on pantheism and the actual state of the world according to their observation. Unfortunately, the experiential approach merely provides experiential evidence for pantheism. While this evidence might be sufficient to outweigh the problem of evil, it does not explain how the gap can be filled.

Second, if pantheists appeal solely to experience to defend the divinity of the world, they face a version of the so-called atheism in disguise objection to pantheism. Recall that by pantheism we mean naturalistic pantheism, which denies the existence of supernatural entities. This is an ontological view that most atheists also accept. If pantheists' attribution of divinity to the world is solely experiential, then there is very little difference, if any, between pantheism and atheism (or at least a version of atheism which postulates the all-inclusive unity). Pantheists experience the world as divine while atheists do not; apart from that, there is no metaphysical difference between their views. Hence, pantheism seems to be a disguised form of atheism.

The difference between pantheism and atheism is small enough if the only difference between them is entirely experiential. The difference may be even smaller, though, because some atheists claim to have experiences that are comparable to pantheists' experiences. Consider the following quote from the atheist Richard Dawkins:

> When I lie on my back and look up at the Milky Way on a clear night and see the vast distances of space and reflect that these are also vast differences of time as well, when I look at the Grand Canyon and see the strata going down, down, down, through periods of time when the human mind can't comprehend, I'm overwhelmingly filled with a sense of, almost worship... it's a feeling of sort of an abstract gratitude that I am alive to appreciate

these wonders. When I look down a microscope it's the same feeling: I am grateful to be alive to appreciate these wonders. (Dawkins 2009)

Dawkins also remarked in his lecture 'The Greatest Show on Earth', delivered at the University of Auckland in 2010, that 'We have cause to give thanks for our highly improbable existence, and the law-like evolutionary processes that gave rise to it. Such gratitude is not owed to, or to be directed towards, anyone or anything'.

Dawkins, as an atheist, recognizes through his own experience that the world is a remarkable and special place which deserves attitudes that are akin to awe, worship, and gratitude. Here, there seems to be very little difference between pantheism and atheism, not only with respect to ontology but also with respect to experience. The only difference seems to be that pantheists hold full-fledged religious attitudes towards the world while atheists like Dawkins hold quasi-religious attitudes towards it.

A similar worry about appealing solely to the experiential approach to divinity is raised by William Mander:

> Most straightforwardly it has been maintained that the One is holy because we feel a particular set of religious emotions towards it. . . . For Rudolf Otto (1917) whatever is holy or 'numinous' is so characterised on the basis of our non-rational, non-sensory experience of it rather than its own objective features and, taking its departure from Otto's work, one approach has been to argue that the feelings of awe which people feel towards God can be, and often are, applied to the universe itself . . . [T]he chief point to make here concerns the extreme subjectivism of this response; it's coming to rest upon feelings which, while sincere enough, indicate nothing whatsoever about the universe itself. On this view, all that distinguishes a pantheist from an atheist is feeling; a certain emotional reaction or connection that we feel to the universe. It would become akin, say, to the difference between one who loves art and another who is relatively indifferent to it. Prima facie, however, this approach puts the cart before the horse; rather than say that the One is divine because we feel a set of religious emotions towards it, it seems more appropriate to suppose that we feel those emotions towards it because we think it is divine. (Mander 2020)

As Mander says, if pantheists hold that it is only a matter of feeling that they consider the all-inclusive unity to be God, then pantheism is only a subjective view without any metaphysical foundation. If this is correct, pantheism

70 THE PROBLEM OF EVIL FOR ATHEISTS

amounts to not much more than atheism with an added assertion, 'the all-inclusive unity is God because we feel it as such'. The point here is not that pantheism is false because the experiential approach is untenable. It is rather that if pantheists appeal *solely* to experience, then pantheism is only a matter of taste without any metaphysical foundation. In sum: if pantheists try to avoid the divinity problem of evil by appealing to experience alone, they face the 'atheism in disguise' objection. Conversely, pantheists can succeed in avoiding the divinity problem of evil only by collapsing their view into atheism.

Pascal famously wrote in *Pensées*, 'If we submit everything to reason, our religion will have no mysterious and supernatural element. If we offend the principles of reason, our religion will be absurd and ridiculous' (Pascal 1670/1958, section IV, 273, p. 78). This quote highlights the limit of appealing solely to experience in defending divinity. Pascal has only traditional theism in mind in the above assertion, but his point applies equally to pantheism.

Pantheists might argue at this point that there is a substantial difference between pantheism and atheism because while pantheists can consider the world to be worship-worthy, atheists cannot. This is evident in the above quote by Dawkins, where he says that he embraces a feeling that is *almost* worship when he appreciates the beauty of nature. However, this only raises a further question for pantheists: on what ground can pantheists consider the world to be worship-worthy if the difference between pantheism and atheism is entirely experiential?[11]

3.8 Pantheists' Non-Experiential Approach

We have seen that pantheists cannot succeed in responding to the divinity problem of evil by appealing to experience alone. This appeal to experience, as we have seen, makes pantheism a disguised version of atheism. Pantheists therefore need a non-experiential approach to divinity which supplements their experiential approach. A non-experiential approach should explain, without appealing to experience, why we should consider the all-inclusive unity to be divine despite the existence of evil.

---

[11] Elsewhere I have argued with Tim Bayne for the difficulty of finding the ground of worship-worthiness (in relation to traditional theism). See Bayne and Nagasawa (2006, 2007). See also Wesley D. Cray (2011), Benjamin Crowe (2007), John Danaher (2012), Jeremy Gwiazda (2011), and Aaron Smuts (2012).

THE PROBLEM OF EVIL FOR PANTHEISTS   71

Recall Levine's claim that pantheists' experiential approach is analogous to traditional theists' experiential approach. Pantheists claim that the all-inclusive unity is divine because they experience it as such, in a manner similar to that in which traditional theists claim that God is divine because they experience God as such. It is worth considering whether pantheists can also develop a non-experiential approach that is analogous to traditional theists' non-experiential approach.

Traditional theists believe that a being's overall greatness is determined in reference to individual great-making properties, such as knowledge, power, and goodness. God is the greatest possible being, according to them, because God has the greatest possible extent of knowledge (omniscience), power (omnipotent), and goodness (omnibenevolence). They believe that God is divine because God is supremely excellent or the greatest possible in this sense. Pantheists may parallel this reasoning and claim that God, as the all-inclusive unity, is divine because it is supremely excellent or the greatest possible albeit based on an alternative, pantheistic understanding of greatness.

What then is the pantheistic understanding of greatness? As we saw earlier, pantheism consists of two theses: the unity thesis, according to which everything that exists constitutes a unity, and the divinity thesis, according to which the all-inclusive unity is divine. The divinity thesis merely states that the all-inclusive unity is divine, so it gives us no hint regarding how greatness should be understood in the pantheistic frame-work. This means that we have to find a hint in the unity thesis. The unity thesis implies that the world is divine not merely because it is a unity, but also because it is an *all-inclusive* unity. In other words, the world is supremely excellent because it is the most encompassing unity—it includes everything. There is nothing beyond the unity and everything is part of the unity. By 'encompassment', we mean the inclusion of an entity as part of one's own being. This unique and extreme form of encompassment is the property which distinguishes the world from everything else. No component of the all-inclusive unity, including any 'proper sub-unity', is as encompass-ing as the all-inclusive unity itself. This idea can inspire pantheists to develop a non-experiential approach to divinity by associating encompass-ment with divinity. According to this approach, greatness should be under-stood not in terms of degrees of such great-making properties as knowledge, power, and goodness, but in terms of the degree of encompassment.

The non-experiential approach based on the notion of encompassment is consistent with how pantheists typically motivate their view. For instance,

72 THE PROBLEM OF EVIL FOR ATHEISTS

Balbus, Cicero's character in *The Nature of Gods* who defRends Stoic pantheism, remarks as follows:

> The various creatures of the universe may meet with many external obstacles to their perfect development. But no obstacle can frustrate the development of the universe itself. The universe moulds and *embraces all things*. Therefore, we must admit the existence of that fourth and final stage of being, which no power can assail. This is the stage of being on which the whole of nature depends. It is thus above all things and nothing has any power against it, and is the universal dwelling-place of reason and of wisdom.
>
> What could be more stupid than to deny that *supreme excellence* to that universal nature which *embraces all things*?. (Cicero 45 BC/1972, p. 137, emphasis added)

Balbus also says:

> [T]he universe itself, which *embraces all things* and apart from which there is nothing, is perfect in every way. How then can it lack the *greatest excellence* of all? And as there is nothing superior to mind and reason, these must be present in the world. (Cicero 45 BC/1972, p. 137, emphasis added)

In the above passages, Balbus suggests that the world or the all-inclusive unity should be considered supremely excellent because it encompasses everything and there is nothing beyond it. By appealing to the concept of encompassment in this way, pantheists can conclude that the all-inclusive unity is divine because it is the most encompassing existence. One may therefore conclude that this non-experiential approach complements the experiential approach, allowing pantheists to respond to the divinity problem of evil without collapsing pantheism into atheism.

Unfortunately, however, there are at least two reasons why the non-experiential approach falls short. First, because of its spatiotemporal limitations, the all-inclusive unity in question is not sufficiently encompassing. Empirical data suggest that our universe, that is, the all-inclusive unity according to pantheism, began to exist approximately 13.5 billion years ago and it is, although expanding, finite in size. Scientists also suggest that our universe will cease to exist eventually as it collapses into the Big Crunch. If they are right, then the world as understood by pantheists is not the most encompassing unity possible. It is limited in space and time.

THE PROBLEM OF EVIL FOR PANTHEISTS   73

Second, the all-inclusive unity is not sufficiently encompassing because it has modal limitations. While it may be the case that nothing *is* more encompassing than the world, it is not the case that nothing *can* be more encompassing than the world. The world encompasses many things, but there are infinitely many other possible things that the world could have encompassed. That is, there are many possible worlds that are more encompassing than our world. Hence, even if we assume that greatness should be determined in terms of encompassment, the world is not the supremely excellent or most fully encompassing possible unity. Even if we agree with pantheists that extreme encompassment can make its bearer divine, the world is still not divine or supremely excellent.

Pantheists may reject the above observation by arguing that the proposed non-experiential approach erroneously mimics the way traditional theists think about divinity. Levine in fact claims that many existing objections to pantheism are based on 'a quasi-theistic notion of deity', which pantheists normally reject (Levine 1994a, p. 145). However, if pantheists give up the 'quasi-theistic notion', they do not seem to be able to find any non-experiential ground of the divinity of the all-inclusive unity.

I conclude that the divinity problem of evil remains a strong challenge for pantheists.

3.9 The Advantage of Traditional Theism Over Pantheism

As I have mentioned above, the divinity problem of evil arises not only for pantheists but also for traditional theists. It would therefore be unfair to raise the divinity problem of evil to challenge pantheists without raising it for traditional theists as well. Traditional theists have to explain how they can maintain the divinity of God as an omniscient, omnipotent, and wholly good being given that God's creation includes evil of considerable quantity and quality. I argue, however, that traditional theists enjoy advantages over pantheists in responding to the divinity problem of evil; conversely, the problem is more pressing for pantheists than for traditional theists.

First, as we saw in Section 3.2, traditional theists hold that the world and God are ontologically distinct. There is certainly a link between God and the world as God's creation, but such a link is only indirect. In the same way that a painter and her painting do not overlap ontologically, God and the world

74 THE PROBLEM OF EVIL FOR ATHEISTS

do not overlap ontologically, according to traditional theism. It is not entirely obvious that a painting must be divine if the painter is divine. Similarly, it is not entirely obvious that the world according to traditional theism has to be divine if God is divine. On the other hand, pantheists hold that the world *is* God, so there is no creator–creation division here. According to pantheism, the world and God cannot be detached because they have the most intimate relationship possible: identity. Evil is part of the world and the world *is* God. It is as if in the pantheistic framework the painting itself *is* the painter. Hence, while traditional theists may be able to avoid the divinity problem of evil by appealing to the ontological gap between God and the world, pantheists may not.

Second, traditional theists have developed many responses to the standard problem of evil, which they can also apply to the divinity problem of evil. For example, they can appeal to the free will theodicy as a solution to the divinity problem of evil by saying that the divinity of God is not in conflict with evil because God wanted to create a world which includes morally significant freedom and that evil is an outcome of humans', rather than God's, misuse of freedom. They can also appeal to the soul-making theodicy by saying that the divinity of God is not in conflict with evil because God intended to create a world in which humans can grow spiritually and evil is necessary for spiritual growth beyond life on earth. They can also appeal to sceptical theism by saying that, while our epistemic limitations do not allow us to comprehend God's reason fully, evil is necessary in God's grand scheme beyond what we can observe. Pantheists cannot respond to the divinity problem of evil by making parallel responses. For instance, they cannot appeal to the free will theodicy because even if, as the theodicy says, evil is an outcome of the human misuse of morally significant freedom, humans themselves are, according to pantheists, part of God. Neither can pantheists appeal to the soul-making theodicy because they hold that there is no life beyond the spatiotemporal universe which humans currently inhabit. Neither can they appeal to sceptical theism because they do not believe in the existence of a personal God with a grand scheme.

I do not mean that it is obvious that traditional theists can succeed in responding to the divinity problem of evil by appealing to the above-mentioned responses. It seems reasonable, however, to say that the divinity problem of evil arises more persistently for pantheists than for traditional theists and that pantheists lack justification for embracing some of the responses to which traditional theists can appeal.

3.10 Multiverse Pantheism

As we saw in Section 3.7, pantheists need to develop a non-experiential approach to the divinity of the all-inclusive unity because otherwise their response to the divinity problem of evil entails that there is no substantial difference between pantheism and atheism. Traditional theists do not face the same problem because they do embrace a non-experiential account of divinity. We then considered in Section 3.8 whether pantheists can develop their own non-experiential account of divinity by appealing to the concept of encompassment. I concluded, however, that the encompassment of the all-inclusive unity is not sufficient for maintaining divinity because it is not the most encompassing unity possible. Even if we grant that greatness should be determined in reference to encompassment, the universe is not deemed supremely excellent or divine.

In the rest of this chapter, I discuss what I call 'multiverse pantheism', according to which the all-inclusive unity is not a single universe but *the multiverse*. I examine this view because it can be construed as a unique attempt to avoid the divinity problem of evil by pressing the notion of encompassment further. Moreover, perhaps providing an additional advantage to pantheists, multiverse pantheism seems to avoid many other versions of the problem of axiological expectation mismatch. I argue below, however, that, ultimately, multiverse pantheism is untenable because it faces its own version of the divinity problem of evil. This means that while multiverse pantheism is an attractive pantheistic option in some respects, it does not succeed in avoiding the divinity problem of evil.

Pantheists normally equate the all-inclusive unity with our universe, the single, spatiotemporally limited universe in which we live. From now until the end of this chapter, let us call this version of pantheism 'standard pantheism' to distinguish it from multiverse pantheism. Like standard pantheism, multiverse pantheism is based on the unity thesis, according to which everything that exists constitutes a unity, and the divinity thesis, according to which the all-inclusive unity is divine. However, multiverse pantheists equate the all-inclusive unity with the multiverse, rather than with a single universe.

In recent years, theoretical physicists and philosophers have developed the multiverse theory, according to which reality consists of multiple universes and our universe is only one of them. Multiverse pantheists appeal to this theory to defend the view that there is nothing more encompassing than the all-inclusive unity. There are many views of the multiverse, but the one

76   THE PROBLEM OF EVIL FOR ATHEISTS

on which we focus here is the most extreme one. According to this view, the multiverse consists of all universes that are metaphysically possible. Moreover, all of these universes are actual. The view says that although distinct universes are causally and spatiotemporally isolated from one another, they are ontologically on a par. Throughout the present chapter, then, by the term 'multiverse' I refer to this extreme form of multiverse. According to the version of multiverse pantheism which I discuss here, such a multiverse exists, and it should be equated with the all-inclusive unity and considered divine.

One might wonder how the multiverse view in question differs from modal realism. Let me set aside the problem of evil for the moment and discuss this issue to clarify what exactly multiverse pantheism is.

Modal realism is the view that all possible worlds exist to the same extent that the actual world does and that all possible worlds, including the actual world, are ontologically on a par (Lewis 1986). On the face of it, there are several differences between modal realism and the multiverse view in question. (i) While modal realism is concerned with possible *worlds* the multiverse view is concerned with possible *universes*. (ii) The multiverse view claims that there are universes that are causally and spatiotemporally isolated from one another. Arguably, this claim is incompatible with modal realism. Bigelow and Pargetter (1987) argue that modal realism cannot allow 'island universes', universes that exist in the actual world but are causally and spatiotemporally isolated. The most prominent proponent of modal realism, David Lewis, himself says, 'I cannot give you disconnected space-times within a single world' (Lewis 1986, p. 72). (iii) Modal realism denies that all possible worlds are *actual*; it says only that all possible worlds *exist* to the extent that our world, that is, the actual world, does. According to modal realism, actuality is merely indexical. There is no ontological difference between the actual world and other possible worlds. The actual world is special for us merely because it is *our* world, just as some other possible world is special for the inhabitants of that world. All possible worlds are ontologically on a par although they are causally isolated from one another. Hence, modal realism says that what distinguishes our world from other worlds is merely indexical. On the other hand, the multiverse view says that all possible universes are indeed actual. The multiverse is actual, and it actually includes all possible universes.

I submit, however, that the differences between modal realism and the multiverse view are mostly terminological. First, what modal realism calls 'worlds' are essentially the same as what the multiverse model calls 'universes'. Universes according to the multiverse view are spatiotemporally isolated realms which jointly exhaust all possible states of affairs, so they are equivalent to possible worlds according to modal realism. Modal realism *is* incompatible with island universes, but what the multiverse model really assumes are not island universes in a single possible world but 'island possible worlds', which are compatible with modal realism. Second, the difference in the treatment of actuality in modal realism and in the multiverse view is also a terminological matter. Modal realism denies that all possible worlds are actual while the multiverse model holds that all universes are actual. However, what Lewis really means by 'the actual world' is only '*this* world in which we live'. He writes, 'Ours is the actual world; the rest are not actual. Why so?—I take it to be a trivial matter of meaning. I use the word "actual" to mean the same as "this-worldly"' (Lewis 1986, p. 92). Given Lewis's understanding of actuality, multiverse pantheists could agree that there is only one actual universe, which is *our* universe, while other universes are non-actual (but existent). So there is no fundamental difference between modal realism and the multiverse view. What the multiverse view calls our universe is what Lewis calls the actual world and what the multiverse view calls other possible universes are what Lewis calls other possible worlds.[12]

3.11 How Multiverse Pantheists Avoid the Shortcoming of Standard Pantheism

Let us return to the divinity problem of evil, which is our main interest, and recap how Levine defends standard pantheism from the divinity problem of evil. Levine argues first that pantheists can avoid the divinity problem of evil by maintaining that the all-inclusive unity is divine because pantheists experience the universe as such and divinity can have 'demonic' aspects. I have argued, however, that this response is unsatisfactory because pantheists' appeal to experience is incomplete. If pantheists consider the universe to be God solely on experiential grounds, pantheism does not fundamentally differ from atheism. Hence, standard pantheists can succeed in responding to the divinity problem only by making their view indistinguishable from

---

[12] I am indebted to John Leslie and an anonymous referee for valuable comments regarding these points pertaining to the multiverse view and modal realism. See Klaas Kraay (2011) for relevant issues.

78 THE PROBLEM OF EVIL FOR ATHEISTS

atheism. To avoid the problem of putting the cart (divinity) before the horse (the ground of divinity); pantheists need a non-experiential approach to fully defend the divinity of the all-inclusive unity. I then considered whether pantheists can develop a non-experiential approach by appealing to the property of encompassment. I argued that, unfortunately, this approach fails because the encompassment of our universe is not significant enough to make it divine. The all-inclusive unity according to standard pantheism is not the most encompassing unity because it is spatiotemporally and modally limited. There are infinitely many other universes that are more encompassing than the actual universe.

Multiverse pantheists avoid the shortcomings of standard pantheism by overcoming both the spatiotemporal and modal limitations of the universe. Consider the spatiotemporal limitation first. Again, standard pantheists believe that God is identical with the universe, that is, *our* universe. This belief entails the unwelcome consequence that God is spatiotemporally finite because our universe is neither infinitely large nor infinitely old. Multiverse pantheists, however, do not face this problem because they identify God with the multiverse. As the most encompassing unity, the multiverse pantheistic God encompasses all possible universes in the past, present, and future. All possible universes that were/are/will be realized were/are/will be part of the multiverse. Multiverse pantheists acknowledge that *our* universe is temporally finite; it began to exist as the Big Bang took place approximately 13.5 billion years ago and it will eventually collapse into the Big Crunch. This does not mean, however, that the multiverse overall is temporally finite. There is no beginning or end to the multiverse on the whole. Similarly, the multiverse in question does not entail the unwelcome thesis that the universe is spatially finite. If it is possible for any universe to be spatially infinite, the multiverse subsumes such a universe because it subsumes all possible universes that are metaphysically possible. Even if no universe can be spatially infinite, the multiverse can still be considered spatially and temporally limitless as it encompasses all universes of all possible sizes and ages. Multiverse pantheism, therefore, overcomes the spatiotemporal finitude of the universe found in standard pantheism.

Consider then the modal limitations of the universe. Standard pantheism says that God is our universe, but clearly our universe is not the most encompassing unity possible. There are many other possible universes that are more encompassing than our universe. Hence, if divinity is understood in terms of encompassment, we cannot deem our universe divine. Multiverse pantheism avoids this problem because it says that God is the

THE PROBLEM OF EVIL FOR PANTHEISTS   79

multiverse, which encompasses all possible universes including all possible beings and all possible states of affairs. If we view greatness as a matter of encompassment rather than of great-making properties, the multiverse pantheistic God *is* the greatest possible being. There is no possible unity that is more encompassing than the multiverse. Therefore, the multiverse pantheistic God is deemed supremely excellent and divine.

Multiverse pantheists do not define greatness in terms of properties that are ascribed to God, such as knowledge, power, and goodness. Interestingly enough, however, multiverse pantheists could argue that the multiverse pantheistic God shares, at least to some degree, many properties with the traditional theistic God.[13] Such properties include omniscience, omnipotence, omnibenevolence, omnipresence, eternity, independence, unsurpassability, and necessary existence.

Again, multiverse pantheism says that God is the totality of all possible universes, a being that encompasses all possible states of affairs, and, moreover, that all such possible universes are actual. This means that all possible forms of knowledge, power, and goodness are actual and encompassed by God. This implies that, at least in one sense, the multiverse pantheistic God is omniscient, omnipotent, and omnibenevolent.[14] The multiverse pantheistic God is also omnipresent and eternal in the sense that it encompasses all spatiotemporal locations in all possible universes. The multiverse pantheistic God is also independent because, as the totality of all possible universes, its existence does not rely ontologically on any other existence. The multiverse pantheistic God is also unsurpassable because there cannot be anything that

---

[13] For a similar point, see István Aranyosi (2013), Graham Oppy (1997), and Eric Steinhart (2004).

[14] The phrase 'at least in one sense' is crucial here. I do not mean, for example, that the multiverse knows things in the way that we do. Multiverse pantheists would be committing the fallacy of composition if they were to hold that the fact that I know that *p* and the fact that the multiverse encompasses me entails that the multiverse knows that *p* in the exact sense in which I know it. Thanks to Klaas Kraay on this point. Notice that, if standard pantheism is true, God encompasses only all forms of knowledge, power, and goodness that are instantiated *in this universe*. This hardly entails that God is omniscient, omnipotent, and omnibenevolent. One might also claim that the multiverse panentheistic God cannot be omniscient, omnipotent, and omnibenevolent because although it encompasses all possible forms of knowledge, power, and goodness it also encompasses all possible forms of ignorance, weakness, and malevolence. The following is a possible response to such a claim: consider, as a parallel example, a group of three people, *A*, *B*, and *C*. *A* knows *x* and *y*, *B* knows *z*, and *C* is totally ignorant. In this scenario, we are inclined to say that the group as a whole knows *x*, *y*, and *z* and that the ignorance of *C* does not cancel out what *A* and *B* know. Similarly, the ignorance/weakness of an individual does not seem to undermine the knowledge/power of the unity to which the individual belongs as a constituent. Omnibenevolence is more difficult to address, but perhaps the same reasoning applies if the privation theory of evil is correct.

80 THE PROBLEM OF EVIL FOR ATHEISTS

is greater than the totality of all possible universes; the totality of all possible universes is the most encompassing being possible. Also, if we consider the totality of all possible universes to be equivalent to logical space, the multiverse pantheistic God is necessarily existent as well.[15]

Perhaps the only prominent attribute of the traditional theistic God that the multiverse pantheistic God lacks is the property of being a free personal agent. Traditional theism says that God is a person or a personal being with intention and volition. Multiverse pantheism does not attribute such a property to God, even though it allows God to subsume all possible persons and personal beings with intention and free will. In this sense, perhaps the multiverse pantheistic God is a partially personal being or a partially free being even though it is not a free person in itself. For personhood there has to be an appropriate bearer of free will and volition, but the totality of all possible universes does not seem to qualify as a bearer of these properties, unless perhaps we defend an extreme form of cosmopsychism which attributes full-fledged consciousness to the multiverse (Jonardon Ganeri and Itay Shani 2022, Yujin Nagasawa and Khai Wager 2017). Nonetheless, as we have seen, the multiverse pantheistic God shares, at least in some sense, many properties with the traditional theistic God. Hence, if multiverse pantheists wish, they could parallel traditional theists' defence of the divinity of God in reference to great-making properties as well as their own defence in reference to encompassment.

Multiverse pantheists seem to be able to defend the divinity of the all-inclusive unity by appealing to a non-experiential account as well as an experiential account, which are analogous to traditional theists' accounts.

---

[15] Another way to see the parallel structure between traditional theism and multiverse pantheism is the following: if the multiverse view is essentially equivalent to modal realism, there seems to be a version of the ontological argument for multiverse pantheism that is comparable to the version of the ontological argument for traditional theism. Again, the being than which no greater can be thought is, according to multiverse pantheism, the totality of all possible universes. Suppose, for the sake of argument, that some of the universes in the multiverse in question, that is, the totality of all possible universes, are not actual (or not existent in Lewis's terminology). It then follows that another totality can be thought that is greater than the totality of all possible universes. Such a totality is thought to encompass all possible universes and all of these universes are thought to be actual (or existent in Lewis's terminology). It is contradictory, however, to say that a being can be thought that is greater than the totality of all possible universes because the totality of all possible universes is that than which no greater can be thought. Hence, it is impossible that some of the universes in the totality of all possible universes are not actual. Therefore, all possible universes in the totality of all possible universes actually exist. Therefore, multiverse pantheism is true.

I do not claim that the above ontological argument is sound, but it shows that multiverse pantheism is indeed analogous to traditional theism; and, hence, multiverse pantheists can develop an analogous non-experiential approach to divinity.

THE PROBLEM OF EVIL FOR PANTHEISTS   81

Therefore, multiverse pantheists seem to have an effective defence of the divinity of the world (despite the existence of evil), a defence which appears to be at least as robust as traditional theists' defence of the divinity of an omniscient, omnipotent, and wholly good God.

3.12 How Multiverse Pantheism Responds to the General Problem of Evil

My aim in this chapter has been to show that the problem of evil arises for pantheists. It is worth pointing out that while multiverse pantheists can establish the divinity of the universe by appealing to encompassment, they still have to explain why there has to be evil in the first place. Multiverse pantheists answer this question as follows. Again, according to multiverse pantheism, the multiverse encompasses all possible universes. This means that every single possible state of affairs is instantiated in the multiverse. States of affairs that include instances of moral evil and natural evil are metaphysically possible. If so, it is unavoidable that evil is realized in the multiverse. In sum, once we accept multiverse pantheism, it is necessarily the case that there is evil. As you will recall, the divinity problem of evil for standard pantheists says that the universe cannot be God as the universe contains evil states of affairs. Multiverse pantheism admits that evil is part of God but insists that this does not undermine the view. On the contrary, it says, given that God is the most encompassing being the multiverse has to subsume all possible states of affairs, including evil states of affairs. Evil does not create any axiological mismatch between our expectation of reality based on multiverse pantheism and our observation of it.

One might wonder, however, why there has to be evil in *our* universe. If God encompasses all possible universes, there should be a universe that is totally free from evil. Why can our universe not be such a universe? Why do *we* have to suffer? Multiverse pantheism responds to this question by saying that there is no reason that our universe, instead of some other universe, has to be free from evil. Multiverse pantheism does not privilege our universe over other universes. Our universe is one of infinitely many universes constituting the multiverse. As we saw earlier, according to modal realism, actuality, which distinguishes the actual world from other possible worlds, is nothing but indexicality. Our universe appears morally or metaphysically special to us merely because *we* happen to exist in this universe. In other universes similar to ours there are our counterparts. If we do not suffer from

82 THE PROBLEM OF EVIL FOR ATHEISTS

evil, then our counterparts in some other universe, who are as real as we are, have to suffer from evil. Given that we and our counterparts are morally equivalent, there is no reason for them to suffer instead of us, and vice versa.

Lewis says that modal realism entails that the net amount of evil in the totality of all possible worlds cannot be increased or diminished (Lewis 1986, p. 127). Similarly, the net amount of evil in the multiverse cannot be increased or diminished. Given that we and our counterparts are morally equivalent, there is no reason for them to suffer instead of us, and vice versa. Perhaps, as Michael Almeida says, this is comparable to a situation in which a rescuer can save either of two drowning children x and y but not both (Almeida 2011, p. 9).[16] In such a situation, it is not legitimate to ask why child x rather than child y has to be rescued. Given the 'ought implies can' principle, it is not the case that one ought to rescue both children because that is not possible. Similarly, it is not legitimate to ask why our universe rather than some other universe has to contain evil.

Summing up what we have seen, multiverse pantheists can answer the following questions effectively:

Q1: How could the all-inclusive unity be divine if it includes evil?

Q2: Why is there evil at all?

Q3: Why is there evil in *our* universe?

The first question corresponds to the divinity problem of evil. Again, the problem of evil consists of three variables: (i) God, (ii) evil, and (iii) the allegedly conflicting relationship between God and evil. Pantheists assign the all-inclusive unity, instead of an omnipotent and wholly good being, to variable (i). The divinity problem of evil arises because pantheists' assumption that the all-inclusive unity is divine is in conflict with the existence of evil, which corresponds to variable (ii). Multiverse pantheists argue that an axiological expectation mismatch does not arise here. The all-inclusive unity is equivalent to the multiverse, which contains evil because of its extreme encompassment. The second question is a general question about the existence of evil in reality. Multiverse pantheists respond to it by claiming that there is evil because every possible state of affairs is instantiated in the multiverse. The third question is concerned with the

---

[16] It should be noted that Almeida makes this point in relation to the compatibility between *traditional theism* and modal realism. His focus is not on multiverse pantheism.

existence of evil in our universe specifically. Multiverse pantheists respond to it by claiming that this is not a legitimate question because all possible universes are ontologically on a par and there is no reason to think that some other universe rather than ours should include evil.

I argued in Chapter 2 that, along with the problem of divine hiddenness, the problem of no best world, and the fine-tuning problem, the problem of evil is only one of many versions of the problem of axiological expectation mismatch discussed in the philosophy of religion. Notice that each of these problems focuses on a 'puzzle' concerning a specific property of the actual universe that appears incompatible with our expectations. Multiverse pantheists can respond to any version of the problem of axiological expectation mismatch within the same logical structure. They can say that the multiverse encompasses all possible universes. Universes are ontologically on a par, and they jointly include all possible states of affairs, so it is not surprising that our universe happens to contain certain properties, such as including a certain amount of evil, having a hidden God, and being fine-tuned to enable life. The converse of this claim is that all of the apparent puzzles or axiological expectation mismatches arise because we assume erroneously that our universe is the only possible universe that exists. Once we give up such an assumption and allow infinitely many universes, these apparent mismatches disappear.

3.13 The Problem of Evil for Multiverse Pantheists

We have seen that multiverse pantheists have answers to Q1–Q3. I argue however that their answer to Q1 (how could the all-inclusive unity be divine if it includes evil?) is limited and this limitation creates an extreme version of the divinity problem of evil. I address this version in the remainder of this chapter.

Multiverse pantheists defend the divinity of the multiverse by appealing to the thesis that encompassment determines a being's greatness. This means that, if multiverse pantheism is true, God encompasses not only some possible evil states of affairs but *all* possible evil states of affairs, including all possible, utterly awful evil states of affairs. This means that multiverse pantheists face evil that is more considerable in quantity and quality than traditional theists and standard pantheists do. This point raises the following question, which is a variation of Q1:

84   THE PROBLEM OF EVIL FOR ATHEISTS

Q4: How could the all-inclusive unity be divine if it includes all possible instances of evil including the most horrendous possible instances of evil?

Multiverse pantheists believe that *all possible instances of evil*, including the worst possible instances of evil, exist. This means that they believe that evil of the most extreme quality and quantity is realized and, moreover, is part of God.

Again, multiverse pantheism adopts the idea that greatness should be understood not in terms of great-making properties, but in terms of the scope of that which it encompasses. According to this interpretation, the more encompassing a being is the higher the greatness of that being is. So the amount of evil that God subsumes actually enhances, rather than diminishes, the greatness of God. Conversely, if the multiverse fails to encompass some evil states of affairs (or any states of affairs at all), it fails to qualify as the greatest possible being.

While multiverse pantheism may not be an incoherent metaphysical view and it depends on one's definition of God whether the totality of all possible universes should be identified with God, such a definition entails disturbing moral or axiological implications which are difficult for many to accept. It is disturbing to think that the all-inclusive unity, which subsumes utterly awful evil states of affairs, such as billions of innocent people being tortured for billions of years for no reason, should be deemed divine. We saw above that the divinity problem of evil shows that standard pantheism is based on an untenable notion of divinity or fails to take the concept of evil seriously. By allowing evil of the most extreme quality and quantity to be part of God, this problem arises for multiverse pantheists more persistently than for any other pantheists. This is a version of the divinity problem of evil specifically for multiverse pantheists.

My point above can be highlighted by considering again the three variables constituting the problem of evil: (i) God, (ii) evil, and (iii) the allegedly conflicting relationship between God and evil. Multiverse pantheists assign the multiverse, instead of an omnipotent and wholly good being or our universe, to variable (i). However, in so doing they reach the situation where the most extreme quality and quantity of evil is assigned to variable (ii). This seems to mean that a gap between (i) and (ii) for multiverse pantheists is more significant than the parallel gap for traditional theists or standard pantheists. In fact, this seems to be the most devastating version of the problem of evil. In the next section, I consider several possible responses to this problem which multiverse pantheists may try to develop. I argue that, unfortunately, none of them is satisfactory.

3.14 Possible Responses to the Divinity Problem of Evil for Multiverse Pantheism

The first response to the divinity problem of evil for multiverse pantheism is hinted at by Cicero's character Balbus:

> [T]here is the influence exerted upon us by the great blessing which we enjoy from a temperate climate, from the fruitfulness of the earth, and from the abundance of other blessings...[T]here is the awe inspired by thunderbolts, storms, cloudbursts, blizzards, hailstorms, floods, plagues, earthquakes or sudden tremors of the earth, showers of stones, and rain-drops red as drops of blood; from the subsidences and sudden fissures in the earth; from monstrosities in man or beast: from fiery portents and comets in the skies, such as recently foretold frightful disasters in the civil war: or from the appearances of twin suns, as happened, so my father told me, in the consulship of Tuditanus and Aquilius, the year in which Scipio Africanus died, himself as glorious as a second sun. Terrified by such events as these, men came to see in them the working of some divine and heavenly power (Cicero 45 BC/1972, p. 129).

Balbus has pantheism in mind in the above passage, but one might try to apply his reasoning to multiverse pantheism as well. Perhaps the evil aspect of the multiverse not only fails to undermine multiverse pantheism but also helps to make the multiverse pantheistic God divine or awe-inspiring. This is compatible with Levine's appeal to Otto's thesis that divinity or holiness can have 'demonic' aspects. Perhaps the multiverse pantheistic God is divine or awe-inspiring precisely because He encompasses all possible forms of evil, including natural disasters. In other words, there is no significant gap between multiverse pantheists' expectation of how reality should be and their observation of how it actually is. It is entirely to be expected, according to this response, that the multiverse includes numerous instances of evil. It is, of course, difficult to regard the multiverse pantheistic God as awe-inspiring if God is entirely evil. However, God also encompasses many, and possibly infinitely many, good states of affairs. Some of them are extremely great possible states of affairs exhibiting goodness beyond our imagination. Hence, one might claim, the multiverse pantheistic God has two contrasting aspects, good and evil, the combination of which makes God awe-inspiring.

Unfortunately, this response does not save multiverse pantheism. Standard pantheists need to countenance only a finite amount of evil

86   THE PROBLEM OF EVIL FOR ATHEISTS

actualized in our universe because the standard pantheistic God does not encompass evil outside our universe. Hence, their claim that the universe is awe-inspiring despite (or even because of) the limited existence of evil around us may not be so extraordinary. Levine writes, again:

> At any rate, there is little reason for the pantheist to argue that what is divine can also be evil, since they can deny that evil falls within the purview of the divine Unity. To say that everything that exists constitutes a divine Unity (i.e. pantheism's essential claim) need not be interpreted in such a way that it entails that all parts and every aspect of the Unity is divine or good. (Levine 1994a, p. 208)

Balbus's and Levine's approach, therefore, might be effective for saving standard pantheism. Perhaps God needs a certain finite amount of evil in the world to be divine or awe-inspiring. Conversely, perhaps a being that encompasses only good is not awe-inspiring and fails to qualify as God. Yet the same reasoning does not apply to multiverse pantheism because the evil that the multiverse pantheistic God encompasses—in quality and quantity— constitutes far too much evil. The multiverse in question encompasses all possible forms of evil including utterly awful ones such as innocent people being tortured for a very long time, possibly an infinite amount of time, for no reason. In other words, it is not merely that the multiverse pantheistic God has some 'demonic' aspects, but it has the worst possible 'demonic' aspects. It is difficult to reconcile this observation with the idea that God is divine. The problem that multiverse pantheists face here is the most extreme form of the problem of evil—or, more specifically, the most extreme form of the divinity problem of evil.

The second response to the divinity problem of evil parallels Lewis's defence of modal realism. As I mentioned above, the multiverse model on which multiverse pantheism relies is essentially identical to modal realism. And modal realism is known to face a moral problem that is relevant to the problem under consideration. The moral problem for modal realism is this: given the claim of modal realism that all possible worlds exist, the total amount of good and evil does not change whether or not we act morally in the actual world. That is, whether or not we act morally to prevent and eliminate evil in the actual world, the same evil is instantiated in some other possible world anyway. Therefore, modal realism appears to discourage us from acting morally. The problem for modal realism is that the view appears to discourage us from acting morally because whether or not we act morally

THE PROBLEM OF EVIL FOR PANTHEISTS 87

and prevent evil in this world, evil is instantiated in some other possible worlds anyway. This is because, given the claim of modal realism that all possible worlds exist, the total sum of good and evil does not change whether or not we act morally in this world.

Lewis's response to this problem is that evil events in other possible worlds should not be our moral concern. He writes:

> For those of us who think of morality in terms of virtue and honour, desert and respect and esteem, loyalties and affections and solidarity, the other-worldly evils should not seem even momentarily relevant to morality. Of course our moral aims are egocentric. And likewise all the more for those who think of morality in terms of rules, rights, and duties; or as obedience to the will of God. (Lewis 1986, p. 127)[17]

One might apply similar reasoning to the divinity problem of evil for multiverse pantheism and say that we should not be bothered that there are utterly awful evil states of affairs in universes other than ours. When we talk about what is good and what is evil, one might say, our main concern is morality in *our* universe and our moral concerns should not extend to other universes that are causally and spatiotemporally distinct from ours.

The above response may be right in saying that we should not be bothered by evil in other universes when considering the moral significance of actions in our own universe. That is, even though the total axiological value and the total amount of good and evil in the sum of all universes do not change whatever action we perform, we should not be discouraged from acting morally in the actual universe. Yet this does not entail that we should not be bothered by evil in other possible universes in light of the thesis that the totality of all possible universes is identical with God. The adoption of an egocentric viewpoint allows us to set aside other universes *in considering our moral actions in our universe*, but it does not allow us to set aside other universes *in considering the divinity of the totality of all universes identified as God*. It is still puzzling how we can deem the totality of all universes divine or worthy of religious veneration if it includes so much evil.

The third response to the divinity problem of evil says that the problem in question should not bother multiverse pantheists because overall the axio-logical value of the multiverse is at least neutral, possibly positive, and

---

[17] For the moral implications of modal realism, see Robert Merrihew Adams (1974) and Mark Heller (2003).

88 THE PROBLEM OF EVIL FOR ATHEISTS

possibly infinitely positive. The multiverse encompasses utterly evil states of affairs, but we should not forget that it also encompasses *all* utterly good states of affairs as well. So, for example, while it includes a state of affairs in which people are tortured for an extended period for no reason, it also includes a state of affairs in which people experience eternal bliss and happiness. Calculating the overall axiological value of a sum of uncountably many universes is challenging. Multiverse pantheists can however optimistically hope that the overall value is, at the very least, neutral—and possibly even positive or infinitely positive.

Unfortunately, this response is not satisfactory either. Even if the total value of the multiverse is infinitely positive, it is still puzzling why some of the most awful events are part of God. Focusing on the worst possible instance of evil that God encompasses, multiverse pantheists face the most acute form of the problem of 'horrendous evil'. As we saw in Chapter 1, Marilyn McCord Adams cites as examples of horrendous evil such events as 'the rape of a woman and axing off of her arms, psycho-physical torture whose ultimate goal is the disintegration of personality, betrayal of one's deepest loyalties, child abuse of the sort described by Ivan Karamazov, child pornography, parental incest, slow death by starvation, [and] the explosion of nuclear bombs over populated areas' (Adams 1999, p. 26). The multiverse pantheistic God encompasses all of these instances, and it also encompasses worse ones, possibly infinitely worse ones. Even those theists who think that the existence of horrendous evil in our universe is justified in a theistic framework are unlikely to think that the existence of horrendous evil of extreme quality and quantity can be justified. Perhaps certain positive aspects of the multiverse can be considered divine, but it is difficult to accept the idea that the whole multiverse, including the most horrendous events, is divine.

The fourth, and final, pantheist response to the divinity problem of evil says that the multiverse does not include all possible universes but all and only possible universes that are overall good. Klaas J. Kraay (2010) argues that if traditional theism is true, God creates a multiverse comprised of all and only those universes that are worthy of creation and sustenance. Multiverse pantheists might apply similar reasoning and hold that God is the multiverse comprising all and only those universes that are worthy of existence and sustenance.

This solution succeeds in eliminating utterly evil states of affairs from God, but it also eliminates some distinctive features of multiverse pantheism. First, if multiverse pantheists exclude from the multiverse universes

THE PROBLEM OF EVIL FOR PANTHEISTS   89

that are not overall good, then the multiverse in question is no longer the most fully encompassing being. If so, multiverse pantheists lose their core idea that the greatness of God resides in encompassment. Second, traditional theists like Kraay can argue that God, as an omnibenevolent being, could and would choose to create all and only possible universes that are overall good. This is because traditional theists believe that God is a morally significantly free agent. In contrast, multiverse pantheists cannot appeal to a similar idea to exclude universes that are not overall good because they do not view God as such a being. Moreover, the multiverse does not have any comparable mechanism to filter out possible universes that are not overall good. (I discuss a related point in Chapter 4 in relation to axiarchism.)

Therefore, none of the four responses to the version of the divinity problem of evil that applies to multiverse pantheists succeeds in fully disposing of the problem. The source of the problem is the tension between multiverse pantheists' understanding of divinity and the significance of evil which the multiverse encompasses. On the one hand, to make the multiverse divine multiverse pantheists need to make it maximally encompassing. On the other hand, however, extreme encompassment entails the extreme quality and quantity of evil. Multiverse pantheists cannot eliminate the axiological expectation mismatch because of the inherent incompatibility between enhancing encompassment and eliminating evil.

3.15 Conclusion

We began our discussion in this chapter by contrasting traditional theism and its alternatives by placing them on a spectrum as follows:

Traditional theism → Panentheism → Pantheism → Axiarchism → Atheism

I set aside panentheism because panentheism, which requires supernaturalism, is not sufficiently distinct from traditional theism for our purposes. In this chapter, therefore, I have focused on pantheism and discussed how the problem of evil arises for pantheists. I have argued that the standard, naturalistic version of pantheism, according to which God is identical with the world, faces the divinity problem of evil because it is not clear why the pantheistic God, that is, the world, should be deemed divine given that it includes evil. I addressed Levine's attempt to respond to the problem which appeals to experience but argued that it does not succeed. I claimed that if pantheists insist that the world is divine solely because we experience it as such, then there is no metaphysical difference between pantheism and atheism.

I argued here that, although the divinity problem of evil applies to traditional theists, pantheists face a more challenging task in addressing it because pantheism lacks several resources that are available to traditional theists. I then discussed multiverse pantheism, which can be construed as an improved form of pantheism. I argued also that, while multiverse pantheism mitigates some of the shortcomings of standard pantheism, it faces its own version of the divinity problem of evil, which is, ironically, the problem in its most extreme form.

In the next chapter, I shift the focus on our spectrum from pantheism to axiarchism and argue that this view also faces a version of the problem of evil.

4

The Problem of Evil for Axiarchists

4.1 Introduction

Pantheists have a naturalistic inclination. Instead of postulating God as an incorporeal, morally significant personal agent beyond the material universe, they consider God to be *identical* with the material universe. I argued in the previous chapter that both standard and multiverse forms of pantheism face the problem of evil. Standard pantheists fail to explain why we should deem the universe divine despite the considerable quantity and quality of evil it realizes. I also argued that their attempt to respond to this problem by referring to their experience of the universe as divine fails because it is unclear how they can differentiate standard pantheism from atheism without providing the metaphysical foundation of divinity. I then discussed how multiverse pantheists may try to mitigate this problem. On the face of it, multiverse pantheism is more compelling than standard pantheism because it can appeal to the extreme encompassment of the multiverse as the metaphysical foundation of divinity. I argued, however, that, ironically, multiverse pantheists face the worst possible version of the problem of evil precisely because of their appeal to extreme encompassment.

Axiarchism is a novel, non-personal alternative to traditional theism and pantheism. According to this view, the world exists because it is better that it be actualized than that it not be actualized; that is, the existence of the world is ethically required. Axiarchists believe that this non-personal, 'creatively effective ethical requirement', rather than God, is the ultimate explanation of the existence of the world.[1] Axiarchism appears initially attractive because, by replacing a personal God with the impersonal ethical requirement, it appears to explain the existence of the world without facing versions of the problem of evil that traditional theists face. I explain in this chapter, however, that there are versions of the problem of evil which arise even

---

[1] John Leslie (2016, p. 16) coined the term 'creatively effective ethical requirement'.

The Problem of Evil for Atheists. Yujin Nagasawa, Oxford University Press. © Yujin Nagasawa 2024.
DOI: 10.1093/oso/9780198901884.003.0005

92   THE PROBLEM OF EVIL FOR ATHEISTS

for axiarchists. I argue, moreover, that traditional theists enjoy advantages over axiarchism in responding to these versions.

This chapter has the following structure. In Section 4.2, I recap two forms of the problem of evil which traditional theists face: the problem of actual evil and the problem of non-actual evil. In Section 4.3, I introduce axiarchism and explain how, initially, it avoids these problems. In Section 4.4, I argue that axiarchists are not better positioned than traditional theists because they face parallel versions of the same problems. In Section 4.5, I introduce one of the four existing responses to the problems and argue that while this response is compatible with both traditional theism and axiarchism, its counterintuitiveness makes the response untenable. In Sections 4.6, 4.7, and 4.8, I introduce the three additional responses and argue that they are compatible with traditional theism but not with axiarchism. In Section 4.9, I consider axiarchists' attempts to develop two unique responses to the problems and argue that neither of them succeeds. I argue, moreover, that if axiarchists try to assimilate traditional theists' approach to address the problems, axiarchism collapses into traditional theism. That is, there is then no point in pursuing axiarchism because it will be identical with traditional theism. In Section 4.10, I conclude.

4.2 The Problem of Actual Evil and the Problem of Non-Actual Evil for Traditional Theists

Traditional theists typically explain the existence of the actual world roughly as follows: as a personal, morally significantly free, wholly good agent, God decided to create a world that contains sentient human beings with whom He can interact. God then instantiated His omnipotence to actualize the world. This is an ultimate explanation of all there is because, as a necessary being, God Himself does not require any explanation of His own existence.

The problem of evil is normally formulated as a challenge for proponents of the above view in light of the existence of evil, as manifested in the crimes, wars, and natural disasters that surround us. The problem of evil, as it is normally considered, is, hence, a problem concerning instances of evil that are *actual*. We saw in Chapter 1, however, that there is a version of the problem of evil which focuses on instances of evil that are not actual. I have called such a version the 'problem of non-actual evil'. The problem of non-actual evil, which was explicitly defended for the first time by Theodore Guleserian (1983), focuses not only on God's omnipotence and unlimited goodness but also on His necessary existence.[2] If traditional theists are correct in saying that God is omnipotent, wholly good, *and* necessarily existent, then there should be no possible world in which there is evil because an omnipotent and wholly good God exists in all possible worlds. There *are*, however, possible worlds in which there is evil. As I explained in Chapter 1, the problem of non-actual evil is arguably more compelling than the problem of actual evil because it can be formulated in such a way that it focuses on a possible but non-actual state of affairs that is more extreme than any state of affairs that we can find in the actual world (for example, a state of affairs in which billions of innocent people are tortured for billions of years for no reason).[3] Let us call them instances of 'appalling evil'. Even if traditional theists can explain away all instances of evil in the actual world, they are likely to struggle to explain away all instances of evil, especially appalling evil, in all possible worlds.

The problem of non-actual evil arises from an apparent conflict between our modal intuitions and traditional theism. Here our modal intuition says that there are all sorts of possible worlds including worlds that contain instances of appalling evil, but the conjunction of the omni-God thesis and the necessary-God thesis appears to imply that there should be no possible world that includes instances of appalling evil. Throughout the present chapter, we focus on both actual evil and non-actual evil.[4]

4.3 Axiarchism as an Alternative to Traditional Theism

Again, Axiarchism is a unique, non-personal alternative to traditional theism.[5] According to this view, the actual world exists because it is better that it be

---

[2] As I mentioned in Chapter 1 of the present book, Guleserian calls the version of the problem of evil in question the 'modal problem of evil'.

[3] Some may disagree and argue that the problem of non-actual evil is less compelling than the problem of actual evil because it appeals to our unreliable speculations about which specific instances of evil are present in possible worlds that are dissimilar to our own and also the contentious thesis that the conceivability (of a specific state of affairs) entails the metaphysical possibility (of such a state of affairs). Thanks to an anonymous referee on this point.

[4] The term 'modal intuition' in this context was introduced by Kraay. He presents the problem of non-actual evil in terms of our modal intuitions and what he calls the '*moral* intuition' according to which 'it is not morally acceptable that, in *w*, God permits the overall bad world *w* to be actual when it is within God's power to prevent this' (Kraay 2011, p. 362).

[5] Mulgan distinguishes two types of axiarchism: 'substantive axiarchism', which posits an impersonal entity or force that makes this physical universe actual, and 'formal axiarchism', which does not posit any new entity or force (Mulgran 2017, p. 2). It is important to note that

94 THE PROBLEM OF EVIL FOR ATHEISTS

actualized than that it not be actualized. In other words, the actualization of the world is an ethical requirement. Axiarchism is not a mainstream view, but it has been defended or favourably considered by such distinguished philosophers as John Leslie (1989, 2001, 2016, 2019), Derek Parfit (1992, 1998), Nicholas Rescher (1984, 2010), and Tim Mulgan (2015, 2017). According to Leslie, Plato was an axiarchist as well. Plato suggests in Book Six of the *Republic* that although the Good lies 'far beyond existence in dignity and power', it gives existence to all known things (Leslie 2019, p. 63).

Mulgan contends that axiarchism can be motivated mainly in three ways (Mulgan 2017, pp. 2–3). First, it can be motivated by appealing to the reasoning typically adopted by traditional theists: God exists because it is better that God be actualized than that He not be actualized. Similarly, axiarchists can claim that the world exists because it is better that the world be actualized than that it not be actualized. In both cases, concrete existence is derived from abstract existence by reference to value (Leslie 2016). Second, axiarchism can be motivated by appealing to science. Science seems inherently axiarchic because such valuable features as simplicity, beauty, and elegance are commonly considered reliable guides to true scientific theories. Here, scientists seem to assume that the world itself is simple, beautiful, and elegant. This assumption can be taken further to develop an axiarchic inference that the world exists because it is simple, beautiful, and elegant (Rescher 2010). Third, axiarchism can be motivated by appealing to reasoning that we typically adopt in metaphysics. Only a *possible* world can be actual. An impossible world cannot be actual because it is *logically*, rather than causally, required that an actual world be a possible world. Axiarchism says analogously that only an overall *good* world can be actual. An overall bad world cannot be actual because it is *ethically*, rather than causally, required that an actual world be an overall good world. I do not assess any of these ways of motivating axiarchism or any general arguments for axiarchism because in the present chapter I focus mainly on the cogency of axiarchism in comparison with traditional theism with respect only to the two problems we have seen above: the problem of actual evil and the problem of non-actual evil.

---

both substantive axiarchism and formal axiarchism deny the existence of a personal axiarchic force. Leslie (2001, 2016, forthcoming) incorporates the concept of God in his axiarchism, but what he means by 'God' differs radically from what traditional theism means by the term.

On the face of it, the problem of actual evil and the problem of non-actual evil are irrelevant to axiarchism because, again, as J. L. Mackie says, the problem of evil as it is standardly formulated is a challenge for those who believe in the existence of an omnipotent and wholly good God (Mackie 1955, p. 200). We can make a parallel claim about the problem of non-actual evil: it arises only for those who believe in the existence of an omnipotent, wholly good, *and* necessarily existent God. Axiarchism does not postulate the existence of God, so it appears to avoid both the problem of actual evil and the problem of non-actual evil.

4.4 The Problem of Actual Evil and the Problem of Non-Actual Evil for Axiarchists

We have seen that axiarchism appears to be an attractive alternative to traditional theism because it explains why the world exists without facing the problem of actual evil or the problem of non-actual evil. Recall, however, that, as I argued in Chapter 2, the problem of evil is not a problem that arises uniquely and specifically for traditional theists. In fact, it is a version of the problem of axiological expectation mismatch, which poses a general problem that is not limited to traditional theism.

The problem of evil understood as a version of the problem of axiological expectation mismatch is concerned with the apparent mismatch between our expectation of how reality should be (which is often based on our worldview) and our observation that, in reality, evil exists. Our expectation here can be based on traditional theism, which implies that an omnipotent and wholly good God would not allow the existence of evil, but it can also be based on axiarchism. Axiarchism says that this world is actual because the actual world is good and the non-personal, creatively effective ethical requirement actualizes what is good. This seems to imply that axiarchism guarantees that there are only good things in the actual world. Clearly, though, the actual world does contain many instances of evil. Hence, there is a mismatch between our expectation of how reality should be and our observation of how it actually is. This is a version of the problem of evil for axiarchists.

Parallel reasoning applies to the problem of non-actual evil. The problem of non-actual evil understood as a version of the problem of axiological expectation mismatch is concerned with the apparent gap between our expectation that there should be no evil, especially appalling evil, in any

96 THE PROBLEM OF EVIL FOR ATHEISTS

possible world and our observation that evil, including appalling evil, exists in many possible worlds.[6] Our expectation here can be based on traditional theism, which implies that an omnipotent, wholly good, and necessarily existent God would not allow evil, especially appalling evil, in any possible world, but it can also be based on axiarchism. Axiarchism is considered a fundamental principle that is necessarily true. If it is only contingently true, it is unclear how it can constitute the ultimate explanation of contingent facts such as the existence of the actual world and the laws of nature. If axiarchism is necessarily true, then there should be no possible world that contains evil, especially appalling evil, because the principle guarantees that there is no evil in any possible world. Clearly, though, many possible worlds do contain evil, including appalling evil. Hence, there is an axiological expectation mismatch. This is a version of the problem of non-actual evil for axiarchists.

I argued in Chapter 1 of the present book that the problem of evil consists of three variables: (i) God, (ii) evil, and (iii) the allegedly conflicting relationship between God and evil. What I have shown here is that the problems of actual evil and non-actual evil arise even if we assign the creatively effective ethical requirement, instead of an omnipotent and wholly good being, to variable (i).

4.5 Response 1: The Actual World *Is* the Best Possible World

We have seen that, although axiarchists do not face either the problem of actual evil or the problem of non-actual evil *for traditional theists*, they do face versions of the same problems. How can axiarchists as well as traditional theists respond to these problems? In this and the following three sections, I introduce and assess four possible responses to these problems. I compare traditional theism and axiarchism in relation to these responses and argue that theists enjoy advantages over axiarchists because the latter cannot consistently pursue any of the responses.

Response 1 makes three claims: (i) Leibnizian optimism, according to which the actual world is the best possible world; (ii) total modal collapse,

---

[6] Note that I use the phrase 'observation' here metaphorically. Obviously we cannot visually observe what exists in possible worlds that are not actual.

THE PROBLEM OF EVIL FOR AXIARCHISTS 97

according to which the best possible world is the only possible world; and (iii) modal actualism, according to which only the actual world exists.

Consider Leibnizian optimism first. Gottfried Wilhelm Leibniz writes:

> It is therefore not a question of a creature, but of the universe; and the adversary will be obliged to maintain that one possible universe may be better than the other, to infinity; but there he would be mistaken, and it is that which he cannot prove. If this opinion were true, it would follow that God had not produced any universe at all: for he is incapable of acting without reason, and that would be even acting against reason... It is thus one must think of the creation of the best of all possible universes, all the more since God not only decrees to create a universe, but decrees also to create the best of all. (Leibniz 1710/1985, p. 249)

Leibniz employs the term 'universe', but it can be understood as equivalent to a 'world' as conceived in contemporary metaphysics. Again, it seems intuitively obvious that there could have been a world that is better than the actual world. Leibniz, however, rejects this claim. Given that God is the greatest possible being, Leibniz contends, He must have chosen to actualize the best among all possible worlds. Hence, Leibniz concludes, the actual world must be the best possible world. Leibniz is a traditional theist, but Leibnizian optimism is compatible with axiarchism. Axiarchists, such as Rescher (2010), argue that the creatively effective ethical requirement allows only the best possible world to be actualized and that, hence, the actual world is the best possible world. Rescher contends that the existence of evil in the actual world does not undermine Leibnizian optimism because this view is strictly speaking opti*malism* rather than bare opti*mism*. While optimism is, according to Rescher, the view that things will go well, optimalism is the view that things will go as well as *possible* (Rescher 2010, p. 41). Optimism demands that the actual world be perfect even if it is impossible for a perfect world to be actualized. On the other hand, optimalism demands only that the actual world be as good as possible. According to the Leibnizian view, the actual world is the best possible world even though it might not be a perfect world.[7] Although I acknowledge the intention behind

---

[7] See Chapter 6 of the present book for a more detailed discussion of optimism. I use the term 'Leibnizian optimism' and discuss Leibniz's work, but I do not insist that my discussion here is strictly faithful to Leibniz's texts. My primary interest in the view is philosophical rather than exegetical.

98   THE PROBLEM OF EVIL FOR ATHEISTS

Rescher's creation of the neologism, I employ the conventional term 'optimism' instead of 'optimalism' in our discussion.

The actual world contains some things that are evil and does not contain everything that is good. This suggests that God and the axiarchic requirement are meant to determine the overall axiological value of *worlds* rather than the axiological values of individual *items* or individual *states of affairs* within worlds. Consider what I call the 'Leibnizian hierarchy', a hierarchy of all (apparently) possible worlds that are ranked in accordance with their overall axiological values. We can picture that, referring to this hierarchy, God or the axiarchic ethical requirement selects the best possible world that sits at the top of the hierarchy and actualizes it. Given that the actual world is, by definition, the world that has been actualized, Leibnizian optimism infers that the actual world must be the very best possible world at the top of the hierarchy. By appealing to this reasoning, traditional theism and axiarchism reject the problem of evil. The actual world is compatible with traditional theism and axiarchism because, according to Response 1, despite its appearance, it *is* the best possible world.

As mentioned above, Response 1 subscribes to total modal collapse, which says that the best possible world is the only possible world and that there are no other possible worlds.[8] Total modal collapse is so called because the space of possibility collapses into a single possible world, that is, the best possible world, which is, according to Leibnizian optimism, the actual world. Traditional theists can defend total modal collapse by arguing as follows: given that God is the greatest possible being, He cannot even in principle actualize a world other than the actual world, that is, the best possible world. Hence, this world is the only possible world. Similarly, axiarchists can defend total modal collapse by arguing as follows: given that the creatively effective ethical requirement is necessarily true, it cannot even in principle actualize a world other than the actual world, that is, the best possible world. Hence, this world is the only possible world. Somewhat paradoxically, total modal collapse makes Leibnizian optimism trivially true: this world is the best possible world not because it is the best among many possible worlds, but because it is the only possible world.

By appealing to total modal collapse as well as Leibnizian optimism, Response 1 purports to eliminate the problem of non-actual evil. Leibnizian optimism entails that the actual world is the best possible world. Total modal

---

[8] Kraay introduced the term 'total modal collapse' (Kraay 2011, p. 364).

collapse entails that the actual world is the only possible world. Therefore, there is no possible world that contains appalling evil or that is not the best possible world.

Response 1 is, however, not compelling because it is doubly counter-intuitive. First, it sacrifices the intuitively plausible thesis that the actual world is not the best possible world. Leibnizian optimism is often considered a desperate attempt to defend traditional theism by denying the self-evident truth: the actual world is not the very best possible world. Second, it sacrifices the intuitively plausible thesis that there are possible worlds other than the actual world. Claiming that the actual world is the only possible world creates problematic consequences for modal semantics. I conclude, therefore, that even though Response 1 is compatible with both traditional theism and axiarchism, it should not be adopted by either of them.

4.6 Response 2: All Possible Worlds, Including the Actual World, Exist

Response 2 makes three claims: (i) anti-Leibnizian optimism, according to which the actual world is *not* the very best possible world; (ii) anti-total modal collapse, according to which the best possible world is *not* the only possible world; and (iii) modal realism, according to which all possible worlds exist to the same extent that the actual world does, even though these worlds are all causally and spatiotemporally isolated from one another.

Response 2 says that Leibnizian optimism and modal collapse are false because it is obvious that this world is neither the best possible world nor the only possible world. We can conceive of possible worlds other than the actual world, some of which are better than the actual world. Response 2 is the extreme opposite of Response 1. Response 1 says that only one world, which is both the best possible world and the actual world, exists. Response 2 says, on the other hand, that all possible worlds, including all sorts of possible worlds that are far from the best possible, exist. Modal realism, to which Response 2 subscribes, says that all possible worlds exist to the same extent that the actual world does. Each possible world is spatiotemporally isolated, but they are all as real as the actual world. There is no ontological difference between the actual world and other possible worlds because actuality is merely indexical. The actual world is special for us only because it is *our* world, just as some other possible world is special for the inhabitants

100 THE PROBLEM OF EVIL FOR ATHEISTS

of that world. The ontological picture this view gives us is analogous to the multiverse scenario that we discussed in Chapter 3 of the present book.

Michael Almeida (2011) defends Response 2, not as an axiarchist but as a traditional theist. Given modal realism, all possible worlds are ontologically on a par. God must coexist with all possible worlds, including possible worlds that contain appalling evil and that are not the best possible. Almeida argues, however, that this does not undermine traditional theism. Lewis says that modal realism entails that the net amount of evil in the totality of all possible worlds cannot be increased or diminished (Lewis 1986, p. 127). If God does not make person p_1 suffer from evil in world w_1, God has to make p_1's counterpart p_2, who is as real as p_1, suffer from evil in w_2, or vice versa. Given that we and our counterparts are morally equivalent and ontologically on a par, there is no reason for one to suffer instead of another. Almeida claims that this is comparable to a situation in which a rescuer can rescue either person p_1 or p_2 but not both. If the rescuer rescues p_1 she cannot rescue p_2, or vice versa. In such a situation, it is not appropriate to blame the rescuer for not rescuing p_1 instead of p_2, or vice versa. Similarly, it is not appropriate to blame God for not eliminating evil for p_1 in w_1 instead of eliminating evil for p_2 in w_2, or vice versa (Almeida 2011, p. 9).

Given modal realism, any instance of evil is eliminable from one world but not eliminable from the totality of all possible worlds. Hence, eliminating such an instance of evil from all possible worlds is not a logical possibility. The so-called ought implies can principle says that if p ought to do q then p can do q. The contrapositive of this is that if p cannot do q then it is not the case that p ought to do q. In the situation under consideration, God cannot eliminate appalling evil from the totality of all possible worlds. It then follows that it is not the case that God ought to eliminate appalling evil from the totality of all possible worlds. This does not compromise the doctrine of divine goodness. This doctrine posits that God does everything that He ought to do—and therefore can do—without requiring Him to do things that are beyond His capabilities and thus fall outside His obligations. This also does not undermine the doctrine of divine omnipotence because a logically impossible action is irrelevant to God's omnipotence. As Nick Trakakis writes:

No matter how much controversy and debate may currently surround the extraordinary attribute of divine omnipotence, there is a virtually complete consensus amongst philosophers and theologians that Aquinas is correct in saying that 'anything that implies a contradiction does not fall under God's omnipotence'... (Trakakis 1997, p. 55)

THE PROBLEM OF EVIL FOR AXIARCHISTS   101

Almeida concludes, therefore, that our modal intuition does not undermine the theistic view. This reasoning applies to the problem of non-actual evil as well. As the problem of non-actual evil says, there are possible worlds that contain appalling evil. This does not undermine traditional theism, according to the reasoning, because God cannot increase the axiological value of the totality of all possible worlds by eliminating appalling evil from specific possible worlds.

We saw above that Response 1 is not compelling because it is doubly counterintuitive. It sacrifices the intuitively plausible theses that the actual world is not the best possible world and that there are possible worlds other than the actual world (or the best possible world). Response 2 does not sacrifice these theses. It affirms that the actual world is not the best possible world and that possible worlds other than the actual world and the best possible world exist. Response 2, however, makes another counterintuitive claim, which is based on modal realism: all possible worlds are as real as the actual world. This is a problem for both traditional theists and axiarchists. Yet a more significant problem for axiarchists here is that Response 2 is not compatible with axiarchism because modal realism contradicts axiarchism. Modal realism says that all possible worlds exist to the same extent that the actual world does. We do not then need here the creatively effective ethical requirement of axiarchism, which filters out less-than-good worlds, because no possible world is filtered out in modal realism. Modal realism says that *all* possible worlds, whether they are good or bad, exist, so the axiological value of a world is irrelevant to the existence or non-existence of that world. Moreover, according to modal realism, there is nothing special about the actual world because actuality is mere indexicality.

Response 2 is a subject of contention because of its counterintuitiveness, which stems from its dependence on modal realism. Nevertheless, whether Response 2 is ultimately defensible or not, it remains an option for traditional theism but not for axiarchism. Consequently, axiarchists are unable to address the challenges posed by the problems of actual evil and non-actual evil by invoking Response 2.

4.7 Responses 3: The Actual World Is One of the Overall Good Possible Worlds

Response 3 makes three claims: (i) anti-Leibnizian optimism, according to which the actual world is *not* the very best possible world; (ii) anti-total modal collapse, according to which the best possible world is *not* the only

102 THE PROBLEM OF EVIL FOR ATHEISTS

possible world; and (iii) modal actualism, according to which only the actual world exists.

Response 3 says that Leibnizian optimism is false because it is obvious that this world is not the very best possible world. Response 3 also rejects total modal collapse and replaces it with 'partial modal collapse', according to which only overall good worlds are possible worlds.[9] Partial modal collapse is so called because it collapses the space of possibility into a set of all possible worlds that are overall good.

Traditional theists defend Response 3 as follows: given that God is an omnipotent and wholly good being, God actualizes only one of many possible worlds that are overall good, such as the actual world. Moreover, given that God exists necessarily there is no possible world that is not overall good. All possible worlds are overall good worlds. Thomas V. Morris is a traditional theist who defends Response 3 in relation to the problem of non-actual evil. He claims that God is 'a delimiter of possibilities'. By this he means that apparently possible states of affairs that 'all non-theistic tests of logic and semantics' deem possible are 'strictly impossible in the strongest sense' if they are 'divinely precluded from the realm of real possibility' (Morris 1985, p. 48). In other words, certain states of affairs and worlds are impossible because they conflict with the nature and existence of God. I am not aware of any axiarchist who defends Response 3, but axiarchists might try to parallel Morris's reasoning. The creatively effective ethical requirement actualizes only a possible world that is overall good, such as the actual world. Moreover, given that axiarchism is necessarily true there is no possible world that is not overall good.

Response 3 appears initially to allow both axiarchists and traditional theists to address the problem of actual evil. The existence of evil or the fact that the actual world is not the best possible world does not undermine traditional theism or axiarchism because the actual world is among the overall good worlds. Response 3 also appears initially to allow both traditional theists and axiarchists to address the problem of non-actual evil. There is no possible world that includes appalling evil because all possible worlds are overall good. There are possible worlds that are not the best possible, but that does not undermine traditional theism or axiarchism because they are still overall good worlds.

---

[9] The term 'partial modal collapse' was introduced by Kraay (2011, p. 364).

Response 3 seems to strike a viable compromise between Response 1 and Response 2, which occupy the opposite ends of the spectrum. Response 1 says that no apparently possible world except the actual world is possible or existent. Response 2 says that all apparently possible worlds are possible and existent. Response 3 says that some but not all apparently possible worlds are possible and only the actual world exists. Possible worlds are, according to Response 3, those that are overall good, and the actual world is among them. Our modal intuition is, hence, only partly correct. Response 3 also does not require the infamous Leibnizian optimism. The actual world is an overall good world, but it is not the very best possible world.

Response 3 says that God or the creatively effective ethical requirement delimits possibilities in such a way that only one among the overall good worlds can be actualized. It is, however, unclear why God or the ethical requirement actualized the actual world rather than the best possible world. To answer this question, we have to consider two scenarios: a scenario in which there is no best possible world and a scenario in which there is the best possible world. I argue that consideration of these scenarios shows that Response 3 is available to traditional theists but not to axiarchists.

In the first scenario, where there is no best possible world, it is easy to answer the question why the actual world rather than the best possible world has been actualized: it is impossible for the best possible world to be actualized because there is no such possible world in the first place. Perhaps for any possible world there is always a world that is better than that world. Again, the contrapositive of the 'ought implies can' principle says that if it is impossible for x to do p then it is not the case that x ought to do p. It is not the case that God or the ethical requirement ought to actualize the best possible world because it is impossible for either of them to actualize such a world. They need only to actualize one of the possible worlds that are overall good.

Traditional theists can say that God randomly selects and actualizes any world among all possible worlds that are overall good. Whichever world God chooses and actualizes, there is always a better world that He could have created, but that does not undermine His goodness because it is impossible for Him to create the best possible world. Insofar as God, according to traditional theism, is a personal being with intention and free will, He can decide to randomly select and actualize one of the overall good worlds. Axiarchists cannot make a parallel claim, however, because the creatively effective ethical requirement alone cannot randomly select one of the overall good worlds. A randomizer is not embedded in the axiarchic requirement,

104 THE PROBLEM OF EVIL FOR ATHEISTS

which is based on a Platonic moral ideal. This means that if there is no best possible world Response 3 is not available to axiarchists. At this point one might argue that axiarchism can adopt a 'satisficing approach' that implies that the creatively effective ethical requirement needs to select only a world that is overall good, not necessarily the best possible world. It remains, however, unclear what mechanism within the Platonic ideal of axiarchism facilitates the actualization of a specific possible world that is merely good enough as opposed to another possible world that is better.

Consider, then, the second scenario, where there *is* the best possible world. In this scenario too, Response 3 is available to traditional theists but not to axiarchists. If, as axiarchists say, the creatively effective ethical requirement works as an axiological filter to select good worlds over bad worlds and better worlds over merely good worlds and so on, then no world other than the best possible world should be actualized. Given the assumption of the scenario that there is the best possible world, the creatively effective ethical requirement should not actualize any possible world other than the best possible world. However, the actual world is not the best possible world. Hence, Response 3 is incompatible with axiarchism.

Traditional theists, on the other hand, can offer a reason that the actual world is not the best possible world even in the scenario in which there is the best possible world. They can appeal to the idea that, unlike a non-personal ethical requirement, a morally concerning *personal* creator can choose not to act as an axiological filter to select and actualize the best possible world. Robert Merrihew Adams's theistic response to the question why the actual world is not the best possible world is an elaboration of such an idea. Adams argues that God can choose to create a world other than the best possible world if the following assumptions are met:

(1) None of the individual creatures in it would exist in the best of all possible worlds.

(2) None of the creatures in it has a life which is so miserable on the whole that it would be better for that creature if it had never existed.

(3) Every individual creature in the world is at least as happy on the whole as it would have been in any other possible world in which it could have existed. (Adams 1972, p. 320)

Given these assumptions, if God actualizes a world that is not the best possible world, God does not thereby wrong any creature in it or treat any

THE PROBLEM OF EVIL FOR AXIARCHISTS   105

creature with less than perfect kindness because none of them would have been benefitted if God had chosen to actualize some other possible world instead of the actual world. If God had actualized the best possible world instead of our world, then He would have actualized creatures other than us. It does not therefore make sense for us to blame God for not actualizing a better world.

Adams defines grace as 'a disposition to love which is not dependent on the merit of the person loved' (Adams 1972, p. 324). 'The gracious *person*', he says, 'loves without worrying about whether the person he loves is worthy of his love' (Adams 1972, p. 324, emphasis added). A gracious God, hence, may well choose to create and love less excellent creatures than He could have created. A gracious God does not choose to create any creatures because of their axiological values. Even if God were to create the best possible creatures, their creation would not hinge on their possessing high axiological value. In this way, we can see that God may not act as an axiological filter to choose the best possible world, even though He is the greatest possible being. Adams writes:

> Grace, as I have described it, is not part of everyone's moral ideal. For instance, it was not part of Plato's moral ideal. The thought that it may be the expression of a virtue, rather than a defect of character, in a creator, not to act on the principle of creating the best creatures he possibly could, is quite *foreign to Plato's ethical viewpoint*. But I believe that thought is *not at all foreign to a Judeo-Christian ethical viewpoint*. (Adams 1972, p. 324, emphasis added)

The above passage suggests that grace is not inherent to axiarchism because axiarchism is considered a variant of Platonism. While the specifics of Adams's account may be subject to debate, it is evident that traditional theists can argue that a personal God does not actualize the best possible world, even if there is such a world. Unfortunately, however, such an option is not accessible to axiarchists.

In summary: Response 3 says that God or the creatively effective ethical requirement delimits possibilities in such a way that only one of the overall good worlds can be actualized. I have argued that, whether or not there is the best possible world, this response can be adopted by traditional theists but not by axiarchists because axiarchists lack the resources necessary to underpin Response 3, such as a personal agent like God who selects one of the overall good worlds on the basis of a random decision or divine grace.

106 THE PROBLEM OF EVIL FOR ATHEISTS

4.8 Response 4: All Overall Good Possible Worlds/ Universes, Including the Actual World/Universe, Exist

On the surface, Response 4 is identical to Response 1 as it makes the same three claims: (i) Leibnizian optimism, according to which the actual world is the best possible world; (ii) total modal collapse, according to which the best possible world is the only possible world; and (iii) modal actualism, according to which only the actual world exists. However, the underlying interpretation of the existing world in Response 4 diverges significantly from the implicit understanding in Response 1. According to Response 4, the actual world is identical with what I call the 'optimal multiverse', a set of *universes* that includes all possible universes that are overall good.[10] The shift in focus from worlds to universes makes Response 4 unique. The optimal multiverse is optimal in the sense that by including all possible universes that are overall good, it yields the highest possible overall axiological value. Response 4 initially appears to be compatible with both traditional theism and axiarchism. Theists can say that, given that God is an omnipotent and wholly good being, He actualizes all and only possible universes that are overall good, which means that He actualizes the optimal multiverse. Axiarchists can similarly say that the creatively effective ethical requirement filters out all possible universes that are not overall good and actualizes the optimal multiverse which includes all and only possible universes that are overall good. In both cases, the actual world, which contains (or which corresponds to) the optimal multiverse, is the best possible world.

Addressing the problem of evil, Response 4 says that the fact that the actual universe contains evil does not undermine either traditional theism or axiarchism. Our universe, which contains evil, is not the very best possible *universe*, but it is still an overall good universe that constitutes the very best possible *world*. The distinction between universes and worlds does the job here. Response 4 can be considered a refined version of Response 1. Klaas Kraay (2011) defends Response 4 as a traditional theist and Leslie (2001, 2016) defends it as an axiarchist.

In response to the problem of non-actual evil, Response 4 says that there is no possible world that contains appalling evil because the actual world,

---

[10] Kraay (2011) calls the multiverse containing all possible universes that are overall good the 'theistic multiverse'. I use the neutral term 'optimal multiverse' as I consider it in relation not only to traditional theism but also to axiarchism.

which contains the optimal multiverse, is the only possible world and the only existing world.

Kraay explicitly equates the optimal multiverse with the actual world. He says that theists 'should maintain that the actual world is a multiverse featuring all and only universes worthy of being created and sustained by God' and that they should 'embrace modal collapse: the claim that this multiverse is the only possible world' (Kraay 2011, p. 361). If the optimal multiverse is indeed identical with the actual world, then Response 4 initially appears to be compatible not only with traditional theism but also with axiarchism. Referring to the Leibnizian hierarchy, which ranks all possible worlds in terms of their overall axiological values, the creatively effective ethical requirement selects and actualizes the best possible world and that best possible world is, according to Response 4, the optimal multiverse, which includes the actual universe.

Unfortunately, however, axiarchists face two problems here. First, it is not clear that there is such a thing as the optimal multiverse, which Response 4 equates with the best possible world. In relation to Response 3, we discussed above a scenario in which the best possible world does not exist because for any possible world there is always another possible world that is better. Similarly, it might be the case that for any possible multiverse there is always another possible multiverse that is better. If so, Response 4, like Response 3, is incompatible with axiarchism, which misses theistic resources such as a personal God who can select one of the overall good multiverses (or worlds) on the basis of a random decision.

Suppose then that, in favour of axiarchism, the optimal multiverse *does* exist. Does this mean that axiarchists can pursue Response 4? My answer is negative because the optimal multiverse should not be equated with a world. Again, the optimal multiverse includes all possible universes that are overall good. As Kraay says, each of these universes 'is a spatiotemporally inter-related, causally closed aggregate'. As we saw in Chapter 3, many metaphysicians, though, reject the possibility of 'island universes', universes that exist in the actual world but are causally and spatiotemporally isolated, within the same possible world (Bigelow and Pargetter 1987; Lewis 1986). If so, it is more appropriate to think that what are considered to be universes here are in fact *worlds*. Hence, we have a set of all possible worlds that are overall good, rather than the optimal multiverse containing all possible universes that are overall good. The three claims comprising Response 4 should consequently be replaced with the following: (i) anti-Leibnizian optimism, according to which the actual world is *not* the very best possible world (the

108 THE PROBLEM OF EVIL FOR ATHEISTS

actual world is one of many overall good possible worlds that exist but it is not the best possible world); (ii) anti-total modal collapse, according to which the best possible world is not the only possible world (all possible worlds that are overall good are possible worlds); and (iii) 'positive modal realism', according to which only all possible worlds that are overall good exist.

We can now see that this revised Response 4 is similar to Response 3 because they both accept (i) and (ii). The only difference between the two responses is found in (iii). Response 3 holds modal actualism while revised Response 4 holds positive modal realism. This means that they disagree over whether Response 3 is correct in saying that only one of all the overall good possible worlds (that is, the actual world) exists or whether revised Response 4 is correct in saying that all of the overall good possible worlds, including the actual world, exist. Under this interpretation, Response 4 is compatible with traditional theism but not with axiarchism. Traditional theism can maintain that, referring to the Leibnizian hierarchy of possible worlds, God chooses to make existent all and only possible worlds that are overall good, that is, all possible worlds on the Leibnizian hierarchy that are above a certain axiological threshold. (I say 'make existent' instead of 'actualize' because only one world can be actual.) On the other hand, the creatively effective ethical requirement of axiarchism, which is based on the Platonic ideal and lacks a randomizer or divine grace, cannot choose to make existent worlds other than the best possible world. The fact that the actual world is not the best possible world hence suggests that axiarchism is false.

At this point, one might reformulate axiarchism as a view about *realities* rather than *worlds* and say that the creatively effective ethical requirement actualizes the best possible reality, which consists of all possible worlds that are overall good. Here 'the actual world' or 'the optimal multiverse' is replaced with 'the actual reality' or 'the best possible reality'. However, this approach faces a familiar problem: the best possible reality might not exist because for any possible reality there might always be another possible reality that is better. Moreover, even if the best possible reality exists, axiarchism still faces a problem. The creatively effective ethical requirement of axiarchism can actualize only a single best possible reality, if not a single best possible world, in the Leibnizian axiological hierarchy. Yet there seems no way to construe a reality, which is understood to consist of distinct possible worlds, as a single organic whole that the creatively ethical require- ment can choose to actualize. There has to be some mechanism for binding distinct possible worlds to form a single reality. If there is a personal God, for

THE PROBLEM OF EVIL FOR AXIARCHISTS   109

example, then one could argue that distinct possible worlds are bound in a single reality through God's psychological unity (Forrest 1997, p. 312). This option is not available to axiarchism, however, because axiarchism does not postulate the existence of a personal being (with psychological states) like God. I conclude, therefore, that Response 4 is, like Responses 2 and 3, available to traditional theists but not to axiarchists.

The responses that we have discussed can be summarized as follows (Table 4.1).

Table 4.1 Responses to the Problem of Actual Evil and the Problem of Non-Actual Evil

	View of the actual world	View of modality	View of possible worlds
Response 1 (The actual world is the best possible world)	Leibnizian optimism	Total modal collapse	Modal actualism
Response 2 (All possible worlds, including the actual world, exist)	Anti-Leibnizian optimism	Anti-modal collapse (plenitude)	Modal realism
Response 3 (The actual world is one of the overall good possible worlds)	Anti-Leibnizian optimism	Partial modal collapse	Modal actualism
Response 4—Initial formulation (All overall good possible universes, including the actual universe, exist)	Leibnizian optimism	Total modal collapse	Modal actualism
Response 4—Revised formulation (All overall good possible worlds, including the actual world, exist)	Anti-Leibnizian optimism	Partial modal collapse	Positive modal realism

4.9 An Axiarchic Rebuttal

We have seen the following: Response 1 is available to both traditional theists and axiarchists, but it is at best highly counterintuitive. Responses 2, 3, and 4 are available to traditional theists but not to axiarchists. This seems to show that traditional theists enjoy an overall advantage over axiarchists with respect to both the problem of actual evil and the problem

110 THE PROBLEM OF EVIL FOR ATHEISTS

of non-actual evil. What can axiarchists do at this point? I consider two options for saving axiarchism but argue that they do not succeed.

The first option for saving axiarchism is to exclude human-centred values from the scope of axiarchism. Tim Mulgan (2015, 2017) proposes a novel version of axiarchism which he calls 'ananthropocentric purposivism'. Mulgan contends that common forms of axiarchism take for granted the assumption that theists make: the best possible world should be the best possible world *for human beings*. According to this assumption, the axiological value of a given world is determined at least in part by how good the world is for human beings. Here the existence of evil is thought to undermine the axiological value of a world. Ananthropocentric purposivism rejects this assumption and holds instead that the universe has a purpose but that humans are irrelevant to that purpose. What matters to the purpose are more general, non-human-centred features of the world, such as beauty, mathematical elegance, complexity, and suitability for the emergence of conscious life (Mulgan 2017, p. 7). Ananthropocentric purposivism can be construed as a unique attempt to save axiarchism from both the problem of actual evil and the problem of non-actual evil. Ananthropocentric purposivism says that Leibnizian optimism, according to which the actual world is the best possible world, is correct but *only with respect to non-human-centred values*. This move is uniquely available to axiarchism because theists cannot detach human values from divine purpose; theists believe that human-centred values play an essential role in God's actualization of the world.

Does ananthropocentric purposivism succeed in saving axiarchism? I think it does as far as avoiding the problem of actual evil and the problem of non-actual evil is concerned. These problems are concerned with a mismatch between the expected level of human-centred values according to axiarchism (or traditional theism) and the actual level of human-centred values according to our observation of the actual world. If human-centred values are not part of our axiology, then we can set aside good and evil and, hence, both the problem of actual evil and the problem of non-actual evil disappear. Yet ananthropocentric purposivism seems uncompelling because the exclusion of human-centred values undermines the initial motivation to pursue axiarchism as an alternative to traditional theism.

Axiarchism is typically introduced as an attempt to explain why our universe is fine-tuned without assuming the existence of God. Broadly speaking, the fine-tuning in question is concerned with the exceedingly small likelihood that sentient beings could have arisen in the universe.

THE PROBLEM OF EVIL FOR AXIARCHISTS   111

More narrowly speaking, it is concerned with the even smaller chance that morally significantly free human agents, who are capable of performing morally significant actions by their own will, could have arisen in the universe. If good and evil are excluded from the explanation of creation, then ananthropocentric purposivism cannot explain the most pressing part of the fine-tuning problem. If ananthropocentric purposivism is correct, then pain and suffering are only by-products of non-human-centred features of the world; they exist only by chance. Ananthropocentric purposivism can then explain the fine-tuning of the universe only on a superficial level where only non-human-centred values are considered. Also, it seems arbitrary that ananthropocentric purposivism includes non-human-centred features, such as simplicity and beauty, but excludes human-centred features, such as moral value, because axiology is normally thought to include moral as well as aesthetic values. Excluding human concerns only for the purpose of avoiding the problem of actual evil would make ananthropocentric purposivism an ad hoc view. Hence, I conclude that axiarchism cannot be fully saved by focusing on non-human-centred features of the world.

Another option for saving axiarchism is to maintain that any resources needed to respond to the problem of actual evil and the problem of non-actual evil, including theistic resources, such as the concept of a personal God who can act as an agent to make a random decision or the doctrine of divine grace, *are* available to axiarchists. According to this strategy, axiarchism is a fundamental creatively effective ethical requirement, which allows virtually *anything*—natural or supernatural, personal or non-personal—to be actualized as long as it is better that it be actualized than that it not be actualized. If, for example, Response 3 is right in saying that God, who selects one of the overall good worlds on the basis of a random decision or divine grace, is necessary and the existence of such a being contributes to the overall axiological value of the world, then the creatively effective ethical requirement guarantees the actualization of God. This means that axiarchists can take advantage of whatever response theists develop to address the problem of actual evil and the problem of non-actual evil. This option, however, is untenable because it makes axiarchism vacuous: we can name any valuable resources we choose and axiarchism guarantees their actualization through the creatively effective ethical requirement. Consider the following claim by Mulgan:

> Many theists argue that, while the physical universe exists because it was created by God, God exists because God's existence is *(perfectly) good*...

112 THE PROBLEM OF EVIL FOR ATHEISTS

> Ontological arguments, and other claims that God cannot fail to exist, can also be given an axiarchic reading. Why does the best possible God exist? Why is there a being than which none greater can be thought? Because that is itself for the best... Ontological arguments use value to move from the abstract existence of the divine nature to the concrete existence of God. (Mulgan 2017, p. 2, emphasis in the original)

We can exaggerate this axiarchic reading of traditional theism. On such a reading, axiarchism is a fundamental principle that underlies even traditional theism and, hence, it can respond successfully to any problems that traditional theism can. Unfortunately, such a claim makes axiarchism no longer an *alternative* to traditional theism.

One might argue that if axiarchism underlies traditional theism we can say that axiarchism, rather than traditional theism, represents the ultimate truth and enjoys priority. I am not sure that such a claim makes sense. Most traditional theists agree that logic forms the foundation of traditional theism; for instance, even an omnipotent God cannot create a married bachelor or draw a square circle. Hence, logic takes precedence over theism. However, it would not be appropriate to treat logic as an alternative to traditional theism. Similarly, if axiarchism underpins traditional theism (as well as all other true metaphysical theories), its relationship with traditional theism should be seen in a manner akin to the relationship between logic and traditional theism. It holds a certain priority over traditional theism, but this does not imply that axiarchism is an alternative to theism or somehow 'truer' than traditional theism. Most importantly, this rebuttal does not save axiarchism because it places axiarchism on a par with traditional theism with respect to addressing the problem of evil. That is, it does not make axiarchism more advantageous than traditional theism in responding to the problem of evil.[11]

---

[11] If axiarchists incorporate traditional theism, they have mainly three ways to understand the relationship between axiarchism and traditional theism:

1. Traditional theism is explanatorily prior to axiarchism.

2. Axiarchism is explanatorily prior to traditional theism.

3. Traditional theism and axiarchism are explanatorily independent.

Options 2 and 3 may be incompatible with traditional theism because they appear to allow for the existence of axiologically significant entities that God does not create. I do not discuss these options here, however, as they are not relevant to my focus on the problem of evil in the present book. It is crucial to note that, regardless of the option axiarchists pursue, they cannot avoid addressing the problem of evil and they do not enjoy a greater advantage than traditional theists in responding to the problem. Thanks to Andrew Bailey for his comments on this point.

4.10 Conclusion

What we have seen in this chapter can be summarized as follows. The problem of actual evil and the problem of non-actual evil pose significant challenges for traditional theists. Axiarchists initially avoid these problems as stated but face alternative versions of the same problems. There are four responses to these problems. Response 1 should be rejected as it is highly counterintuitive. Responses 2, 3, and 4 are available to traditional theists but not to axiarchists. There are two unique strategies that are aimed at salvaging axiarchism but neither of them proves successful. One of them in particular implies that axiarchism is not even an alternative to traditional theism.

I conclude therefore that it is better to embrace traditional theism than axiarchism with respect to both the problem of actual evil and the problem of non-actual evil.

PART III

THE PROBLEM OF EVIL FOR ATHEISTS/NON-THEISTS

5
The Problem of Systemic Evil

5.1 Introduction

In Part II of the present book, I argued that the problem of evil does not uniquely and specifically challenge traditional theists because there are versions of the problem which arise for pantheists and axiarchists. I argued, moreover, that traditional theists enjoy advantages over pantheists and axiarchists in responding to those versions of the problem. Even if my argument succeeds, however, my achievement so far is relatively limited because pantheists and axiarchists do not represent the majority of non-theists. The majority of non-theists would reject not only the existence of God according to traditional theism, but also the existence of God according to pantheism and the existence of a creatively effective ethical requirement according to axiarchism. Hence, the majority of non-theists may not be bothered by my claim that evil creates a challenge for pantheists and axiarchists as well as traditional theists. In the rest of the present book, therefore, I try to develop a more expansive version of the problem of evil, one which arises for atheists and other non-theists.

Let me explain how I aim to develop my argument. Recall that in Chapter 1 I offered a comprehensive analysis of the problem of evil, arguing that this problem consists of three variables: (i) God, (ii) evil, and (iii) the allegedly conflicting relationship between God and evil. In what follows, I introduce a radically new version of the problem, which I call the 'problem of systemic evil', by tweaking variable (ii) while keeping the value of variable (i) that traditional theists normally assign to it—an omnipotent and wholly good being as conceived in traditional theism. This means that, as the first step, in this chapter I develop the problem of systemic evil as a new challenge for *traditional theists*. In the following chapters, however, I try to 'neutralize' the problem of systemic evil by adjusting variable (i). That is, I transform the problem in such a way that systemic evil poses a challenge not only for traditional theists, but also for atheists and other non-theists.

The Problem of Evil for Atheists. Yujin Nagasawa, Oxford University Press. © Yujin Nagasawa 2024.
DOI: 10.1093/oso/9780198901884.003.0006

118 THE PROBLEM OF EVIL FOR ATHEISTS

This chapter has the following structure. In Section 5.2, I shed light on pain and suffering that sentient animals, including humans, experience in the process of natural selection and evolution. In Section 5.3, I argue that the system of natural selection and evolution, which underlies such pain and suffering, constitutes the problem of systemic evil for traditional theists. I then discuss the uniqueness of systemic evil in detail by referring to the list of varieties of evil which I introduced in Chapter 1. In Section 5.4, I explain that the problem of systemic evil that I present in this chapter poses a substantial *challenge* for traditional theism rather than an *argument against* traditional theism. In Section 5.5, I discuss the notion of a challenge by addressing Voltaire's criticism of Leibniz's theistic response to the problem of evil. Section 5.6 concludes.

5.2 Pain and Suffering in Nature

Consider variable (ii) in our scheme of the problem of evil. The problem of systemic evil assigns a value to this variable by focusing on the pain and suffering that are necessitated in the process of natural selection and evolution.

Nature is governed by natural selection, which involves competition for survival. Uncountably many organisms have competed and struggled for survival over the last four billion years, and this process is still ongoing. No biological organisms in nature can escape this process entirely, no matter how intelligent they are. In this cruel, blind system, the weaker are eliminated, and even the survivors will eventually die, often painfully and miserably. It seems intuitively obvious that this observation creates a challenge for traditional theists who believe that nature was created by an omnipotent and wholly good God.

The claim that pain and suffering in nature constitute a challenge for traditional theists is not new. In fact, Charles Darwin himself expressed his perplexity about the cruelty of nature when he introduced the theory of evolution. Darwin considers this problem explicitly in reference to the Ichneumonidae, a family of parasitic wasps. These wasps paralyse grasshoppers and caterpillars without killing them. They take the prey into their nests and deposit eggs into the bodies in such a way that the hatchlings can feed on the live bodies of the prey. Darwin finds it difficult to reconcile such cruelty in nature with the theistic worldview. In his letter to Asa Gray dated 22 May 1860, Darwin writes:

THE PROBLEM OF SYSTEMIC EVIL   119

With respect to the theological view of the question; this is always painful to me.—I am bewildered.—I had no intention to write atheistically. But I own that I cannot see, as plainly as others do, & as I should wish to do, evidence of design & beneficence on all sides of us. There seems to me too much misery in the world. I cannot persuade myself that a beneficent & omnipotent God would have designedly created the Ichneumonidae with the express intention of their feeding within the living bodies of caterpillars, or that a cat should play with mice. (Darwin 1887, p. 311)

Some may argue that caterpillars do not experience significant suffering, or at least that their capacity for suffering is minimal given their limited cognitive, sensory, and neural systems, which would not allow them to experience pain in the same way as humans. Even if that is true, there are many other examples of cruelty in nature that involve sentient animals. For example, as Darwin mentions in the above quote, there have been and there will be uncountably many mice that are severely injured and die slowly and painfully as cats play with them. There are many other examples involving the pain and suffering of higher life forms.

In an earlier letter to J. D. Hooker dated 13 July 1856, Darwin famously writes: 'What a book a Devil's chaplain might write on the clumsy, wasteful, blundering low & horridly cruel works of nature!'[1] If we focus on pain and suffering in the process of natural selection, we can analogize nature to a small cage in which many animals are locked in together so that they fight desperately and kill each other to obtain and hold limited resources until a handful survive. In fact, Darwin's theory of evolution was inspired by Thomas Malthus's book, *An Essay on the Principle of Population* (1798), in which Malthus argues that the human population would cease growing exponentially after reaching a certain number because the propensity of populations to produce more offspring than can possibly survive with the limited resources available to them causes war, famine, and disease, which would effectively reduce population size. Darwin applies Malthus's insight to the larger biological domain.

Many contemporary scholars share Darwin's sentiment regarding the cruelty of nature. The philosopher Holmes Rolston III, for example, writes, 'Though there is no sin in amoral nature, there is quite a list of candidate evils from which nature might need to be redeemed: predation, parasitism,

---

[1] See Paul Draper (2012) for a detailed discussion of Darwin's view of pain and suffering in nature. I note that my view of evil and natural selection is inspired by Draper's important work.

120 THE PROBLEM OF EVIL FOR ATHEISTS

selfishness, randomness, blindness, disaster, indifference, waste, struggle, suffering, death' (Rolston 1994, p. 212). Similarly, in an interview with Frank Miele, Richard Dawkins, one of the best-known contemporary champions of the theory of evolution, says:

> [N]atural selection is out there and it is a very unpleasant process. Nature is red in tooth and claw. But I don't want to live in that kind of a world. I want to change the world in which I live in such a way that natural selection no longer applies. (Miele 1995)

Dawkins's claim that he does not want to live in a world governed by natural selection is illuminating because it makes us realize vividly how cruel nature is. Imagine a society in which legal and political systems are designed to mimic natural selection. People in such a society would have to fight constantly for limited resources; assault and murder to obtain food and other goods would be everyday events. Those who survive are likely to be selfish and physically strong individuals whose main concern is their own survival. Those who are disadvantaged, such as the elderly, the poor, and the sick, would have no hope of surviving. Nature seems comparable to such a violent, unfair, and immoral society, in which few would wish to live.

One might think that these descriptions of nature are exaggerated. The seventeenth-century philosopher Pierre Bayle makes pessimistic claims about the world: 'that man is wicked and miserable; that there are everywhere prisons and hospitals; that history is simply a collection of crimes and calamities of the human face'. Leibniz, who is known for his optimistic worldview, rejects Bayle's pessimism by contending that it is an overstatement.

> I think that there is exaggeration in that: there is incomparably more good than evil in the life of men, as there are incomparably more houses than prisons. With regard to virtue and vice, a certain mediocrity prevails. Machiavelli has already observed that there are few very wicked and very good men, and that this causes the failure of many great enterprises. I find it a great fault in historians that they keep their mind on the evil more than the good. The chief end of history, as also of poetry, should be to teach prudence and virtue by examples, and then to display vice in such a way as to create aversion to it and to prompt men to avoid it, or serve towards that end. (Leibniz 1710/1985, p. 216)

One might follow Leibniz's optimism and point out that the pain and suffering that animals experience are mostly irrelevant to us because, even in the worst cases, modern humans have never lived in a cruel survival game of beasts. Even if such a claim is correct, though, it should be acknowledged that billions of other sentient animals have lived and will live in hostile and violent environments. Moreover, from a larger historical point of view, humans *are* products of a long evolutionary process, which has involved a long series of violent, cruel, and unfair competitions among our animal ancestors. Moreover, these sentient animals constitute natural resources on which our human existence depends heavily. The fact that we, privileged humans, are fortunate enough to avoid the most violent consequences of natural selection does not mean that we transcend the biological system.

5.3 The Nature of Systemic Evil

We have seen that nature is filled with pain and suffering, which are outcomes of natural selection and evolution. This, however, is not news for philosophers. In fact, philosophers have discussed the problem of evil in relation to natural selection and evolution intensively. For example, contemporary scholars, such as Paul Draper (1989, 2012) and Quentin Smith (1991), have developed and defended the use of natural selection as an argument against traditional theism, and such theistic scholars as Michael A. Corey (2000), Trent Dougherty (2014a), Michael J. Murray (2008), and Christopher Southgate (2008) have tried to respond to them. What is, then, unique about the problem of systemic evil that I raise here?

The problem of evil standardly focuses on specific *events* that are considered evil (for example, World War II, the Holocaust, the Boxing Day Tsunami) or specific *types of events* that are considered evil (for example, wars, genocides, natural disasters). Indeed, when the above philosophers address the problem of pain and suffering in nature, they focus on specific events or specific types of events in nature. The most well-known case that is relevant here is perhaps William L. Rowe's example of a fawn that is burnt badly in a bushfire and dies slowly and painfully (Rowe 1979, p. 337). As we saw in Chapter 1, Rowe discusses this as an instance of gratuitous evil which can serve as evidence against the existence of God.

I do not exclude the possibility that specific events or specific types of events can pose a problem for traditional theists. In advancing the problem

122   THE PROBLEM OF EVIL FOR ATHEISTS

of systemic evil, however, I do not repeat the same point. My point is rather that the entire biological *system* on which nature is based poses a challenge for theists' belief in the existence of an omnipotent and wholly good God. That is why I call this the problem of *systemic* evil. I believe that the problem of systemic evil is more profound than other versions of the problem of evil because it suggests a conflict between God and evil on a deep level: it appears that God chose to install a specific system that nomologically necessities pain and suffering.

Typically, when theists face the problem of evil they try to explain away specific events or specific types of events that are deemed evil by advancing theodicies. Take the free will theodicy. This theodicy is an attempt to shift the apparent responsibility for realizing evil from God to humans. For instance, the existence of crimes is not a threat to belief in the existence of God because, according to this theodicy, crimes are outcomes of human abuse of morally significant freedom; humans, rather than God, are responsible for evil. However, this kind of theodicy does not seem to be applicable to the problem of systemic evil. Even if specific instances or types of evil are outcomes of human freedom, the biological system which necessitates pain and suffering is not an outcome of human freedom. Humans are not responsible for the existence of the system. Specific instances or types of evil may be freak accidents or consequences of personal wrongdoings. Yet the system of natural selection and evolution, which guarantees pain and suffering for uncountably many sentient animals, is not a matter of accidents or individual responsibility. Under the system pain and suffering are nomological necessities.

Consider again the abovementioned analogy to society. We may be able to explain, either legally or politically, why certain events or types of events—such as crimes, violence, and wars, all considered evil—occur in society, and how individuals are held responsible for them. These explanations are analogous to theodicies. However, the more fundamental question remains: why must these specific legal and political systems, which give rise to such events or types of events, exist in the first place?

In Chapter 1, we saw a variety of evil summarized by reference to quantity and quality in the following list:

Quality
- Nature of Evil
  - Axiological Evil vs Deontological Evil
  - Unspecific Evil vs Specific Evil

- Causes of Evil
  - Moral Evil vs Natural Evil
  - Individual Moral Evil vs Collective Moral Evil
- Victims of Evil
  - Humans vs Non-Human Sentient Animals
- Kinds of Evil
  - Gratuitous Evil vs Non-Gratuitous Evil
  - Varieties of Pain and Suffering

Quantity

- Intensity of Evil
- Extensity of Evil
  - Individual Victims vs Group Victims
  - Space
  - Time
  - Modality

To understand the uniqueness of systemic evil more precisely, let us review the above categorization. Consider first the distinction between axiological evil and deontological evil. When the problem of systemic evil is presented as a challenge for traditional theists, it can be formulated either axiologically or deontologically. If it is formulated axiologically it says that the axiological level of a world that contains a biological system which necessitates pain and suffering for uncountably many organisms does not seem to match the level that we reasonably expect from theistic belief in an omnipotent and wholly good God. If the problem is formulated deontologically, on the other hand, it says that the moral status of a world that contains a biological system that necessitates pain and suffering for uncountably many organisms does not seem to match the moral status that we reasonably expect from theistic belief in an omnipotent and wholly good God.

Consider now the distinction between unspecific evil and specific evil. According to the problem of unspecific evil, the existence of evil in general is incompatible with the existence of God. According to the problem of specific evil, on the other hand, the existence of a specific type of evil (for example, wars, genocides, natural disasters) or a specific instance of evil (for example, World War II, the Holocaust, the Boxing Day Tsunami) is incompatible with the existence of God. As I observed above, the problem of systemic evil falls into neither of these categories. It is certainly not a version of the problem of specific evil because it does not focus on any specific instance or type of evil. Neither, however, is it a version of the problem of unspecific

124   THE PROBLEM OF EVIL FOR ATHEISTS

evil because it does not focus on the existence of evil in general. It focuses instead on the specific *system* which necessitates instances or types of evil. In other words, systemic evil is not a specific or unspecific instance of evil; it is rather the foundation of such instances.

Consider now the cause of systemic evil. The problem of systemic evil is a version of the problem of natural evil because it focuses on a biological system for which humans are not responsible. Unlike common versions of the problem of natural evil, though, it does not refer to any specific natural disasters, such as tornados, earthquakes, and flooding. Again, the focus of the problem is on the system of natural selection and evolution. One might argue that if we assume that the system was created by a morally responsible God we could in principle consider systemic evil a variation of moral evil, rather than natural evil. Yet systemic evil remains radically distinct from ordinary instances of moral evil such as wars and crimes, which stem from the actions of free humans.

The distinction between individual evil and collective evil depends on whether a given wrongdoing arises from the intent or negligence of an individual or a collective of individuals. If we construe the problem of systemic evil as a version of the problem of moral evil, where God is alleged to be responsible for the existence of the biological system, then one could argue that the problem of systemic evil is a version of the problem of individual evil. Here, the individual in question is God. Whether or not such an argument is compelling, it seems clear that, given monotheism and given that free human agents are not morally responsible for the existence of the biological system, the problem of systemic evil cannot be a version of the problem of collective evil.

Consider now the victims of evil. Philosophers have focused primarily on types of evil, such as wars, crimes, and earthquakes, in which humans are victims. Some however have also discussed types of evil, such as bushfires and environmental degradation, in which non-human animals are victims. The problem of systemic evil subsumes pain and suffering for all sentient animals, including both humans and non-human animals, which are subject to the process of natural selection and evolution. In other words, victims of systemic evil include all sentient animals that are subject to natural selection and evolution. In this sense, the problem of systemic evil is an all-encompassing form of the problem of evil.

Regarding types of evil, we can begin with the distinction between gratuitous evil and non-gratuitous evil. This distinction applies to specific types or instances of evil. For example, the suffering of a fawn being burnt

THE PROBLEM OF SYSTEMIC EVIL   125

alone in a bushfire seems gratuitous because it does not realize any greater good while the moderate pain experienced when stubbing a toe seems non-gratuitous because it is necessary for realizing the greater good of avoiding more serious bodily damage. This distinction does not apply to systemic evil because systemic evil is not a specific type or instance of evil in a relevant sense. There is, however, an effective way to articulate the problem of systemic evil by focusing on gratuitous evil rather than non-gratuitous evil that arises in the process of natural selection. The existence of natural selection seems to be particularly problematic for traditional theists when we focus on the gratuitous pain and suffering that are necessitated by the biological system. In Chapter 1, in relation to the distinction between gratuitous evil and non-gratuitous evil, I discussed Mackie's notion of first-order evil and second-order evil (Mackie 1982, p. 154). Mackie calls basic instances of pleasure instances of first-order good and basic instances of pain and suffering instances of first-order evil. Instances of compassion and heroism, for example, can be considered instances of second-order good because they are realized through first-order evil; and instances of disinterest and cowardice can be considered instances of second-order evil because they are realized through first-order good. It is interesting to point out that systemic evil is fundamental in the sense that the system in question underlies even evil of the lowest order.

In Chapter 1, I also discussed distinct types of pain and suffering. We saw that particular attention to horrendous evil, an intense and most horrific form of evil, makes us wonder whether it constitutes a prima facie reason to doubt that the lives of those who suffer such evil can be considered good on the whole. The problem of systemic evil does not focus on any specific types of pain or suffering, but it can be presented most vividly when we focus on the fact that the most horrendous instances of evil are also outcomes of the process of natural selection and evolution.

Let us move on to discuss the quantity rather than the quality of evil. Consider first the intensity of evil in terms of the degree of pain and suffering the victims experience. Not only all kinds of evil but also all degrees of pain and suffering are relevant to the problem of systemic evil because, again, pain and suffering of all kinds are outcomes of the evolutionary process. The extensity of evil—how many victims there are and how evil is distributed spatially and temporally—is also relevant to systemic evil. Every instance of pain and suffering realized in any spatial region on Earth at any

126 THE PROBLEM OF EVIL FOR ATHEISTS

point in time in the planet's biological history is an outcome of the process of natural selection and evolution.

The problem of systemic evil does not arise if there are no sentient organisms in the world. For instance, there was no problem of systemic evil at the time the Big Bang took place. It is important to note, however, that the focus of the problem does not have to be limited to Earth, because theists believe that God created the whole world, not just this specific planet. Hence, it may well be the case that the problem of systemic evil existed before sentient organisms appeared on Earth and may continue to exist after their disappearance because there may be other planets where sentient organisms evolve through natural selection or a similar process. In the present book, however, I focus on systemic evil realized specifically on Earth.[2]

Again, systemic evil itself does not correspond to any specific events that involve pain and suffering, but the system in question that underlies all such events. In this sense, the problem of systemic evil is possibly the most fully encompassing form of the problem of evil. Name any instance of evil that seems particularly egregious. It is part of the problem of systemic evil.

Consider, finally, modality. Traditional theists typically believe that God is a necessary being. That is, God exists in all possible worlds. That is why, as we saw in Chapters 1 and 4, the problem of evil can be formulated not only in terms of actual evil, that is, evil that is realized in the actual world, but also non-actual evil, that is, evil that is realized in possible worlds other than the actual world. The problem of non-actual evil is particularly intractable when we consider extreme instances of evil that seem metaphysically possible but not actual, such as a state of affairs in which billions of innocent people are tortured for billions of years for no reason. Like the standard problem of evil, the problem of systemic evil could also be 'modalized' by considering a possible world in which natural selection or some other system necessitates extreme instances of evil which are worse than instances found in our world. For the sake of simplicity, however, I focus on systemic evil in the actual world, or, more specifically, systemic evil on our planet.

The uniqueness of the problem of systemic evil, which distinguishes it from other problems of evil, lies in its fundamental and all-encompassing nature. Natural selection is a fundamental matter because it serves as a fundamental biological process shaping our entire natural environment, from which no organism can escape. Moreover, it is an all-encompassing

---

[2] See Guy Kahane (2022) and Chapter 8 of the present book on the spatial and temporal aspects of the problem of systemic evil.

matter because it subsumes all instances of evil experienced by sentient beings, both human and non-human, across the entire biological spectrum throughout natural history.

5.4 The Allegedly Conflicting Relationship between God and Systemic Evil

Again, the problem of evil consists of three variables: (i) God, (ii) evil, and (iii) an allegedly conflicting relationship between God and evil. So far in this chapter I have focused on formulating the problem of systemic evil for traditional theists. Here, I have assigned a value to variable (i) as traditional theists normally do. That is, I have assumed that God is an omnipotent and wholly good being who created the actual world.

When formulating the problem of systemic evil, variable (ii) is given a unique value. The following are some key points about systemic evil that I established in the previous section.

- Systemic evil can be understood either axiologically or deontologically.
- Systemic evil is neither specific nor unspecific.
- Systemic evil can be considered a type of natural evil, but it does not correspond to any specific natural events such as natural disasters.
- Systemic evil can be construed as individual evil but not as collective evil.
- Systemic evil involves both human and non-human sentient animals as victims.
- The distinction between gratuitous evil and non-gratuitous evil does not apply to systemic evil, even though the system of natural selection and evolution underlies both.
- Systemic evil itself is not an instance of horrendous evil, but the system in question underlies all instances of horrendous evil that emerge as part of natural selection and evolution.
- The intensity and extensity of all instances of evil realized in the process of natural selection and evolution are linked to systemic evil.
- Instances of systemic evil on other planets or in other possible worlds are also relevant even though they are set aside in our discussion here.

We are now left with variable (iii), which is concerned with the relationship between variable (i) and variable (ii). How should this relationship be

128　THE PROBLEM OF EVIL FOR ATHEISTS

understood in formulating the problem of systemic evil? As discussed in Chapter 1, the following are common options for assigning values to variable (iii):

- The Logical Problem of Evil (Mackie 1955)
- The Evidential Problem of Evil
  - The Inductive Version (Rowe 1988, 1991)
  - The Deductive Version (Rowe 1996)
  - The Abductive Version (Draper 1989)

The above categorization is based on the assumption that the problem of evil should be presented as an '*argument* from evil' against traditional theism. That is, it is assumed that there is a logical or evidential (as well as inductive, deductive, or abductive) inference from the existence of evil to the non-existence of God. It is indeed possible to adapt the notion of systemic evil to formulate the argument from evil. However, defending the problem of evil as a successful refutation of traditional theism is not an easy task.

First, it is difficult to show that God and evil are *logically* incompatible. Even if there is a way to show this, it would involve many extra steps and assumptions that are inevitably contentious because, as Plantinga observes, if there is any contradiction at all between the proposition that God exists and the proposition that evil exists, it is neither explicitly nor formally contradictory (Plantinga 1974a, p. 16). Many philosophers, including those of an atheistic persuasion, concur that there exists no purely logical proof demonstrating the impossibility of God's existence in the presence of evil. The atheist Rowe, for example, writes, 'Some philosophers have contended that the existence of evil is *logically* inconsistent with the existence of the theistic God. No one, I think, has succeeded in establishing such an extravagant claim' (Rowe 1979, p. 335).

Second, it is not easy to pursue the evidential route either, because it is difficult to make inductive, deductive (probabilistic), or abductive inferences when considering God, who, by definition, is distinct from ordinary beings and eludes our full comprehension. It is difficult, if not impossible, to make an uncontentious inference concerning what God ought or ought not do or to assign probabilistic values to such a proposition as that God exists given that evil exists, even if we have subjective probability in mind here.

I acknowledge that we can attempt to frame the problem of evil as a logical or deductive argument, but I agree with Rowe that no matter what evidence we may have it is unlikely that the problem of evil conclusively

THE PROBLEM OF SYSTEMIC EVIL 129

refutes traditional theism (Rowe 1996, p. 266). I believe that the same claim applies to alternatives to traditional theism. When I say that there are versions of the problem of evil for atheists and other non-theists, I do not mean that there are versions of the argument from evil which I believe conclusively refute atheism/non-theism. I mean instead that certain versions pose powerful challenges for atheists and other non-theists, just as certain versions pose powerful challenges for traditional theists. Hence, in this chapter, I have not aimed to present the problem of systemic evil as an *argument* against traditional theism. Instead, I have presented it in a somewhat less formal manner as a *challenge* for traditional theists.

I do aim to avoid entangling myself in the ongoing and highly contentious debate between traditional theists and their critics concerning the argument from evil and its various responses. It would be a formidable endeavour to establish the problem of systemic evil as an unequivocal refutation of traditional theism before applying it to challenge atheism/non-theism. Therefore, the success of this chapter lies in persuading the reader that the problem of systemic evil at least presents a substantial challenge for traditional theists.

Hence, the conclusion of my discussion of the problem of systemic evil in the present chapter is not that traditional theism is false or unlikely to be true in light of the existence of systemic evil. It is rather that traditional theists must take the problem of systemic evil seriously because it poses a particularly significant challenge for them.

5.5 Systemic Evil as a Challenge

In discussing Voltaire's response to Leibniz's optimism, Peter Kivy (1979) makes an interesting point that is relevant to my claim that the problem of systemic evil is a challenge for, rather than an argument against, traditional theism.

Voltaire's *Candide: Optimism* (1759/1947) features a character named Pangloss, who is a caricature of Leibniz. Pangloss is an optimistic philosopher who confidently believes that despite the existence of evil the actual world is the best of all possible worlds. His slogan is 'All is for the best in the best of all possible worlds'. According to Kivy, Pangloss would not be moved by any argument against optimism because he believes optimism to be entailed by his firm belief that there is an omnipotent and wholly good God. Pangloss does not believe that the coherence of such a belief can be

130   THE PROBLEM OF EVIL FOR ATHEISTS

disputed because, according to him, it is established on a priori grounds. Hence, Kivy writes, 'We cannot, therefore, do anything in the way of ratiocination to dislodge his [Pangloss's] optimism, short of beginning at the beginning, with his a priori proof (or in Leibniz's case, proofs) of God's existence and attributes, and showing the proof invalid or the premises false' (Kivy 1979, p. 218). In other words, there is no *argument* against optimism that would move Pangloss. Kivy claims, however, that there is an alternative way of challenging Pangloss and that is precisely what Voltaire pursues through the story of Candide, a student of Pangloss who encounters numerous instances of evil over the course of his journey. Kivy writes:

> We can, however, get at Pangloss' optimism directly, without making this 'end run,' in another way. We can, by bombarding him, so to speak, with the evil of the world, by, in other words, sticking his nose in it, force his belief in optimism closer and closer to zero point, and, in so doing, put such a strain on his theological belief system that it may crack, thus impelling him to a reexamination of its a priori grounds. This is not 'refutation' in the sense defined above: it is not, that is, a logical demonstration of falsity. So let us call it instead 'confounding'... (Kivy 1979, p. 218)

Candide encounters a multitude of horrific events in the world, such as wars, earthquakes, and slavery. Voltaire's aim in citing these events is not to develop a logically structured argument against Pangloss's optimism. Instead, he intends to challenge Pangloss's unwavering adherence to optimism by exposing him to the gruesome aspects of reality that contrast starkly with his optimistic expectations rooted in theistic belief. Lloyd Strickland claims that in the following passage Arthur Schopenhauer adopts the same strategy as Voltaire (Strickland 2010, p. 19):[3]

> If, finally, we should bring clearly to a man's sight the terrible sufferings and miseries to which his life is constantly exposed, he would be seized with horror; and if we were to conduct the confirmed optimist through the hospitals, infirmaries, and surgical operating-rooms, through the prisons, torture-chambers, and slave-kennels, over battle-fields and places of execution; if we were to open to him all the dark abodes of misery, where it hides itself from the glance of cold curiosity, and, finally, allow him to

[3] Strickland (2010, p. 19) notes that this approach was also adopted by Nicholas Malebranche and several other philosophers.

THE PROBLEM OF SYSTEMIC EVIL   131

glance into the starving dungeon of Ugolino, he, too, would understand at last the nature of this 'best of possible worlds.' For whence did Dante take the materials for his hell but from this our actual world? And yet he made a very proper hell of it. And when, on the other hand, he came to the task of describing heaven and its delights, he had an insurmountable difficulty before him, for our world affords no materials at all for this. (Schopenhauer, 1844/1909, p. 420)

My approach aligns with that of Voltaire and Schopenhauer in the sense that I do not aim to construct a formal refutation of traditional theism based on the existence of evil. I focus on illuminating the gruesome foundation of the existence of sentient animals by referring to systemic evil and presenting it as a formidable challenge for traditional theists.[4]

I wish to emphasize, however, that my approach differs from Voltaire's and Schopenhauer's in important respects. First, I do not, and indeed do not need to, bombard traditional theists with numerous examples of evil. The problem of systemic evil is parsimonious because the system in question is the basis of all instances of pain and suffering realized through the process of natural selection and evolution. Therefore, there is no need to list many specific examples of evil as Voltaire and Schopenhauer do. Second, even though Voltaire and Schopenhauer do not intend to present a structured argument against traditional theism, their aim is still to undermine traditional theism. Yet I do not advocate for the dismissal of traditional theism as a consequence of the problem of systemic evil. On the contrary, as explained in Chapter 8 of the present book, I believe that traditional theists can be more optimistic than atheists and other non-theists regarding the potential for developing a successful response to the problem.

5.6 Conclusion

In this chapter I have introduced the problem of systemic evil, which arises for traditional theists who believe in the existence of God as an omnipotent and wholly good being. I have argued that the problem of systemic evil is

---

[4] Voltaire's and Schopenhauer's points can be developed into a Bayesian argument if we construe their gruesome examples of evil as cumulative evidence against the existence of an omnipotent and wholly good God. As I explained in Chapter 2, however, I do not pursue this route in the present book because I wish to free our discussion of any unnecessary technicality and complexity.

more pressing than other versions of the problem of evil because it is linked to all instances of pain and suffering that sentient human and non-human animals experience. I have also argued that the problem of systemic evil is fundamental because it is concerned with the entire biological system underlying our existence—a system for which we bear no responsibility.

6
Optimism

6.1 Introduction

In the previous chapter, I introduced the problem of systemic evil, a version of the problem of evil which focuses on the system of natural selection and evolution, a system which necessitates pain and suffering for countless sentient animals. I presented this problem as a significant challenge for traditional theists who believe in the existence of an omnipotent and wholly good God. It is important to recall, however, that I argued in Chapter 2 that the problem of evil is not exclusive to traditional theists; rather, it is a broader problem concerning axiological expectation mismatch, a discrepancy between one's expectation of how the world should be and one's observation of how it actually is. In the next chapter, I apply this argument to the problem of systemic evil to show that this version of the problem of evil can be 'neutralized' in such a way that it raises a challenge for most 'optimists', which include most traditional theists, pantheists, axiarchists, and even atheists. More broadly, I argue that the problem of systemic evil arises for anyone who, irrespective of their stance on traditional theism and its alternatives, finds their optimistic expectation of reality failing to match their observation of reality.

Before developing my approach to neutralizing the problem of systemic evil, I clarify exactly what I mean by optimism in our context. My ultimate goal is to develop a version of the problem of systemic evil that applies to as many optimists as possible, including many atheists and other non-theists as well as traditional theists. In this chapter, therefore, I try to arrive at a version of optimism that is very modest yet optimistic enough to create a relevant axiological expectation mismatch.

This chapter has the following structure. In Section 6.2, I discuss the origin of the term 'optimism' and present its philosophical background. In Section 6.3, I specify the scope of optimism in reference to the axiological value of reality rather than the moral status of actions. In Section 6.4, I discuss Leibniz's optimism and its alternatives and argue that we should focus on what I call 'modest optimism'. In Section 6.5, I discuss several

The Problem of Evil for Atheists. Yujin Nagasawa, Oxford University Press. © Yujin Nagasawa 2024.
DOI: 10.1093/oso/9780198901884.003.0007

134 THE PROBLEM OF EVIL FOR ATHEISTS

characteristics of optimism in detail and try to specify the scope of modest optimism. In Section 6.6, I argue from both philosophical and psychological perspectives that most non-theists (as well as traditional theists) are likely to accept modest optimism. Section 6.7 concludes.

6.2 The Origin of Optimism

Today, the term 'optimism' is used in a variety of contexts, including medicine, psychology, economics, politics, and even the weather. However, the term is historically linked to a debate in the philosophy of religion. In fact, it is one of the very few terms that have been coined in the philosophy of religion and are now commonly used beyond academia.

The term 'optimism' is derived from the Latin term *optimum*, which means 'best'. Leibniz published *Essays of Theodicy on the Goodness of God, the Freedom of Man and the Origin of Evil*—or *Theodicy* in short—in 1710. In this work, Leibniz used the phrase *optimum* to describe his own thesis that this world is the best possible world. In 1737, the French Jesuit mathematician Louis-Bertrand Castel coined, in his review of *Theodicy*, the term 'optimism' in describing Leibniz's work as 'the system of the best [l'Optimum], or optimism [l'optimisme]' (Castel 1737, p. 207; Strickland 2019, p. 9). Voltaire published his satire *Candide: Optimism* in 1759. This is a fictional story about Candide, a nephew of a German baron. Candide is taught that this world is the best possible world by an optimistic scholar, Pangloss, who is a caricature of Leibniz. Candide is kicked out of his home when he falls in love with the baron's young daughter. Over the course of his journey he encounters a myriad of evil, including wars, earthquakes, and slavery. In the end, he meets an old Turkish man living a simple life and concludes that 'we must go and work in the garden' (Voltaire 1759/1947, p. 143). The story, which represents Voltaire's critique of Leibniz's optimism, popularized the term 'optimism'.

6.3 Optimism and Axiology

In Chapter 1, we discussed the distinction between the problem of axiological evil and the problem of deontological evil. According to the problem of deontological evil, evil is understood in terms of the moral status of actions, such as whether one ought to do x or one ought not to do x.

Atheists who adopt this approach argue that, roughly speaking, the deontological assessment shows that there are states of affairs in the actual world such that an omnipotent and wholly good God ought not to bring them about or ought not to let them happen. According to the axiological approach, on the other hand, evil is understood in terms of the undesirability or negative value of pain, which is intrinsically bad (as well as the desirability or positive value of pleasure, which is intrinsically good). Atheists who adopt this approach argue that, roughly speaking, the suboptimal axiological value of a certain state of affairs in the actual world or the overall suboptimal axiological value of the actual world implies that there is not an omnipotent and wholly good God. (In what follows, I use such terms as 'goodness', 'greatness', and 'pleasure' interchangeably and such terms as 'badness', 'evil', and 'pain' interchangeably.)

Here (and in the rest of the present book), I adopt the axiological, rather than the deontological, approach, for two reasons. First, in philosophical discourse optimism is conventionally understood as an axiological thesis. It is a positive claim about the axiological values of pain and pleasure realized in the actual world, rather than a positive claim about the moral status of actions performed in the actual world. Second, the axiological approach is more closely aligned than the deontological approach with our attempt to develop versions of the problem of evil which apply to non-theists. The deontological approach applies to traditional theists, who believe in the existence of God as a moral agent who ought or ought not to bring about certain states of affairs. This approach is not, however, relevant to atheists and other non-theists who do not believe in the existence of any significant moral agent that is comparable to God. The axiological approach, which is concerned with the general expectation regarding the presence of pleasure and pain, or good and evil, in the actual world, is better suited to developing a version of the problem of evil that applies to as many people as possible.

6.4 Leibnizian Optimism and Modest Optimism

Consider a version of optimism which Leibniz defends in *Theodicy*:

> Leibnizian optimism: The actual world is the best possible world.

This is the same thesis that we addressed in Chapter 4 of the present book in our discussion of axiarchism. Leibnizian optimism provides a good starting

136 THE PROBLEM OF EVIL FOR ATHEISTS

point for considering distinct forms of optimism because it is arguably the most extreme form of optimism. According to this view, there is an axiological hierarchy of all possible worlds, including the actual world. God, as the greatest possible being, selected and created the actual world, which sits at the top of this hierarchy. Leibnizian optimism can be considered a consequence of traditional theism. If, as traditional theists say, God is the best possible being and the creator of the actual world, then it seems natural to expect that the actual world is the best possible world, reflecting God's supremacy. Conversely, it would be surprising if the actual world was not the best possible world given the assumption that it was created by God.

Let me clarify exactly what Leibnizian optimism is by addressing some common misunderstandings of the view.[1] First, Leibnizian optimists do not necessarily mean that their view implies that everything in the actual world, that is, the best possible world, is the best possible of its kind. They do not normally claim, for instance, that trees in the actual world are the best possible trees. If they had maintained that everything in the actual world is the best possible of its kind, then they would have to assume that everything in the actual world has an intrinsic value. This is a contentious thesis to which Leibnizian optimists are not committed.[2] Also, it is not obvious that the fact that the whole world has the property of being the best possible world entails that everything in it also has the property of being the best possible of its kind. Assuming such an entailment seems to commit the fallacy of decomposition. The Leibnizian view in *Candide* is often presented in the slogan, 'all is for the best in this world of ours'. Notice that this is formulated as 'all is *for* the best' rather than 'all *is* the best' (Voltaire 1759/1947, p. 27). The fact that not everything in the actual world is the best possible of its kind, therefore, does not immediately undermine Leibnizian optimism. It is not a necessary condition for the actual world's being the best possible world that everything in the actual world be the best possible of its kind.

Second, most Leibnizian optimists are not committed to the belief that the actual world, that is, the best possible world, cannot contain evil. They certainly do not think that the absence of evil is a sufficient condition for a given world's being the best possible world. As Lloyd Strickland points out, Leibniz contends in *Theodicy* that 'one must confess that there is evil in this

---

[1] For an in-depth discussion of common misconceptions surrounding Leibniz's views, see Lloyd Strickland (2010).

[2] For a defence of the view that everything is intrinsically valuable, see Scott Davison (2012).

world which God has made, and that it would have been possible to make a world without evil or even not to create any world, since its creation depended upon the free will of God' (Leibniz 1710/1985, p. 378; Strickland 2019, p. 22, footnote 8). For instance, God could have created a world in which there is only a rock and, accordingly, there is no evil. Such a world would not, however, be the best possible world. It would not even be a good world because goodness is not instantiated (unless one thinks that the existence of a rock has positive axiological value). The mere absence of evil, therefore, does not make the world the best possible world. Also, Leibnizian optimists normally believe that the absence of evil is not a necessary condition for a given world's being the best possible world. On the contrary, they would claim that the absence of evil is a sign that a given world is not the best possible world (even though they would not also claim that the presence of evil is a sign that it is the best possible world). This is because they believe that the presence of a certain quantity of evil is necessary to realize the greater good. As Strickland contends, Leibniz himself claims that instances of evil in the actual world are either linked to the greater good or by-products of such instances (Strickland 2010, p. 27). Leibniz writes:

> But I deny [the thesis that 'whoever makes things in which there is evil, and which could have been made without any evil, or need not have been made at all, does not choose the best course'] and I might content myself with asking for its proof. In order, however, to give a clearer exposition of the matter, I would justify this denial by pointing out that the best course is not always that one which tends towards avoiding evil, since it is possible that the evil may be accompanied by a greater good. For example, the general of an army will prefer a great victory with a slight wound to a state of affairs without wound and without victory. (Leibniz 1710/1985, p. 378)

Leibniz also writes:

> God has a far stronger reason, and one far more worthy of him, for tolerating evils. Not only does he derive from them greater goods, but he finds them connected with the greatest goods of all those that are possible: so that it would be a fault not to permit them. (Leibniz 1710/1985, p. 200)

Hence, the absence of evil is neither a necessary nor sufficient condition for a given world's being the best possible world and the presence of evil is a necessary but not sufficient condition for its being the best possible world.

138 THE PROBLEM OF EVIL FOR ATHEISTS

Third, Leibnizian optimists do not think that their thesis implies that the actual world, that is, the best possible world, includes the minimum amount of evil even in comparison with other good possible worlds. There are good possible worlds which include less evil than the actual world does. It is not obvious, though, that those worlds are better than the actual world because perhaps a more significant amount of evil is necessary to achieve the maximum level of overall goodness. Hence, the minimum amount of evil is not a necessary (or sufficient) condition for a given world's being the best possible world (even though it is also unlikely that the maximum amount of evil is a necessary or sufficient condition).

We have seen that Leibnizian optimism is not as extreme as it may initially appear. It is compatible with the existence of evil, and it does not even require that the quantity of evil in the actual world be minimal. In fact, it is *in*compatible with the absence of evil and it requires a certain quantity—most likely a significant quantity—of evil in the actual world. Nicholas Rescher—as noted in Chapter 4—for this reason calls Leibniz's view 'optimalism' rather than 'optimism', noting that 'being the very best of the possibilities need not and will not call for being perfect' (Rescher 2010, pp. 118–119).

Even though Leibnizian optimism is less extreme than the impression that it initially gives, it remains a highly contentious view. First, Leibnizian optimism requires that there is a hierarchy of all possible worlds based on greatness. Again, traditional theists normally believe that God is the best possible being, which implies that there is an axiological hierarchy of all possible *beings*.[3] It is not obvious, however, that this entails that there is also an axiological hierarchy of all possible things within a specific category, such as worlds. Second, assuming that there is an axiological hierarchy of all possible worlds it remains contentious that there is *the* best possible world, or even *a* best possible world. As we discussed in Chapters 2 and 4 of the present book, some argue that for any possible world w there is always a possible world such that it is better than w. Third, it seems implausible that the actual world is the best possible world because we can conceive of a world that is greater than the actual world. For example, we can conceive of a world such that it is nearly identical to the actual world except that a certain negative state of affairs in the actual world is absent from it or that a certain additional positive state of affairs is present in it. I do not intend to suggest

---

[3] See Ch. 2 of Yujin Nagasawa (2017) for a discussion of an axiological hierarchy of possible beings.

that Leibnizian optimism is definitively refuted by these criticisms. Given its highly contentious nature, however, it is prudent to temporarily set aside Leibnizian optimism and strive to formulate a more modest form of optimism that would likely find broader acceptance among both traditional theists, atheists, and other non-theists.

Consider, then, a more modest form of optimism:

Modest optimism I: The actual world is a good world.

Modest optimism I is compatible with Leibnizian optimism. One can consistently hold that, as modest optimism I says, this world is a good world and, moreover, as Leibnizian optimism says, it is the best possible world. However, it is also compatible with the negation of Leibnizian optimism. One can consistently hold that while, as modest optimism I says, the actual world is a good world, it is not, contrary to what Leibnizian optimism says, the best possible world. Modest optimism I is based on the rejection of the following three views: (i) the converse of Leibnizian optimism, according to which the actual world is the worst of all possible worlds; (ii) pessimism, according to which the actual world is a bad world, and (iii) neutralism, according to which the actual world is neither good nor bad.[4] Modest optimism I says that, overall, there is more good than evil in the actual world. Modest optimism I is not as straightforward as Leibnizian optimism because it includes an infinite spectrum of optimism—from the version according to which the actual world is barely good to the Leibnizian version according to which it is the best possible world. As my aim here is to develop a modest form of optimism which can be accepted by as many optimists as possible, encompassing a variety of optimistic views gives modest optimism an advantage. However, I wish to go one step further and consider a view that is even more modest than modest optimism I.

Notice that the axiological expectation mismatch on which the problem of evil is based arises from our *negative* observation of how the actual world is in the presence of evil. To create a conflict with this negative observation, we do not necessarily need a *positive* expectation of how the actual world should be; a *non-negative* expectation would suffice. I propose, therefore, the following view:

Modest optimism II: The actual world is not a bad world.

---

[4] Pessimism subsumes the converse of Leibnizian optimism, according to which the actual world is the worst of all possible worlds.

140 THE PROBLEM OF EVIL FOR ATHEISTS

Modest optimism II is even more modest than modest optimism I because it does not offer any positive assessment of the world; it offers only a non-negative assessment. Instead of saying, as optimism does, that the actual world is good, it says that the actual world is not bad.

Modest optimism II is consistent with Leibnizian optimism and modest optimism I, but it is also consistent with 'neutralism', according to which the actual world is neither good nor bad. However, it is worth noting that neutralism remains silent regarding the specific manner in which the actual world is considered neither good nor bad. One possible explanation is that worlds lack axiological values entirely. Another possible explanation is that the quantities of goodness and badness realized in the actual world are in perfect balance. If the actual world had contained more goodness, then it would have been a good world; or, if it had contained more badness, it would have been a bad world. Yet the actual world contains an equal quantity of goodness and badness and, hence, the world is neither good nor bad. Like modest optimism I, modest optimism II subsumes the whole spectrum of optimism in addition to neutralism. Modest optimism II is therefore suitable for our purpose—creating a version of the problem of evil which applies to as many people as possible. The above formulation of modest optimism II is however still too vague for our use. In the following section, therefore, I discuss and specify the scope of modest optimism II.

6.5 The Scope of Modest Optimism II

We have seen that Leibnizian optimism, which says that the actual world is the best possible world, does not necessarily imply that everything in the actual world is the best possible of its kind. Parallel reasoning applies to modest optimism II. When modest optimism II says that the actual world is not bad, it does not necessarily imply that everything in the actual world is not bad. Modest optimism II is compatible with the existence of states of affairs that are considered bad. This suggests that if we are to formulate modest optimism precisely, we have to explicitly specify in what sense modest optimists consider the actual world not to be bad. I submit that the following revision addresses this concern:

> Modest optimism III: Overall and fundamentally, the actual world is not a bad world.

Perhaps this formulation is analogous to the claim that, overall and fundamentally, x is not a bad person. Person x may not be perfect, and x may have some negative traits, but, overall, x is not a bad person and there is nothing fundamentally bad about x as a person. Similarly, according to the above formulation of modest optimism III, while the actual world may not be a perfect world and it may contain some bad states of affairs, overall, it is not a bad world and there is nothing fundamentally bad about it as a world. By employing the term 'fundamentally', modest optimists do not necessarily imply that the actual world is not bad on the most fundamental metaphysical level, such as the quantum level. Instead, they suggest that the world is not fundamentally bad on levels deeper than those typically engaged in everyday discourse, such as the personal, social, or political levels. To illustrate this point, consider two hypothetical worlds: W_1, which is very bad owing entirely to freak accidents or bad luck, and W_2, which is equally bad but because of a fundamental biological system that necessitates this badness. My contention here is that W_2 is fundamentally bad, whereas W_1 is not.

Let us now consider the scopes of modest optimism III and its alternatives. Leibnizian optimism is an optimistic view about the actual world. That is, its axiological claim covers the entirety of the actual world, rather than a specific region of the actual world. This is because Leibnizian optimism is normally presented as a corollary of traditional theism, according to which an omnipotent and wholly good God created the entire world. There is no need for Leibnizian optimists to limit the scope of their view given that God is responsible for the creation of the whole world. We set traditional theism aside here, however, because our ultimate aim is to detach traditional theism from the problem of evil and develop a version of the problem which arises for most people, including most atheists and other non-theists. Do atheists and other non-theists also have reason to think that modest optimism should apply to the entire world? Some may. Take, for example, non-theists who subscribe to axiarchism, which we discussed in Chapter 4. Again, axiarchism is a non-personal alternative to traditional theism which says that the world exists because it is good that it exists. That is, according to axiarchism, the existence of the world is ethically required. Axiarchism says that this non-personal, 'creatively effective ethical requirement', rather than God, is the ultimate explanation of the existence of the actual world. If axiarchism is true, non-theists, like theists, have good reason to think that optimism and, accordingly, modest optimism apply to the entire world, rather than some parts of it.

142 THE PROBLEM OF EVIL FOR ATHEISTS

Many atheists and other non-theists would however be unwilling to apply modest optimism about the entire world.[5] It is theoretically possible, for example, that there are many planets in remote galaxies that are filled with enormous quantities of evil. If non-theists cannot exclude such a possibility and do not endorse a comprehensive axiological view like axiarchism, then they cannot hold modest optimism about the entire world, even though they may be comfortable in holding modest optimism about their own local environments.[6] Hence, given that we aim to develop a modest form of optimism which even many atheists would be willing to accept, we have to limit the spatial scope of modest optimism significantly. Accordingly, I propose the following further revision of modest optimism III:

Modest optimism IV: Overall and fundamentally, the environment in which we exist is not bad.

According to this view, while we may or may not know the axiological value of the entire world, we are confident that a relatively local environment to which we belong is overall and fundamentally not bad. It is difficult to specify precisely what 'the environment in which we exist' means, but our natural environment on Earth seems to be a good candidate. In the following discussion, for the sake of simplicity, by the term 'modest optimism' I refer to modest optimism IV, not modest optimisms I–III.

6.6 Why We Should Think That Atheists/Non-Theists Would Accept Modest Optimism

We have arrived at modest optimism, the thesis that, overall and fundamentally, the environment in which we live is not bad. Although modest optimism is very modest, not all atheists and other non-theists would accept it. There are atheistic/non-theistic pessimists who make claims which seem to negate modest optimism. Arthur Schopenhauer, for instance, claims that the actual world is the worst of all possible worlds. That is, he thinks that

---

[5] As I explain in Section 6.6 of the present chapter, Platonists, pantheists, and Aristotelians may also represent non-theists who apply modest optimism to the whole actual world.

[6] I am grateful to Guy Kahane who raises this point in his response to my earlier work on the problem of evil for atheists. See Kahane (2022).

there is no possible world that is worse than the actual world or is as bad as the actual world. He writes:

> But indeed to the palpably sophistical proofs of Leibniz that this is the best of all possible worlds, we may seriously and honestly oppose the proof that it is the worst of all possible worlds. For possible means, not what one may construct in imagination, but what can actually exist and continue. Now this world is so arranged as to be able to maintain itself with great difficulty; but if it were a little worse, it could no longer maintain itself. Consequently, a worse world, since it could not continue to exist, is absolutely impossible: thus this world itself is the worst of all possible worlds. (Schopenhauer 1844/1909, pp. 395–396).

In the above passage, Schopenhauer seems to suggest that the actual world is fine-tuned in such a way that it is the worst of all possible worlds. The actual world is so bad, according to him, that if we tried to make it worse it would no longer exist. There is therefore no possible world that is worse than the actual world. This view appears to mirror Leibnizian optimism, according to which the actual world is the best possible world.

Contrary to initial appearance, though, it is not entirely obvious that Schopenhauer's thesis that the actual world is the worst of all possible worlds is inconsistent with modest optimism. In Section 6.4, we saw that Leibniz's thesis that the actual world is the best possible world is compatible with the existence of evil in the actual world. The fact that the whole world is the best possible does not imply the absence of evil. Likewise, Schopenhauer's thesis that the actual world is the worst of all possible worlds is compatible with the existence of the good (or the neutral) in the actual world. The fact that the whole world is the worst possible world, therefore, does not imply that all regions in the world are bad. Hence, Schopenhauer could in principle maintain that, while the actual world is the worst of all possible worlds, as modest optimism says, the environment in which we exist is not bad. Schopenhauer would however not make such a claim because his pessimism stems from his observation of the very environment in which we live:

> In fact, the conviction that the world and man is something that had better not have been is of a kind to fill us with indulgence towards one another. Nay, from this point of view, we might well consider the proper form of address to be, not *Monsieur, Sir, mein Herr*, but *my fellow-sufferer, Socî malorum, compagnon de misères!* (Schopenhauer 1851/1913, p. 29)

144 THE PROBLEM OF EVIL FOR ATHEISTS

Schopenhauer thinks that this is a fundamental problem, not a problem that can be fixed:

> If the world were a paradise of luxury and ease, a land flowing with milk and honey, where every Jack obtained his Jill at once and without any difficulty, men would either die of boredom or hang themselves; or there would be wars, massacres, and murders; so that in the end mankind would inflict more suffering on itself than it has now to accept at the hands of Nature. (Schopenhauer 1851/1913, p. 13)

Hence, we can conclude that Schopenhauer and his followers are likely to reject modest optimism.

As another example of a pessimist, David Benatar argues that coming into existence is always a serious harm. He writes:

> Although the good things in one's life make it go better than it otherwise would have gone, one could not have been deprived by their absence if one had not existed. Those who never exist cannot be deprived. However, by coming into existence one does suffer quite serious harms that could not have befallen one had one not come into existence. (Benatar 2006, p. 1)

Benatar derives from this consideration the proposition that it is morally wrong to procreate and, hence, that the optimal size of the human population is exactly zero. It would be better, he says, all things being equal, if human extinction were to happen sooner rather than later. Benatar does not talk explicitly about optimism and pessimism in relation to the problem of evil specifically, but given that there are billions of people on Earth and that he thinks that harm is fundamentally linked to existence he would, like Schopenhauer, reject modest optimism.

Non-theists, especially atheists, are often caricatured as negative, nihilistic, pessimistic people who think that life is miserable or absurd. Their ontology is limited to the material universe and, according to the caricature, they think that there is nothing about our mortal existence that we should feel happy or grateful about. Perhaps atheists like Schopenhauer and Benatar fit this stereotype.[7] However, it is a mistake to assume that they represent most non-theists.

---

[7] For empirical research on stereotypes of atheists and non-religious people, see: Will M. Gervais et al. (2017), Richard C. Grove, Ayla Rubenstein, and Heather K. Terrell (2019), Marcel Harper (2007), and Jordan W. Moon, Jaimie Arona Krems, and Adam B. Cohen (2021).

It seems evident to me that modest optimism is so modest that most people, including most atheists and other non-theists, are likely to accept it. To establish my argument on firm ground, however, in what follows I provide concrete reasons to think that most atheists/non-theists are likely to accept modest optimism. The first set of reasons is based on philosophical considerations and the second set of reasons is based on empirical findings. These reasons are limited in the sense that they do not show that all atheists/non-theists must accept modest optimism, but it suggests that at least a substantial number of them should or would accept it.

6.6.1 Philosophical Reasons

There is a close link between traditional *theism* and modest optimism. As I have explained, traditional theists commonly believe that we and our environment were created by an omnipotent and wholly good God. Given this belief, it seems reasonable for them to expect that, as modest optimism says, overall and fundamentally, the environment in which we exist is not bad (and is likely to be very good). Hence, traditional theism implies modest optimism.[8]

On the other hand, there is no straightforward link between atheism/non-theism and modest optimism because atheists/non-theists do not believe that we and our environment were created by an omnipotent and wholly good God. Take, however, axiarchism. Again, axiarchists believe that the actual world exists because it is good that it exists. That is, the world was actualized through the creatively effective ethical requirement. This means that, overall and fundamentally, the entire world is good (and, hence, not bad). This, of course, does not immediately imply that our environment in particular is overall and fundamentally good. Like traditional theism and Leibnizian optimism, axiarchism is compatible with the existence of evil and, hence, it is in principle possible for axiarchists to hold that our own environment is overall and fundamentally bad even though the actual world is overall good. However, most axiarchists are likely to reject such a thesis because they tend to infer the truth of axiarchism from their observation of

---

[8] For a recent discussion of the relationship between traditional theism and optimism, see Justin J. Dealey (2021).

146 THE PROBLEM OF EVIL FOR ATHEISTS

our own environment.[9] More broadly, atheists/non-theists who are attracted to Platonism are also likely to accept modest optimism because Platonists typically believe that everything aspires to be good (Leslie 2019; Steinhart 2023). To take a further example, pantheists believe that the world is divine or holy. They may infer from this belief that the world and our environment in it are overall and fundamentally not bad.[10] Aristotelians and Epicureans are also likely to accept optimism (and, accordingly, modest optimism) (Simon Blackburn 1994, p. 261; Mor Segev 2022). Furthermore, there are more straightforward atheists who believe that the actual world is not bad in the sense that it is neither good nor bad, rather than in the sense that it is good or neutral. Nietzsche, for instance, writes:

> Whether it is hedonism or pessimism, utilitarianism or eudaemonism—all these ways of thinking that measure the value of things in accordance with pleasure and pain, which are mere epiphenomena and wholly secondary, are ways of thinking that stay in the foreground and naïvetés on which everyone conscious of creative powers and an artistic conscience will look down not without derision, not without pity. (Nietzsche 1966, p. 225)

Nietzsche's view in the above passage seems to be compatible with the version of neutralism that we discussed above. If we cannot assign any axiological value to our environment in reference to pain and pleasure, or good and evil, then, overall and fundamentally, our environment seems to be neither good nor bad and, accordingly, modest optimism seems to be correct in saying that, overall and fundamentally, it is not bad.

Proponents of the views that I have mentioned here, such as axiarchism, Platonism, pantheism, and neutralism, may not constitute the majority of atheists/non-theists. Yet it is important to acknowledge that there is a non-negligible number of atheists/non-theists whose views imply modest optimism in much the same way as traditional theism implies modest optimism.

---

[9] Tim Mulgan may be one of the very few exceptions. As seen in Chapter 4 of the present book, he defends a version of axiarchism which he calls 'ananthropocentric purposivism'. This view is a non-human-centred version of axiarchism, which excludes pain and pleasure (or good and evil) *for human beings* from its axiarchic considerations (Mulgan 2015). According to this view, while the universe has a purpose humans are irrelevant to that purpose. This view does not imply any mechanism that ensures that our environment is, overall and fundamentally, not bad in the sense relevant to our discussion here. See Chapter 4 of the present book on this view.
[10] For relevant discussions of pantheism, see Chapter 3 of the present book and Levine's works (1994a, 1994b).

6.6.2 Psychological Reasons

Setting aside the above philosophical reasons for atheists/non-theists to accept modest optimism, there are empirical findings indicating that most atheists/non-theists are modest optimists. These findings do not suggest that atheists/non-theists are obligated to embrace modest optimism, nor do they suggest that atheists/non-theists actively promote modest optimism on philosophical grounds. However, as a matter of observed behaviour, most people, including most atheists/non-theists, consciously or unconsciously accept modest optimism. Psychological studies focus on general optimism rather than modest optimism in particular. Insofar as general optimism implies modest optimism, however, we can infer from these findings that most people, including most non-theists, are likely to accept modest optimism.

In criticizing Leibnizian optimism, Pierre Bayle writes 'that man is wicked and miserable; that there are everywhere prisons and hospitals; that history is simply a collection of the crimes and calamities of the human race' (Leibniz 1710/1985, p. 216). In response to this remark, Leibniz contends, 'I think that there is exaggeration in that: there is incomparably more good than evil in the life of men, as there are incomparably more houses than prisons. With regard to virtue and vice, a certain mediocrity prevails' (Leibniz 1710/1985, pp. 216–217). In agreement with Leibniz, Strickland writes:

> If one only reads books by Bayle, or watches only the news, one surely gets an unbalanced and distorted picture of things. Murders, tortures, kidnappings, earthquakes, floods etc. may make good news, and excellent subjects for books on the problem of evil, but they are hardly that commonplace, and for most people the worst they will ever do, or have done to them, is much lower down the scale of unpleasantness. Evils are not rare, but they are rarer than is sometimes supposed, and when they do occur they are, more often than not, relatively minor. (Strickland 2010, pp. 23–24)

Strickland continues:

> As indicated above, I think Leibniz is right to say that we routinely overestimate the quantity of evil on this planet. Anyone who claimed that there is 'a lot' of evil in the world as we know it, if by 'a lot' they mean there is considerably more evil than good in it, would be making a

claim that is difficult to square with the experience of the majority. For although there are many horrors in this life, they do seem to spare most of its inhabitants (i.e., most rational beings are not murdered, kidnapped, tortured or utterly crushed by evils in other ways.) Misery, wretchedness and vice are commonplace, but are not obviously more common than their opposites. I think it plausible, on the evidence available to us, to say that there is 'a fair amount' of evil in our world, but that it does not exceed the quantity of good. (Strickland 2010, p. 25)

When critics argue that there is a lot of evil in the world, they do not have to mean that there is more evil than good. The problem of evil is a version of the problem of axiological expectation mismatch, so all that needs to be shown is that there is more evil in the world (or in our environment) *than expected*. Hence, if we formulate the problem of evil for modest optimists it needs to be shown only that there is a quality or quantity of evil that is significant enough to suggest that, overall and fundamentally, the environment in which we live is not good.

Empirical findings are important and relevant because they suggest the opposite of what Leibniz and Strickland seem to think. That is, people tend to exaggerate *optimism* rather than pessimism. Let us consider these findings. There have been numerous empirical studies indicating a strong link between religiosity and optimism. Joseph W. Ciarrocchi et al. remark that '[r]ecent work on optimism and religiosity has consistently found a positive relationship between them' (Ciarrocchi et al. 2008, p. 122). According to these studies, religious people are generally happier and more optimistic than non-religious people (Amy L. Ai et al. 2003; William N. Dember 2002; David R. Hayward et al. 2016; Rezvan Homaei et al. 2016; Mattis et al. 2004; Ryan S. Ritter et al. 2014; Luciano Magalhães Vitorino et al. 2022). By non-religious people, these studies typically mean non-believers in Abrahamic religions, which constitute a large group of non-theists in the West (Ciarrocchi et al. 2008, p. 122). There are also some comparisons between religious people. For instance, according to Neal Krause and R. David Hayward (2014), conservative Protestants are more optimistic than those who affiliate with other denominations. According to Morgan Green and Marta Elliott's research (2010), people with liberal religious beliefs tend to be healthier but less happy than those with fundamentalist religious beliefs.

If religious people are generally more optimistic than non-religious people, they are likely to accept a more optimistic view of the world than non-religious people. It is important to note, however, that this does not suggest that non-religious people (or atheists/non-theists) are not optimistic. On the contrary, psychological studies consistently find that regardless of religious or non-religious affiliations people are generally optimistic; in fact, they are unrealistically optimistic. Tali Sharot writes:

> Humans, however, exhibit a pervasive and surprising bias: when it comes to predicting what will happen to us tomorrow, next week, or fifty years from now, we overestimate the likelihood of positive events, and underestimate the likelihood of negative events. For example, we underrate our chances of getting divorced, being in a car accident, or suffering from cancer. We also expect to live longer than objective measures would warrant, overestimate our success in the job market, and believe that our children will be especially talented. (Sharot 2011, p. 941)

As far as I know, there are no empirical studies of personal bias towards optimism (or modest optimism) in a strictly philosophical sense. There are, however, numerous psychological studies that are relevant to the philosophical debate over the problem of evil. These studies suggest that people generally exhibit optimism bias towards the risk of being victims of natural evil as well as moral evil. The following is a list of studies confirming optimism bias concerning moral or natural evil.

Natural Evil
- Natural Disasters
  - Earthquakes: Julia S. Becker et al. (2013); Jerry M. Burger and Michele L. Palmer (1992); Marie Helweg-Larsen (1999); John McClure et al. (2011); John McClure et al. (2016); Matthew Spittal et al. (2005)
  - Hurricanes: W. Douglass Shaw and Justin Baker (2010); Kathleen Sherman-Morris and Idamis Del Valle-Martinez (2017); Craig Trumbo et al. (2011, 2014, 2016)
  - Tornados: Jerry Suls et al. (2013); Neil D. Weinstein et al. (2000)
  - Environmental Risks: Robert Gifford et al. (2009); Julie Hatfield and R. F. Soames Job (2001); P. Wesley Shultz et al. (2014)
- Illness
  - Heart Attack: Nancy E. Avis, Kevin W. Smith, and John B. McKinlay (1989); Vera Hoorens and Bram P. Buunk (1993); Nathan M. Radcliffe and William M. P. Klein (2002); Neil D. Weinstein (1980, 1983)

150 THE PROBLEM OF EVIL FOR ATHEISTS

- Cancer: Jeffrey Jensen Arnett (2000); Valerie A. Clarke, Tracy Williams, and Stephen Arthey (1997); Kevin R. Fontaine and Sylvia Smith (1995); Vera Hoorens and Bram P. Buunk (1993); Marianna Masiero et al. (2018); Neil D. Weinstein (1983); Tracy Williams and Valerie A. Clarke (1997)
- Sexually Transmitted Disease: John Chapin (2000, 2001a); Vera Hoorens and Bram P. Buunk (1993); Neil D. Weinstein (1983)
- Pandemics: Pascual-Leone Alvaro et al. (2021); Hichang Cho, Jae-Shin Lee and, Seungjo Lee (2012); Elena Druică, Fabio Musso, and Rodica Ianole-Călin (2020); Benjamin J. Kuper-Smith et al. (2021)
- Food Poisoning: Doigo Thimoteo Da Cunha et al. (2015); Sharon M. Parry et al. (2004); Kelly Lameiro Rodrigues et al. (2020); Maria de Sousa Carvalho Rossi et al. (2017).

Moral Evil

- Mugging: Neil D. Weinstein (1980)
- Burglary: Neil D. Weinstein (1980)
- Youth Violence and Sexual Assault: John Chapin (2001b); John Chapin and Grace Coleman (2010); John Chapin, Stacy de las Alas, and Grace Coleman (2005); John Chapin and Mari Pierce (2011); Amy Saling Untied and Cynthia L. Dulaney (2015)
- Terrorism: Elaine Gierlach, Bradley Belsher, and Larry Beutler (2010); Josianne Kollmann et al. (2022); Charles T. Salmon, Hyun Soon Park, and Brenda J. Wrigley (2003)
- Car Accidents: Clara Alida Cutello et al. (2021); James R. Dalziel and R. F. Soames Job (1997); David M. DeJoy (1987); Neil D. Weinstein (1980, 1983); Melanie J. White, Lauren C. Cunningham, and Kirsteen Titchener (2011)

As the above list indicates, people display optimism bias towards a wide range of instances of evil. Moreover, their optimism bias is persistent. Those who have previously experienced relevant events, particularly those who have experienced significant loss or damage in such events, tend to show little optimism bias immediately after the events, but the bias normally comes back within several months. In Jerry M. Burger and Michele L. Palmer's study of the 1989 Northern California earthquake, optimism bias was not present immediately after the earthquake, but it was present three months later. Also, according to the same study, even the reduction in optimism that was observed immediately after the earthquake was limited to natural disasters, not other adverse events. Optimism bias is therefore considered stable and persistent over the long term (Burger and Palmer 1992).

Temporal distance from a previous adverse event, that is, how much time has passed since previous experiences of relevant events, is obviously linked to the temporal suppression of optimism bias. Whether *geographical* distance can also make any difference is a more hotly debated issue. Craig Trumbo et al. (2011) studied the risk perception of residents of the Gulf Coast of the United States after Hurricanes Katrina and Rita in 2005 and concluded that any correlation between proximity to a natural disaster and risk perception is, if there is any, weak. Optimism bias is not necessarily linked to ignorance or carelessness. A study of residents of Wellington City, New Zealand, where earthquakes had taken place, by Matthew J. Spittal et al. (2005) suggests that optimism bias can be positively linked to a population's preparedness for natural disasters.

As Nathan M. Radcliffe and William M. P. Klein (2002) note, we can distinguish three types of optimism: 'dispositional optimism', 'unrealistic optimism', and 'comparative optimism'. Dispositional optimism is the general, relatively stable orientation to hold positive expectations. Unrealistic optimism is inaccurate belief that one's own risk is lower than it actually is. Comparative optimism is the belief that one's own risk is below average. Comparative optimism is not always problematic because given one's circumstances it may be rational for one to believe that one's risk is below average. Radcliffe and Klein (2002) find that, in relation to heart attack risks, dispositional optimism is correlated with comparative optimism but not with unrealistic optimism.

Whether there are cultural differences reflected in levels of optimism bias is disputed. For example, Elaine Gierlach et al. (2010) studied differences among Argentinean, Japanese, and North American mental health workers concerning their risk perceptions of natural disasters (tsunamis and earthquakes) and terrorism. They found that risk perceptions were highest among the Japanese for natural disasters and terrorism while risk perceptions of terrorism were lowest among North Americans and Argentineans. They also found, however, that all the participants from all three countries had lower perceptions of risk to the self than to others in both disasters. Additionally, participants across all cultures rated risk to self as lower than risk to others across all disaster types. These findings seem to suggest that cultural factors can have a significant influence on risk perception and that the belief that one has stronger immunity to disasters than others is a

152 THE PROBLEM OF EVIL FOR ATHEISTS

cross-cultural phenomenon.[11] To take another example, according to a study by Steven J. Heine and Darrin R. Lehman (1995), Canadians exhibit greater unrealistic optimism than the Japanese. Some researchers have explored the hypothesis that North Americans are more optimistic than Asians with respect to dispositional optimism (Edward C. Chang 1996a, 1996b; Edward C. Chang et al. 2010; Li-Jun Ji et al. 2004). We have focused on adverse events, but optimism bias is known to occur in connection with positive events, such as financial success and happy marriages, as well.[12] Despite apparent cultural differences regarding levels, optimism bias is widespread and enduring.

There is no consensus as to why optimism bias is universal and persistent. Some researchers have considered evolutionary foundations of optimism bias. According to the multi-agent-based computer model developed by Dylan Evans et al., under certain environmental conditions agents with optimism bias, somewhat counterintuitively, outperform rational agents who act only to maximize expected utility (Evans et al. 2003). Also, according to the computational model developed by Dominic D. P. Johnson and James H. Fowler, a given population tends to be optimistic over time because overconfidence maximizes individual fitness. Their model also suggests that, in the process of evolution, population-wide optimism is stable in a variety of environments (Johnson and Fowler 2011). Some researchers have utilized evolutionary game theory to explain the persistence and stability of optimism bias (Oren Bar-Gill 2006; Burkhard C. Schipper 2021). There have also been neurophysiological studies of optimism. According to David Hecht, optimism is linked to neurophysiological processes in the left hemisphere of the brain while pessimism is associated with neurophysiological processes in the right hemisphere of the brain (Hecht 2013). Additionally, a number of meta-analytic studies have corroborated the presence of optimism bias (Cynthia T. F. Klein and Marie Helweg-Larsen 2002; Marie Helweg-Larsen and James A. Shepperd 2001; Lise Solberg Nes and Suzanne C. Segerstrom 2006).

In sum, whether or not optimism (or modest optimism) is true or rational, empirical studies suggest that, as a matter of fact, people have a strong tendency to embrace optimism. While the extent of their optimism

---

[11] For cross-cultural studies of optimistic bias, see also Elaine Gierlach, Bradley Belsher, and Larry Beutler (2010); Steven J. Heine and Darrin R. Lehman (1995); Li-Jun Ji et al. (2004); P. Wesley Schultz et al. (2014); and Mary Sissons Joshi and Wakefield Carter (2013).

[12] For optimism bias concerning positive events, see Susana O. Gouveia and Valerie Clarke (2001), and Tali and Sharot (2011).

bias may vary across regions and cultures, its existence is evident. This bias is most likely to manifest with respect to events in the environment that are relevant to the problem of evil, such as natural disasters and illness, which represent natural evil, as well as burglary and terrorism, which represent moral evil. Optimism bias can be suppressed when people experience relevant events, but it is so persistent that it generally returns after only a short period of time. Scientists believe that optimism bias has evolutionary and neurophysiological foundations. Marie Helweg-Larsen and James A. Shepperd, therefore, remark that '[a]mong the most robust findings in research on social perceptions and cognitions over the last two decades is the *optimism bias*' (Helweg-Larsen and Shepperd 2001, p. 74, emphasis in the original).

The empirical findings that we have addressed do not imply any conceptual link between atheism/non-theism and modest optimism. They do however support the thesis that most people, including most atheists/non-theists, accept modest optimism as a matter of fact.

6.7 Conclusion

My aim in this chapter has been to develop a modest version of optimism which can be accepted by most people. I have argued that modest optimism, according to which, overall and fundamentally, the environment in which we live is not bad, is such a version. I have tried to show that there are philosophical reasons to think that many atheists/non-theists accept modest optimism. I have explained, in particular, that there are many non-theists, such as axiarchists, Platonists, and pantheists, whose views imply modest optimism. I have also tried to show that there are psychological reasons to think that most atheists/non-theists endorse modest optimism. Psychologists have found that optimism is widespread, cutting across both religious and non-religious demographics. Because optimism entails modest optimism, we can infer from these findings that modest optimism is also widespread. I conclude, therefore, that a significant number of atheists/non-theists (as well as traditional theists) are modest optimists.

7

The Problem of Systemic Evil for Atheists/Non-Theists

7.1 Introduction

I hope to have established so far in this part of the book the following two key theses: (i) the problem of systemic evil raises a more significant challenge for traditional theists than other versions of the problem of evil and (ii) there are good reasons to think that most people, including most traditional theists and most atheists/non-theists, are modest optimists. In this chapter, I combine these two theses and argue that there is a version of the problem of systemic evil which raises a challenge for all modest optimists. This, I believe, is a significant finding because it effectively suggests that there is a version of the problem of evil that should trouble many atheists and other non-theists, who are normally considered immune to the problem of evil. In other words, if my argument succeeds, atheists and non-theists can no longer dismiss the problem of evil by claiming that it is a problem which only traditional theists need to worry about.

This chapter has the following structure. In Section 7.2, I recap theses (i) and (ii) and explain that the problem of systemic evil arises for modest optimists because there is a discrepancy between their axiological/onto-logical expectation of how our environment should be and their observation of how it actually is. In Section 7.3, I argue that the problem can also be presented by focusing on the emotive aspect, rather than the propositional aspect, of modest optimism. The emotive aspect pertains to the pleasure and gratitude we experience in connection with our own existence. In Section 7.4, I compare the problem of systemic evil for modest optimists with a problem which Janna Thompson calls the 'apology paradox'. I argue that while these two problems are structurally similar, the problem of systemic evil is more persistent than the apology paradox. In reference to that paradox, I also explain that the problem of systemic evil can be presented in terms of hope about the prospects for our future. Section 7.5 concludes.

The Problem of Evil for Atheists. Yujin Nagasawa, Oxford University Press. © Yujin Nagasawa 2024.
DOI: 10.1093/oso/9780198901884.003.0008

THE PROBLEM OF SYSTEMIC EVIL FOR ATHEISTS/NON-THEISTS   155

7.2 The Problem of Systemic Evil for Modest Optimists

Let us recap the two key theses that we have established so far. The first key thesis is concerned with the problem of systemic evil *for traditional theists* which we addressed in Chapter 5 of the present book. This problem focuses on the system of evolution and natural selection which necessitates pain and suffering for uncountably many sentient animals. This problem raises a significant challenge for traditional theists because, instead of merely pointing out that there are specific instances of evil or specific types of evil in the world, it reveals that the fundamental biological system on which our existence is founded nomologically necessitates a significant amount of pain and suffering in the world.

The second key thesis is concerned with modest optimism. According to this view, despite the existence of evil around us, overall and fundamentally the environment in which we exist is not bad.[1] This is probably the most modest version of optimism, and it is compatible with a wide range of optimistic views. As we saw in Chapter 6 of the present book, there are philosophical and psychological reasons to believe that most people, including most traditional theists and most atheists/non-theists, accept this view.

By combining the above two theses we can establish the following problem. On the one hand, according to modest optimism, overall and fundamentally, the environment in which we exist is not bad. On the other hand, however, our observation of systemic evil suggests that it is not the case that our environment is, overall and fundamentally, not bad. The environment is based on the system of natural selection and evolution, which entails pain and suffering for uncountably many sentient animals. Natural selection is a *fundamental* matter because it is a basic biological system that underlies our environment as a whole and no organism can escape it. It is also an *overall* matter because it covers the entire biological sphere throughout natural history. Hence, modest optimists face an axiological expectation mismatch: there is a gap between their modestly optimistic expectation of how our environment should be and their observation of how it actually is that fails to match their modest optimism. Notice that this problem is structurally in parallel with the problem of systemic evil *for traditional theists*: there is a gap between traditional theists' optimistic expectation of how the world should be and their observation of how it actually is that fails to match *their* optimism.

---

[1] This is modest optimism IV, a version that we reached in Chapter 6 of the present book. By the term 'modest optimism' I refer here to modest optimism IV, not modest optimisms I–III.

156 THE PROBLEM OF EVIL FOR ATHEISTS

The version of the problem of systemic evil that we discussed in Chapter 5 is designed to challenge only traditional theists. The above version, however, challenges both traditional theists and atheists/non-theists. First, it challenges traditional theists because most traditional theists are modest optimists. They assume that the world is overall and fundamentally good because they believe that the world was created by an omnipotent and wholly good God. Second, the target of the above version also includes some atheists/non-theists who endorse such views as axiarchism and Platonism, which entail that the world is overall and fundamentally good. Third, more generally, the target includes most people, including most atheists/non-theists as well as most traditional theists, because, as I explained in Chapter 6, empirical research suggests that optimism bias, particularly with respect to adverse events that are considered evil, is persistent and widespread, regardless of one's religious belief or cultural background.

As I discussed in Chapter 1, the problem of evil for traditional theists consists of three variables: (i) God, (ii) evil, and (iii) an allegedly conflicting relationship between (i) and (ii). When I introduced the problem of systemic evil in Chapter 5, I kept variable (i) as it is and assigned systemic evil to variable (ii). This is because, again, I presented the problem specifically for traditional theists. The problem of systemic evil *for modest optimists*, on the other hand, does not mention God; it is based solely on the conflict between systemic evil and modest optimism. This version can, therefore, be considered a 'neutralized' version of the problem of systemic evil, which applies to most atheists/non-theists as well as traditional theists. The above version assigns our environment—which modest optimists regard as having a non-negative overall and fundamental value—rather than God as the omnipotent and wholly good being, to variable (i).

I focus in the rest of the present book on the neutralized version of the problem of systemic evil, which arises for all modest optimists. From now on, for the sake of simplicity, I will call this version simply 'the problem of systemic evil', rather than 'the problem of systemic evil for modest optimists', and the version which arises specifically for traditional theists—that is, the version which I addressed in Chapter 5—the 'problem of systemic evil for traditional theists'.

Who can avoid the problem of systemic evil? Since the problem is designed to arise for all modest optimists, anyone who rejects modest optimism can avoid the problem. In other words, the axiological expectation mismatch on which the problem is based does not arise for pessimists, who

THE PROBLEM OF SYSTEMIC EVIL FOR ATHEISTS/NON-THEISTS   157

are willing to affirm that our environment *is* overall and fundamentally bad. They are not surprised by our observation of the environment in the face of natural selection and evolution. Such philosophers as Arthur Schopenhauer, who believe that the actual world is the worst possible world, would not find systemic evil a threat to their worldview.[2] Yet, as I explained in Chapter 6, there are compelling grounds to believe that pessimists are, in fact, quite scarce.

When I introduced the problem of systemic evil for traditional theists, I presented it as a *challenge* for traditional theists rather than an *argument* against theism. I adopt the same approach here. We understand variable (iii) in our scheme—a variable which is concerned with the allegedly conflicting relationship between the overall and fundamental value that modest optimists assign to our environment and their observation of how the environment actually is in the face of systemic evil—as a source of 'challenge' rather than an 'argument'. When I say that the problem of systemic evil arises for modest optimists, therefore, I do not mean that systemic evil logically contradicts modest optimism or that systemic evil is evidence that is strong enough to refute modest optimism. I instead deem systemic evil a substantial obstacle which modest optimists must address. As I discuss in Chapter 8, I do not exclude the possibility that a certain type of modest optimist can indeed offer a successful response to the problem of systemic evil. Yet the fact that our existence is fundamentally based on the system of natural selection and evolution, which entails the temporal and spatial prevalence of a variety of intense pain and suffering over a very long time, gives us prima facie reason to question modest optimism. And, if modest optimism is on shaky ground, then systemic evil is a problem for most atheists/non-theists as well as for traditional theists. Hence, traditional theists and atheists/non-theists face the same version of the problem of evil. I argue in Chapter 8, moreover, that this problem is potentially more significant for atheists/non-theists than for traditional theists.

I have argued that the problem of systemic evil is based on the axiological mismatch between modest optimism and our observation of the environment, which seems to suggest the contrary. We can encounter this axiological expectation mismatch in the following three distinct ways depending on our starting point. In the first way, we start with modest optimism.

---

[2] For Schopenhauer's pessimism, see Chapters 5 and 6 of the present book.

158 THE PROBLEM OF EVIL FOR ATHEISTS

We assume that the environment in which we live is overall and fundamentally not bad; that is, modest optimism is true. Perhaps our endorsement of modest optimism here is based on our optimism bias or commitment to theism, axiarchism, or Platonism, which entails modest optimism. Upon close examination of the pain and suffering caused by natural selection and evolution, however, we realize that our expectation based on modest optimism does not seem to match the actual state of our environment, and, hence, the problem of systemic evil arises.

Charles Darwin is a plausible example of a modest optimist who encountered a similar problem in this way. In his twenties, as a student at Cambridge, he read and was deeply impressed by William Paley's *Natural Theology or Evidence of the Existence and Attributes of the Deity* (1802/2006). He later wrote, 'I do not think I hardly ever admired a book more than Paley's "Natural Theology". I could almost formerly have said it by heart' (Darwin 1887, p. 219). However, as we saw in Chapter 5 of the present book, he started to question, as he studied biology, Paley's view that nature was designed by an omnipotent and wholly good God. At the age of 51, Darwin wrote:

> With respect to the theological view of the question; this is always painful to me.—I am bewildered.—I had no intention to write atheistically. But I own that I cannot see, as plainly as others do, & as I should wish to do, evidence of design & beneficence on all sides of us. There seems to me too much misery in the world. I cannot persuade myself that a beneficent & omnipotent God would have designedly created the Ichneumonidae with the express intention of their feeding within the living bodies of caterpillars, or that a cat should play with mice. (Darwin 1887, p. 311)

The above quote suggests that Darwin effectively encountered the problem of systemic evil through the first way that I mentioned above. He was initially attracted to the theistic, optimistic worldview but later faced his own axiological expectation mismatch when he realized through his study of biology that natural selection necessitates horrendous pain and suffering in nature. His bewilderment corresponds to the gap on which the problem of systemic evil sheds light.

The second way in which the axiological expectation mismatch arises is the opposite to the first way. We start with observing our environment and affirm, through our scientific study, that natural selection and evolution necessitate pain and suffering. We subsequently encounter and accept

THE PROBLEM OF SYSTEMIC EVIL FOR ATHEISTS/NON-THEISTS   159

modest optimism perhaps through religious teaching. We then struggle to reconcile this optimism with our scientific observation of pain and suffering in nature. Perhaps this way of encountering the axiological expectation mismatch is the least commonplace because, again, most people are predisposed to embrace modest optimism, with or without reflection.

The third way to encounter axiological expectation mismatch begins with both modest optimism and our observation of the environment. We embrace, again, upon reflection or intuitively, modest optimism believing that our environment is overall and fundamentally not bad. Meanwhile, we also form a belief, perhaps by studying biology, that our environment is founded on the system of natural selection and evolution, which necessitates pain and suffering. However, we do not initially recognize the axiological gap because we do not consider these two mismatched components together. When we do consider them together, however, we realize that there is a discrepancy between our expectation of how our environment should be and how it actually is. It seems reasonable to think that many educated people today encounter the problem of systemic evil in this way. While most people embrace modest optimism intuitively and they are made aware, through biological education, of pain and suffering caused by natural selection and evolution, they do not normally recognize the apparent axiological mismatch until it is pointed out, perhaps by philosophical work like the present book.

The problem of systemic evil can arise in any of the above three distinct ways because, again, the problem consists of three variables: (i) the overall and fundamental value that modest optimists assign to our environment, (ii) systemic evil, and (iii) the allegedly conflicting relationship between (i) and (ii). If we start with (i) and encounter (ii), we encounter the problem understood in the first way; if we start with (ii) and encounter (i), we encounter the problem understood in the second way; and if we start with (i) and (ii) at the same time, we encounter the problem understood in the third way. These distinct ways lead us to the same axiological expectation mismatch.

7.3 The Emotive Element of the Problem of Systemic Evil

Optimism has propositional and emotive elements. The propositional element corresponds to one's positive assessment of the state of our environment and the emotive element corresponds to one's emotional reaction to such an

160   THE PROBLEM OF EVIL FOR ATHEISTS

assessment.[3] So far we have developed the problem of systemic evil by focusing on the propositional element. In this section, however, I argue that the problem of systemic evil can be presented by focusing on the emotive element as well.

Recall our formulation of modest optimism as follows: overall and fundamentally, the environment in which we exist is not bad. While this statement represents the propositional element, it also seems to imply the following thesis concerning the emotive element:

> The existential gratitude thesis: It is appropriate that we feel pleased about and grateful for our existence in the environment in which we live.[4]

Gratitude can be directed towards specific aspects of life, such as being born in a democratic society or having enough food to sustain ourselves. The focus of the existential gratitude thesis lies, however, in expressing gratitude for our existence within the broader context of the natural environment. The word 'we' in the existential gratitude thesis refers to many or most of us, who live ordinary lives. The thesis leaves open the possibility that there are some people whose lives are so awful that those lives do not merit the expression of gratitude.[5]

The existential gratitude thesis is commonly held by traditional theists. They normally believe that God's creation is good and that we should be pleased about and grateful for our existence. This idea is expressed throughout the Bible. For instance, the first chapter of the Book of Genesis describes God's creation of humans and animals and reports, 'God saw all that he had made, and it was very good' (Genesis 1:31). The first chapter of the Epistle to the Hebrews reads, 'Since we are receiving a kingdom that cannot be shaken, let us be thankful, and so worship God acceptably with reverence and awe' (Hebrews 12:28). In the New Testament we can also find such verses as 'Every good and perfect gift is from above, coming down from the Father of the heavenly lights, who does not change like shifting shadows' (James 1:17) and 'Let them give thanks to the Lord for his unfailing love and his wonderful deeds for mankind' (Psalm 107:21–22). Contemporary theistic

---

[3] Jane E. Gillham et al. discuss the following distinct elements of optimism: (1) the belief that the world is the best of all possible worlds and (2) a hopeful disposition or a conviction that good will ultimately prevail (Gillham et al. 2002, p. 53).

[4] Guy Kahane calls this 'attitudinal optimism' (Kahane 2021, p. 3).

[5] See John Bishop (2010), Joshua Lee Harris, Kirk Lougheed, and Neal DeRoo (2023), and Michael Lacewing (2016) for recent discussions of existential gratitude.

THE PROBLEM OF SYSTEMIC EVIL FOR ATHEISTS/NON-THEISTS 161

philosophers commonly echo these expressions and embrace the existential gratitude thesis. They think that we owe thanks and worship to God for creating and sustaining our existence. Thomas V. Morris, for example, contends that 'We...have a duty to worship God and be thankful for his benefits' (Morris 1984, p. 261). Richard Swinburne even goes as far as saying that worship is not only an appropriate expression of gratitude but an obligation for God's sake: 'Worship is obligatory—it is the proper response of respect by man to his creator' (Swinburne 1981, p. 126).

However, atheists and other non-theists can in principle also endorse the existential gratitude thesis because it does not require belief in the existence of God. In fact, many, if not most, atheists/non-theists appear to endorse it. Those atheists/non-theists maintain that even though they do not believe in the existence of God, it is still appropriate for them to feel pleased and grateful that they are alive in our environment. For instance, the atheist philosopher Roland Aronson remarks:

> Feelings of dependence and of belonging are appropriate attitudes of response by the secular person...So are feelings of reverence and awe. None of these need be vague or fuzzy—if their worldly sources are not ignored and they are not projected beyond our universe, they become specific modes of living and experiencing our actual situation (Aronson 2006, p. 36)

Richard Dawkins, another prominent atheist, also expresses his gratitude for being alive, which he feels when he experiences the magnificence of nature. As we saw in Chapter 3 of the present book, he remarks:

> When I lie on my back and look up at the Milky Way on a clear night and see the vast distances of space and reflect that these are also vast differences of time as well, when I look at the Grand Canyon and see the strata going down, down, down, through periods of time when the human mind can't comprehend, I'm overwhelmingly filled with a sense of, almost worship... it's a feeling of sort of an abstract gratitude that I am alive to appreciate these wonders. When I look down a microscope it's the same feeling: I am grateful to be alive to appreciate these wonders. (Dawkins 2009)

As I also noted in Chapter 3 of the present book, Dawkins also contended in his lecture 'The Greatest Show on Earth', delivered at the University of Auckland in 2010, that 'we have cause to give thanks for our highly

162 THE PROBLEM OF EVIL FOR ATHEISTS

improbable existence, and the law-like evolutionary processes that gave rise to it. Such gratitude is not owed to, or to be directed towards, anyone or anything'. Another atheist, Greta Christina, writes:

> I have a strong awareness of having good things in my life that I didn't earn. Including, most importantly, my very existence. And it feels wrong to not express this awareness in some way. It feels churlish, or entitled, or self-absorbed. I don't like treating my good fortune as if it's just my due. I think gratitude is a good thing. (Christina 2011)

Finally, the atheist philosopher Masahiro Morioka endorses what he calls 'birth affirmation'. He writes, 'Birth affirmation means the state of mind in which I can say from the bottom of my heart that I am truly glad that I have been born. In short, it means to be able to say "Yes" to my having been born' (Morioka 2021, p. 43). It seems reasonable to construe these quotes as expressions of endorsement of the existential gratitude thesis. Dawkins, Christina, and Morioka present their endorsements in terms of 'I', but on a charitable interpretation they are not simply stating that they are among a small number of privileged people who should express feelings of pleasure and gratitude towards their lives. The existential gratitude thesis should not be understood as the plain assertion that '*I* am pleased and grateful to be alive (but I do not know about others)'. It is rather the thesis that it is appropriate at least for most of us to feel pleased and grateful that we are alive because, overall and fundamentally, the environment in which we exist is not bad.

Atheists/non-theists do not direct their gratitude towards God because, of course, they do not believe in the existence of God. Instead, they typically present their gratitude in terms of how wonderful our environment is and how extraordinarily fortunate we are to be able to exist in and appreciate it, especially given the extremely low probability that any particular individual comes into existence. As noted above, Dawkins writes, 'We have cause to give thanks for our highly improbable existence, and the law-like evolutionary processes that gave rise to it'. Whether or not atheists can coherently express gratitude without assuming any agent, such as God, to whom to direct their gratitude is an important question, but I do not address it here.[6] What is important for our purposes is that the existential gratitude

---

[6] See, for example, John Bishop (2010), Richard J. Colledge (2013), and Michael Lacewing (2016).

THE PROBLEM OF SYSTEMIC EVIL FOR ATHEISTS/NON-THEISTS   163

thesis is commonly embraced not only by theists but also by atheists and other non-theists.

We have seen, then, that both atheists/non-theists and theists hold the existential gratitude thesis, which is an emotive implication of modest optimism. Nevertheless, when we consider that our existence depends nomologically on evolutionary processes, which guarantee pain and suffering for countless humans and sentient animals, it becomes challenging to wholeheartedly embrace the existential gratitude thesis with sincerity and authenticity. In the presence of such systemic evil, expressing feelings of pleasure and gratitude genuinely becomes a struggle for modest optimists. This difficulty represents the emotive dimension rather than the propositional dimension in the context of the problem of systemic evil.

The emotive version of the problem shows that there is a tension between pleasure and gratitude that we feel appropriate to express in reference to our existence in our environment and the actual state of our environment. More precisely, the core of the formulation is the apparent incompatibility between the following two points: (a) the existential gratitude thesis, according to which it is appropriate that we feel pleased about and grateful for our existence in the environment in which we live and (b) the scientific fact that our existence depends fundamentally on a violent, cruel, and unfair biological system which guarantees pain and suffering for many people and other sentient animals. Metaphorically speaking, holding (a) while acknowledging (b) is like expressing pleasure about and gratitude for living in our environment with smiley faces while, at the same time, recognizing that we are standing on the corpses of countless people and sentient animals that had to die painfully and miserably to allow us to survive. The costs that these people and animals had to pay for our survival appear unjustifiably high.

Psychologists define *cognitive dissonance* as a state of discomfort which one experiences as a result of one's conflicting beliefs, attitudes, or behaviours (Joel Cooper 2007; Eddie Harmon-Jones 2019; Eddie Harmon-Jones and Judson Mills 1999). For example, cognitive dissonance arises when one finds it difficult to stop smoking even though one is fully aware that smoking is harmful, or when one finds it difficult to stop stealing even though one firmly believes that stealing is morally wrong. One way of understanding the problem of systemic evil (and, more broadly, the problem of axiological expectation mismatch) is to take it as an example of cognitive dissonance. Cognitive dissonance arises for modest optimists when they are in a state of discomfort resulting from the conflict between their expectation of how their environment should be and their observation of how it actually is. This is in

164 THE PROBLEM OF EVIL FOR ATHEISTS

line with expectation confirmation theory, which I addressed in Chapter 2 of the present book. According to the theory, cognitive dissonance can arise when there is inconsistency between one's expectations and the newly obtained information. For example, if we have a certain positive expectation of a product and our interaction with the product disconfirms our expectation, there can be negative cognitive or emotional effects, resulting in cognitive dissonance.

Recall that Darwin uses such expressions as 'painful' and 'bewildered' when he considers his 'theological view' in the face of the cruelty and violence that he finds in nature. This supports my claim that the problem of systemic evil is an example of cognitive dissonance. We can also see that the emotive aspect of the problem of systemic evil corresponds to cognitive dissonance. Modest optimists can be in a state of discomfort when they feel pleasure and gratitude about their existence while, at the same time, realizing that our environment is overall and fundamentally not good.

7.4 The Apology Paradox and the Hope Thesis

One might point out that the emotive version of the problem of systemic evil is akin to the 'apology paradox', which Janna Thompson (2000) introduces in ethics.[7] Let me compare these two puzzles because the comparison allows us to highlight the strength of the problem of systemic evil.

Thompson formulates the apology paradox as a challenge for people who sincerely wish to express apology for or regret about the fact that historical injustices, such as slavery, war crimes, and the dispossession of indigenous people, have taken place while acknowledging that we benefit from them. Suppose, for example, that your grandparents met in Poland during World War II. Suppose further that, given their circumstances, they would not have met had the Holocaust not taken place. This means that, as their descendant, you would not have existed without the Holocaust. That is, your existence depends causally on the Holocaust. Of course, you believe that the Holocaust is an awful event which should have never taken place. If you are a political leader, you might wish not only to express regret but also to apologize for the historical injustice. At the same time, you may also wish to affirm that you are happy and grateful to be alive. Yet, given the causal link

---

[7] According to Neil Levy (2002), the apology paradox is a version of the non-identity problem originally introduced by Derek Parfit (1984).

THE PROBLEM OF SYSTEMIC EVIL FOR ATHEISTS/NON-THEISTS   165

between the Holocaust and your existence, it seems inconsistent or inappropriate to express pleasure about and gratitude for your life while regretting or apologizing for the fact that the Holocaust took place.

The apology paradox and the problem of systemic evil (especially its emotive formulation) have similar structures. The apology paradox focuses on the link between our existence, for which we feel fortunate and grateful, and historical injustices involving pain and suffering for victims. The problem of systemic evil, on the other hand, focuses on the link between our existence, for which we feel fortunate and grateful, and natural selection, which necessitates pain and suffering for people and other sentient animals. There are, though, many reasons to think that the problem of systemic evil is radically distinct from the apology paradox.

I submit that the challenge that the problem of systemic evil poses is more fundamental and pressing than the challenge that the apology paradox poses. First, like the traditional problem of evil, the apology paradox focuses on specific historical *events* such as the Holocaust (or specific types of historical event, such as genocide) that are deemed evil or morally wrong, while the problem of systemic evil focuses on the entire biological system, such as natural selection, which is deemed evil. Needless to say, the biological system is more fundamental than historical events that take place within the system. Second, the apology paradox focuses on a *contingent* causal link between a specific historical event and our existence, while the problem of systemic evil focuses on a *nomologically necessary* link between the biological system and our existence. Of course, nomological necessity is a stronger notion than contingency. (I will explain a related point in detail below.) Third, the apology paradox focuses on historical injustices, for which free humans are responsible, while the problem of systemic evil focuses on the biological system, for which humans are not responsible. Fourth, the apology paradox is concerned with the existence of specific individuals or groups of individuals, while the problem of systemic evil is concerned with the existence of humanity (and sentient animals) as a whole.

Thompson introduces the apology paradox, but she also proposes a solution to it. We can confirm that the problem of systemic evil is more fundamental and pressing than the apology paradox also by applying Thompson's solution to the apology paradox to the problem of systemic evil. Thompson describes her 'best solution' to the apology paradox as follows:

> Many people feel uncomfortable or even apologetic about benefiting from an injustice even when they had no responsibility for it. They are sorry that

166   THE PROBLEM OF EVIL FOR ATHEISTS

the good things that they now possess came to them because of a past injustice. They do not regret that they have these things, but that they came to have them in the way they did. An apology could be interpreted as an expression of this kind of regret. So interpreted it is not, strictly speaking, an apology *for* the deeds of our ancestors or an expression of regret that they happened. Rather it is an apology *concerning* deeds of the past, and the regret expressed is that we owe our existence and other things we enjoy to the injustices of our ancestors. *Our preference is for a possible world in which our existence did not depend on these deeds.* (Thompson 2000, p. 475, emphasis added to the last sentence)

Thompson's point in the above passage is the following: we can consistently say that we are fortunate and grateful to be alive while regretting or apologizing for the fact that a historical injustice, which is causally linked to our existence, took place because it is coherent to wish that our existence had been realized through some other causal link. This point can be clarified by analysing it in terms of possible worlds. The apology paradox is based on the following assumption:

(1)   If a certain historical event, say, the Holocaust, had not taken place, then we would not have existed.

According to possible world semantics, this does *not* entail the following:

(2)   There is no possible world in which the Holocaust did not take place and we (or our counterparts) exist.

Instead, (1) entails the following:

(3)   In the closest possible world to the actual world in which the Holocaust did not take place, we (or our counterparts) do not exist.

And this is compatible with the following:

(4)   There is a possible world in which the Holocaust did not take place and we (or our counterparts) exist.

Such a world might be quite different from the actual world because it is not the *closest* possible world to the actual world in which the Holocaust did not

THE PROBLEM OF SYSTEMIC EVIL FOR ATHEISTS/NON-THEISTS 167

take place. But the consistency of (1) (and equivalently (3)) with (4) shows that one can coherently wish that we (or our counterparts) had existed without the Holocaust. So, according to Thompson, what we do when we wish that the Holocaust had not taken place while holding the existential gratitude thesis is express our preference for a world described in (4) rather than the actual world. I submit, however, that even if Thompson's response successfully resolves the apology paradox we cannot apply a parallel response to the problem of systemic evil. This point highlights the strength of the problem of systemic evil.

The problem of systemic evil is based on the following assumption:

(1')   If natural selection had not governed nature, then we would not have existed.

This does *not* entail the following:

(2')   There is no possible world in which natural selection does not govern nature and we (or our counterparts) exist.

Instead, (1') entails the following:

(3')   In the closest possible world to the actual world in which natural selection does not govern nature, we (or our counterparts) do not exist.

And this is compatible with the following:

(4')   There is a possible world in which natural selection does not govern nature and we (or our counterparts) exist.

But a world described in (4') is fundamentally different from the actual world because the laws of nature in such a world differ significantly from those that apply to the actual world. Changing the laws of nature is much more radical than removing a certain historical injustice from the actual world. Wishing that the laws of nature had been different is so fundamental that it would undermine the existential gratitude thesis, according to which it is appropriate that we feel pleased about and grateful for our existence in the environment in which we live. If we say, when acknowledging the pain and suffering in our environment, that our world should be radically modified to the extent that the current laws of nature are replaced with

168 THE PROBLEM OF EVIL FOR ATHEISTS

some other laws, then we are essentially saying that it is *not* appropriate that we feel pleased about and grateful for our existence in our environment. What sort of environment is it in which we exist without natural selection? Perhaps it is a world in which we (or our counterparts) are silicon-based beings created by a higher intelligence, or immaterial spirits that do not arise through evolution. Wishing that such an environment, instead of *our* environment, was actual, and wishing that we lived in such an environment, would be equivalent to rejecting modest optimism.

We have focused on the past and the present in considering the apology paradox and the problem of systemic evil. We have addressed how we can understand our present state, which is a consequence of the pain and suffering that have taken place in our environment. However, we can also formulate the problem of systemic evil by referring to the future. Such a version is formulated in terms of hope rather than the feeling of fortunateness or gratitude. Consider the following thesis:

The hope thesis: It is appropriate that we feel hopeful about the prospects for our existence in the environment in which we live.

Optimism is often understood as a positive expectation of future outcomes. Optimism about the weather or the economy is a good example. If modest optimism is correct in saying that overall and fundamentally the environment in which we live is not bad, then it seems reasonable to embrace the hope thesis; given the non-negative state of our environment it is appropriate to be hopeful (or at least not to be pessimistic) about the future.

The existence of systemic evil suggests, however, that modest optimists cannot coherently maintain the hope thesis because our existence depends nomologically on the system of natural selection and evolution, which guarantees that there is always a significant quantity of pain and suffering in our environment. Given the system it is not appropriate to feel hopeful about the prospects for our future. We cannot escape the system of natural selection and evolution because it underlies our existence and guarantees the constant realization of pain and suffering for uncountably many sentient animals.[8] This is analogous to a situation where one lives in a social or

---

[8] Paul Prescott (2021) defends a related point by raising what he calls the 'secular problem of evil'. According to this problem, evil is a challenge for secularists because people who meet their basic prudential interests are committed to a good-enough world and the quantity of evil in the world indicates that the actual world is not a good-enough world.

THE PROBLEM OF SYSTEMIC EVIL FOR ATHEISTS/NON-THEISTS 169

political system that is fundamentally unfair, violent, and harmful. We cannot coherently feel hopeful about the prospects for our future in a society based on such a system. The problem of systemic evil is, moreover, worse than this situation because while we can at least in principle replace or escape a social or political system, we cannot do the same with the system of natural selection and evolution.

7.5 Conclusion

In this chapter, I have argued that the problem of systemic evil raises a challenge for modest optimists. To illustrate the depth of the problem, I have presented it in two distinct ways. First, I have presented it by focusing on the propositional aspect of modest optimism. I have argued that the axiological expectation mismatch arises for modest optimists when they realize the discrepancy between their belief that our environment is overall and fundamentally not bad and their recognition of the pain and suffering necessitated by the system of natural selection and evolution. Second, I have focused on the emotive aspect of modest optimism. I have argued that modest optimists struggle to affirm that it is appropriate that we feel pleased about and grateful for our existence when they realize that the system of natural selection and evolution underlies our existence. I have argued, moreover, that modest optimists struggle to affirm that it is appropriate that we feel hopeful about the prospects for our future. The thesis that the problem of systemic evil is a significant challenge for modest optimists is important because most traditional theists *and* most atheists/non-theists are modest optimists. This means that the problem of evil is no longer a problem only for traditional theists. It is a problem for nearly everyone, including most atheists/non-theists.

8

The Advantages that Traditional Theists Enjoy

8.1 Introduction

I have argued that the problem of systemic evil is a challenge for most atheists/non-theists as well as most traditional theists because it arises for anyone who, at a minimum, accepts modest optimism. The crucial question then is the following: between traditional theists and atheists/non-theists, which is more likely to succeed in overcoming the challenge? In this chapter, I argue that traditional theists enjoy a distinct advantage over atheists/ non-theists because they have enormous supernaturalist resources they can tap to respond to the challenge, resources to which atheists/ non-theists do not have access. This means, in other words, that the problem of systemic evil is a more significant challenge for atheists/ non-theists than for traditional theists. This finding is important because the problem of evil is often seen as a rationale for rejecting traditional theism in favour of atheism/non-theism. My argument suggests that the situation is almost the other way around: if one seeks a successful response to the problem of systemic evil, it is better to be a traditional theist than an atheist or non-theist.

This chapter has the following structure. In Section 8.2, I introduce an example of a painting which illustrates my thesis that the problem of systemic evil poses a more significant challenge for atheists/non-theists than for traditional theists. In Section 8.3, I defend the thesis further by scrutinizing the comparative advantage that traditional theists enjoy over atheists/non-theists. In Section 8.4, I defend my argument against several objections, including those raised and discussed by Guy Kahane and Francis Jonbäck. In Section 8.5, I conclude.

The Problem of Evil for Atheists. Yujin Nagasawa, Oxford University Press. © Yujin Nagasawa 2024.
DOI: 10.1093/oso/9780198901884.003.0009

8.2 The Painting Analogy

We can describe the problem of systemic evil through the following painting analogy. Imagine an abstract painting which corresponds to the environment in which we exist. Within the painting, areas corresponding to positive things in the environment are coloured yellow and areas corresponding to negative things in it are coloured grey. While modest optimists allow that some parts of the painting are coloured grey, they do not believe that the whole painting is more grey than yellow. Apart from a few, including those who believe that the painting is coloured in yellow and grey in perfectly equal proportion, all modest optimists believe that the painting is overall more yellow than grey. Now, the problem of systemic evil suggests that modest optimists' view here is inaccurate because if we peel off the yellow surface of the painting we can find a large grey layer, which corresponds to the violent, cruel, and unfair system of natural selection underlying our biological existence and necessitating pain and suffering for uncountably many sentient organisms. Hence, according to the problem of systemic evil, contrary to the initial appearance, the painting is in fact more grey than yellow. That is, modest optimists are mistaken in believing that, overall and fundamentally, the environment in which we exist is not bad.

How can traditional theists respond to the problem of systemic evil illustrated in the above example? A promising response is to say that our assessment of the painting is incomplete because the painting has an even more complex structure. Traditional theists are typically supernaturalists, so they believe that the environment in which we exist is not limited to the material, biological domain; we also belong to a non-material, supernatural domain. For example, they think that there is a God, an incorporeal being who exists beyond the material universe and interacts with us, and that there are also souls which survive death and transcend material existence. To defend modest optimism, traditional theists can ascribe a positive axiological value to this non-material, supernatural domain and claim that there is a vast fundamental yellow layer underneath the grey layer. Thanks to this yellow layer, ultimately the painting is not dominated by the grey colour. In other words, modest optimists are correct in believing that, overall and fundamentally, the environment in which we exist is not bad.

Let us strengthen the above point by linking it to existing theistic responses to the traditional problem of evil. The soul-making response, for instance, says that our pain and suffering are compatible with the existence of an omnipotent and wholly good God because these experiences are

172 THE PROBLEM OF EVIL FOR ATHEISTS

necessary for spiritual growth. Such spiritual growth is useful even for people who die young because, according to this response, our existence is not limited to the lifespans of our physical, biological bodies; there is an afterlife. The sceptical theistic response, to take another example, says that we cannot fully comprehend why God allows pain and suffering to occur in our environment. This does not mean, however, that God does not have good reason for doing so; it simply means that we are cognitively or morally limited with respect to the deeper justice that God exhibits. To take yet another example, Marilyn McCord Adams's response to the problem of evil says that intimacy with God would engulf even the most horrendous forms of evil and overcome any prima facie reasons for doubting the value of human life (Adams 1989). Using Adams's term, God 'defeats' evil even if there might not be a humanly accessible answer to the question why there has to be evil. These theistic, supernaturalist responses can be applied, with necessary adjustments, to the problem of systemic evil. Such an approach suggests that even if areas in the painting corresponding to large portions of our material and biological domain are grey, traditional theists have enormous resources which can be utilized to show that the painting is not, overall, more grey than yellow. None of these responses is available to atheists because the atheist ontology is limited to the material and biological domain.[1]

In the present book, I do not have space to discuss whether or not any of these specific theistic responses succeeds in solving the problem of systemic evil. Yet it is clear that traditional theists are significantly better situated than atheists/non-theists are to respond to the problem. Traditional theists have in their ontology much greater, and possibly infinitely greater, resources than atheists/non-theists to which they can appeal. By drawing upon items that exist beyond the material and biological domain, such as God and the afterlife, traditional theists can develop a variety of approaches to the problem, approaches to which atheists/non-theists do not have access.[2] Hence, the problem of systemic evil poses a more significant challenge for atheists/non-theists than for traditional theists.

---

[1] Atheistic/non-theistic ontology normally also includes abstract objects. It is hard, however, to see how the existence of abstract objects can help them develop a plausible response to the problem of systemic evil. See Chapter 4 of the present book for relevant issues.

[2] Atheism/non-theism here includes mainly three prominent views that we have discussed: pantheism, axiarchism, and atheism. Recall, as I explained in Chapter 2, that by pantheism I mean naturalistic pantheism, which does not postulate anything supernatural.

8.3 Comparing Traditional Theism with Atheism/Non-Theism: Which One Wins?

Let me explicate further the comparative advantage of traditional theism over atheism/non-theism in relation to the problem of systemic evil by considering the following four possible scenarios:

- Atheists/non-theists succeed in developing a compelling response to the problem.
- Atheists/non-theists do not succeed in developing a compelling response to the problem.
- Traditional theists succeed in developing a compelling response to the problem.
- Traditional theists do not succeed in developing a compelling response to the problem.

The first scenario, in which atheists/non-theists succeed in developing a compelling response to the problem of systemic evil, is unlikely to obtain. For atheists/non-theists, the painting consists of only two layers: the first layer, which corresponds to the initial appearance of the environment in which we exist, and the second layer, which corresponds to the systemic evil that underlies it. It seems impossible for atheists/non-theists to show that the painting is not overall more grey than yellow despite the second layer, which is predominantly grey, because, given their limited, naturalist ontology they cannot, unlike traditional theists, postulate the presence of any further layer. Assume, for the sake of argument, however, that atheists/non-theists do somehow succeed in showing that the painting is not predominantly grey. That is, atheists/non-theists succeed in establishing, without requiring supernaturalist ontology, a compelling response to the problem showing that modest optimism is true. In this case, it is likely that traditional theists can simply borrow the atheistic/non-theistic response because traditional theists' supernaturalist ontology subsumes the naturalist ontology of atheists/non-theists and, hence, traditional theists have at their disposal all the resources that atheists/non-theists have. This means that in the first scenario, metaphorically speaking, the competition between traditional theists and atheists/non-theists in tackling the problem of systemic evil will result in a draw. *If* atheists/non-theists can develop a successful response to the problem, so can traditional theists.

174 THE PROBLEM OF EVIL FOR ATHEISTS

In the second scenario, atheists/non-theists do not succeed in developing a compelling response to the problem of systemic evil. This scenario is likely to obtain because, again, given that the ontology of atheists/non-theists is limited to the material and biological domain it seems impossible for them to show that the painting is not predominantly grey. This means that there is no naturalistic response to the problem which traditional theists can borrow from atheists/non-theists. This is not necessarily, however, bad news for traditional theists. Traditional theists can still try to develop their own response because, as we have seen, they have enormous supernaturalist resources which atheists/non-theists lack. This means that in this second scenario the competition between traditional theists and atheists/non-theists in tackling the problem of systemic evil will result in a loss for atheists/non-theists or, at best, a draw.

In the third scenario, traditional theists succeed in developing a compelling response to the problem of systemic evil. It is most likely that such a response requires supernaturalism because to show that the painting is not predominantly grey it is necessary to postulate the third layer underlying the second, grey layer. This means that it is most likely that a compelling response to the problem is available only to traditional theists and not to atheists/non-theists. Hence, in this scenario, traditional theists are likely to win (and they draw in a less likely case in which the response is compatible with naturalism).

In the fourth scenario, traditional theists do not succeed in developing a compelling response to the problem of systemic evil. That is, they cannot overcome the challenge that the problem poses even if they appeal to supernaturalist resources. In this scenario, it is almost certain that atheists/non-theists do not succeed either because, again, their naturalist ontology is more limited than theists' supernaturalist ontology. (Conversely, if atheists/non-theists do succeed in overcoming the challenge then so do traditional theists, which means that this scenario collapses into the first scenario.)

What I have shown above can be summarized as follows:

- It is unlikely that atheists/non-theists can succeed in developing a compelling response to the problem of systemic evil, but if they do succeed traditional theists can simply borrow the responses developed by atheists/non-theists.
- If atheists/non-theists do not succeed in developing a compelling response, traditional theists may still be able to develop a compelling response.

- If traditional theists succeed in developing a compelling response, it is unlikely that atheists/non-theists can simply borrow it.
- If traditional theists do not succeed in developing a compelling response, it is most likely that atheists/non-theists do not succeed either.

Hence, traditional theists enjoy an advantage over atheists/non-theists when responding to the problem of systemic evil. While they can win or draw, atheists/non-theists can only lose or draw. This implies that if one wishes to maintain modest optimism it is better to subscribe to traditional theism than to atheism/non-theism. In other words, the problem of systemic evil is a more significant challenge for atheists/non-theists than for traditional theists. This finding is important as it undermines the prevailing view that the problem of evil provides sufficient reason to reject traditional theism and accept atheism/non-theism.

8.4 Responding to Objections

I introduced a version of the problem of systemic evil in an earlier work (Nagasawa 2018b). Since the publication of that work, some objections have been raised against my argument. In this section, I defend my argument against those objections. In fairness to the critics, I note that some of the objections in effect do not apply to my argument in the present book in part because I have improved the argument advanced in the earlier work in response to those objections. I am grateful to the critics for raising the objections, which have helped me to strengthen the argument. I focus on objections introduced by Guy Kahane (2022) and Francis Jonbäck (2021), but I also address additional objections that might be raised.

8.4.1 Objection 1: There is something odd about rejecting atheism/non-theism in response to the problem of systemic evil

The thrust of my argument is that given the problem of systemic evil modest optimists enjoy a greater advantage if they subscribe to traditional theism rather than to atheism/non-theism. Kahane claims, however, that it would be odd for modest optimists to conclude that traditional theism is true or

176 THE PROBLEM OF EVIL FOR ATHEISTS

atheism/non-theism is false because of the problem of systemic evil. He writes:

> If atheists discover that EE [systemic evil] is in tension with EO [modest optimism], how could that be, on its own, a reason to conclude that the argument from evil, and their other arguments against theism, are mistaken? That would be like concluding, from a failed exam, not that you're not as good as you thought but that the teacher must be conspiring against you. In most cases, when we encounter strong evidence that things are worse than we had assumed, that's a bad reason to reject that evidence and hold on to our rosy assumption. To be motivated to adopt theism on these grounds would be an instance of wishful thinking—an epistemic vice. Moreover, it is a vice that atheists often accuse theists of succumbing to. So surely what atheists should conclude instead is that EO [modest optimism] is false.[3] Kahane (2022, p. 704)

I agree with Kahane's claim that '[i]n most cases, when we encounter strong evidence that things are worse than we had assumed, that's a bad reason to reject that evidence and hold on to our rosy assumption'. However, this claim seems to be almost trivially true. Of course, when one encounters *strong* evidence against one's view it is usually not a good idea to reject that evidence merely to retain the view. In our discussion of the problem of systemic evil, however, we do not compare only two items, evidence (systemic evil) and the target view (modest optimism). There is a third item (traditional theism, atheism, or a version of non-theism). My claim is that if one accepts the existence of systemic evil but remains convinced by modest optimism, it is more advantageous to be a traditional theist than an atheist because traditional theism is better positioned than atheism/non-theism for responding to the problem. In other words, traditional theists seem to have a better chance than atheists/non-theists of weakening the evidential force of systemic evil against modest optimism. Hence, I maintain that the problem of systemic evil can be presented as an

---

[3] By 'EE', Kahane means the following thesis: 'Evolutionary Evil (EE): Terrestrial evolutionary history contains a vast amount of badness (and evolution may also be a systemic evil)'. By 'EO' he means the following thesis: 'Existential Optimism (EO): The world is, overall, a good place and we should be grateful for our existence in it' (Kahane 2022, p. 702). To make it easier for readers to follow my discussion I have replaced 'EE' with 'systemic evil' and 'EO' with 'modest optimism'.

indirect motivation for modest optimists to prefer traditional theism to atheism/non-theism.

It is important to emphasize, however, that I do not claim that the problem of systemic evil is an argument for traditional theism or an argument against atheism/non-theism in a strict sense. As I have explained throughout the book, it is appropriate to consider the problem of evil a *challenge* for traditional theists and atheists/non-theists, rather than an *argument* against traditional theism or atheism/non-theism. The problem of systemic evil alone does not indicate the falsity of either traditional theism or atheism/non-theism. Hence, I do not advocate the following: atheism/non-theism is false (or traditional theism is true) because modest optimism is true and systemic evil exists.

Modest optimism is an axiological assessment of the environment in which we exist while traditional theism and atheism/non-theism are ontological theses about what exists or does not exist. At this point, critics might argue that the thrust of Kahane's objection is that it does not make sense to infer the truth or falsity of an ontological thesis from an axiological thesis.

An inference from an axiological thesis to an ontological thesis is likely to be more complex than an inference from an ontological thesis to an ontological thesis. I am not sure, however, whether it is always a mistake to make an inference from an axiological thesis to an ontological thesis. For instance, one could make an inference from one's strong intuition about the axiological status of the world to the existence or non-existence of a particular being. The theistic argument from beauty is an inference from a positive axiological assessment of the world to the existence of God, and the atheistic argument from evil is an inference from a negative axiological assessment of the world to the non-existence of God. Whether or not these arguments succeed is, of course, a matter of dispute, but an inference from an axiological thesis to an ontological thesis does not seem to be as contentious as the critics make it out to be. Having said that, I have no intention in the present book to make any such inference. I will be pleased if readers of the present book are persuaded at least that the problem of systemic evil arises for both traditional theists and atheists/non-theists, and I will be even more pleased if they are persuaded that traditional theists enjoy advantages over atheists/non-theists when responding to the problem. I do not, however, mean to refute atheism/non-theism or establish traditional theism here.

178 THE PROBLEM OF EVIL FOR ATHEISTS

8.4.2 Objection 2: The spatiotemporal scope of my argument is problematic

My argument is based on the idea that, given the presence of systemic evil, if the naturalist ontology of atheists/non-theists is correct, the painting, which corresponds to our environment, is overall more grey than yellow. Kahane argues, however, that this is far from obvious. He writes:

> Humanity might go extinct soon or go on for many millions of years. The future may be utopian or dystopian or anything in between. We simply don't know. And if we have in mind the universe as a whole, the Earth is anyway an incredibly tiny part of that. Now, if we are alone in the universe then *and* sentient beings are the only source of value, then this doesn't matter: whatever conclusions we reach about the Earth also apply to the universe as a whole. But these are large assumptions. For all we know, there may be a multitude of advanced intergalactic civilizations, meaning that what happens on little planet Earth is of negligible significance in deciding the value of the universe as a whole. (Kahane 2022, p. 708)

In my earlier work to which Kahane directs this objection, I formulated optimism in terms of 'the world' (Nagasawa 2018b). If this term is construed as denoting the actual world according to possible world semantics, it includes the entire spatiotemporal reality that is actualized. I argued above that while traditional theists may be able to show that the painting, which corresponds to our environment, is not overall more grey than yellow, atheists/non-theists would struggle to do so. This is because while traditional theists have enormous supernaturalist resources at their disposal, atheists/non-theists are limited to their naturalist—that is material and biological—resources. Kahane seems however to suggest in the above passage that this assessment is incorrect because if modest optimism is formulated in terms of the actual world, atheists/non-theists can appeal to material, biological resources to show that the painting may not overall be more grey than yellow. For instance, they can argue that while there are many sentient animals *on Earth* whose lives are filled with pain and suffering, there may be millions of more planets in distant galaxies on which there are many more sentient animals whose lives are filled with pleasure and happiness. Alternatively, they can argue that while the history of Earth has so far been filled with pain and suffering for sentient animals, there may be a utopian future ahead of us in which their descendants' lives are filled with pleasure and happiness.

THE ADVANTAGES THAT TRADITIONAL THEISTS ENJOY   179

I have two responses to the objection in question. First, I acknowledge that Kahane makes a valid point in response to the formulation of optimism in my earlier work. I should not have formulated optimism in terms of the world, which is misleading. That is why, in the present book, I focus on 'the environment in which we exist' instead of the world. As I discussed in Chapter 6, while it is difficult to specify precisely what this term should mean our natural environment on Earth seems to be a good candidate and it is specific enough for our purposes. In regard to temporality, we can restrict our focus to the past, the present, and the foreseeable future in Earth's natural history. These suggestions are in fact what optimists and pessimists normally assume. When optimists present an optimistic worldview or pessimists present a pessimistic worldview, they do not intend to include in their scope happy aliens that may or may not exist in remote galaxies or happy earthlings in a utopia that may or may not exist in the remote future.

Second, having said all the above, my essential claim about the comparative advantage that traditional theists enjoy over atheists/non-theists holds even if we formulate optimism in terms of the world. Suppose, for the sake of argument, that atheists/non-theists succeed in defending modest optimism and responding to the problem of systemic evil by appealing to happy aliens in distant galaxies or happy earthlings in the distant future. In this case, traditional theists also succeed in defending modest optimism and responding to the problem of systemic evil because they can simply borrow the response developed by atheists/non-theists. This is because, again, traditional theists' supernaturalist resources subsume atheists' and non-theists' naturalist resources.

8.4.3 Objection 3: Natural selection adds nothing to the overall value of our environment

The essential ingredient of the problem of systemic evil is natural selection, which is a fundamental system underlying the existence of sentient animals including humans. I have argued that natural selection poses a challenge for modest optimists because it seems to undermine their claim that, overall and fundamentally, the environment in which we exist is not bad. Kahane contends, however, that natural selection does not add anything to the overall value of our environment. He writes:

180 THE PROBLEM OF EVIL FOR ATHEISTS

> Of course, natural selection is causally more fundamental than its products. But that just makes it a prodigious instrumental bad. However, that's irrelevant: merely instrumental value adds nothing to the overall value of the world. (Kahane 2022, p. 6)

Kahane may be correct in saying that natural selection itself does not add anything to the overall (intrinsic) value of the world; only the pain and suffering it causes do. The fundamentality of natural selection plays an important role here, however, because modest optimists believe that, overall and *fundamentally*, the environment in which we exist is not bad. The fundamental nature of natural selection nomologically necessitates over a long period of time the presence of pain and suffering for a large number of sentient animals; hence, the system contributes to overall value by significantly affecting the duration and number of victims. Given this nature, we cannot pretend that pain and suffering will eventually vanish from our environment or that we can change our social or political system to eradicate them. In this sense, natural selection is unique and important even though the system itself may not add any intrinsic axiological value.

8.4.4 Objection 4: Humanity may make natural history overall good

Kahane argues that even if we agree that natural history on Earth was overall bad for a long time, it is not obvious that it has remained bad since humans appeared on the planet. He writes:

> Whether evolutionary history contains more bad than good is a difficult empirical question. However, several authors argue that the lives of most animals in the wild contain more bad than good. If this argument about suffering in the wild is correct then it could be generalized into a general claim about evolutionary history.
>
> But even that is just a claim about one part of the past. Once humans arrive on the scene, they potentially bring into play distinctive goods—such as the value of rational agency, moral virtue, deep personal relationship, knowledge, achievement and aesthetic creation and appreciation—that are widely held to possess far greater value than mere sentience. So to show even just that terrestrial history is overall bad *until now*, Nagasawa will

THE ADVANTAGES THAT TRADITIONAL THEISTS ENJOY   181

need to show either that human history is itself overall bad, or that even if it
is good, it's not enough to outweigh the prior bad. (Kahane 2022, p. 7)

It seems anthropocentric to think that the arrival of humanity turns natural
history from being overall bad to being overall good despite the continuous
existence of pain and suffering for uncountably many sentient animals. It is
also worth noting that, today, many believe the exact opposite: the arrival of
humanity has worsened the natural environment to a catastrophic extent as
it contributes to degradation and creates more harm to sentient animals.
Setting that point aside, it is not easy to persuade critics who do not share the
same axiological intuition because it is practically impossible to calculate
precisely the overall axiological value of our environment.

Traditional theists can, however, respond to the objection in question
from another perspective. In the above passage, Kahane suggests that the
arrival of humans may make natural history overall good because of distinctive goods that they realize, such as the value of rational agency, moral
virtue, and so on. If this is a successful non-theistic response to the problem
of systemic evil, then traditional theists can simply borrow it. This response
is not available exclusively to atheists/non-theists because, again, traditional
theists' supernaturalist resources subsume the naturalist resources of atheists/
non-theists. Interestingly, and perhaps ironically, the naturalist response
here echoes the greater-good theodicy which atheists/non-theists often
dismiss when traditional theists posit it in response to the problem of evil.

8.4.5 Objection 5: It is not obvious that the theistic world is better

Again, I have argued that traditional theists enjoy an advantage over
atheists/non-theists because they have supernaturalist resources to which
atheists/non-theists cannot appeal. Kahane argues, however, that it is not
clear that supernaturalist resources would really help here. He writes:

[The claim that 'if atheism is true, nothing exists beyond the material
universe'] is merely a negative claim. It tells us nothing about the value
that the world would contain if atheism is true. It just tells us that the only
entities and properties which determine that value are those contained in the
natural world. No supernatural cavalry can come to the rescue to redeem all
those millions of years of agony. Still, in itself, that's neither bad nor good

182 THE PROBLEM OF EVIL FOR ATHEISTS

news—it may exclude God and His immense value, but also Satan and all kind[s] of malignant supernatural forces. (Kahane 2022, p. 705)

Kahane's objection is linked to 'anti-theism', which he and several other philosophers have discussed in recent years (Kahane 2011, 2021; Klaas J. Kraay 2018, 2021; Kirk Lougheed 2020). Anti-theism is silent about whether or not God exists. It says, however, that, contrary to what traditional theists believe, it would be worse if God did exist. Kahane writes, 'For example, [if God exists] your eternal bliss in the afterlife might be outweighed by the badness of the never-ending violation of your privacy [by an omniscient God]. If so, then under theism, the world might not be an "overall good place"' (Kahane 2022, p. 711). Pro-theism, on the other hand, says that it would be better if God did exist.

By putting forwards the problem of systemic evil and arguing for the comparative advantage of traditional theism, I do not intend to make the following grand ontological claim: traditional theism is true and atheism/non-theism is false given the existence of systemic evil. Equally, I do not intend to make the following grand axiological claim: pro-theism is true and anti-theism is false. That is, I do not advocate that the world would be a better place if God existed than otherwise. All I claim is that traditional theists enjoy an advantage over atheists/non-theists when responding to a specific challenge: the problem of systemic evil. Whether the overall axiological value of our world (or environment) would be greater if God did or did not exist is a further question, which requires a highly complex axiological assessment that I lack the space to discuss in the present book.

The following analogy may help to illustrate my point. Suppose that there is a problem of poverty (which is analogous to systemic evil) in a certain country under a specific economic policy X (which is analogous to traditional theism). Critics who support another economic policy Y (which is analogous to atheism/non-theism) claim that this is a serious challenge for X. I argue, however, that the problem persists even if we replace X with Y and, moreover, that the resources that X offers subsume the resources that Y offers and some of X's resources that are not available to Y may be helpful in tackling the problem. My main claims here are the following: (i) poverty is a problem for both policies X and Y; (ii) X may enable policymakers to develop a solution to the problem by appealing to resources that are not available to Y; and, hence, (iii) X enjoys a relative advantage over Y when tackling the problem. I do not however make a grand claim here that this hypothetical country is overall financially better off under policy X than

THE ADVANTAGES THAT TRADITIONAL THEISTS ENJOY 183

under Y; establishing such a claim requires a complex, comparative assessment of the impact and implications of X and Y along numerous dimensions of the country's economy. This is beyond my focus on the problem of poverty itself.

Returning to the problem of systemic evil, in putting forwards my argument I make the following claim only: traditional theists enjoy a relative advantage over atheists/non-theists *with respect to responding to the problem of systemic evil*; I certainly do not claim to have established the truth of pro-theism or the falsity of anti-theism.

8.4.6 Objection 6: The emotive version of the problem of systemic evil has an unreasonably wide scope

In Chapter 7, I introduced the emotive version of the problem of systemic evil. This version centres on the tension between the following two theses embraced by traditional theists and atheists/non-theists who accept modest optimism: (a) the existential gratitude thesis, according to which it is appropriate that we feel pleased about and grateful for our existence in the environment in which we live and (b) the fact that our existence depends fundamentally on a violent, cruel, and unfair biological system which guarantees pain and suffering for many people and other sentient animals. I argued that this set of theses evokes a form of cognitive dissonance, a state of discomfort which one experiences as a result of one's conflicting beliefs. Kahane argues, however, that the scope of my argument is problematic. He contends that when people express gratitude they do so from a personal, rather than cosmic, perspective. He writes, 'We rarely . . . see things from such a high altitude. When we are glad about our own lives, or the lives of those we care about, we do so from our own personal standpoint' (Kahane 2022, p. 9). He also contends that it is not obvious that (a) and (b) are in conflict because 'our gladness shouldn't be all-in' (Kahane 2022, p. 9). He writes:

> [Gladness] needs to be conditional: *given* that things have gone so badly, we are still personally pleased that, against the odds, we somehow still arrived and are doing reasonably well. While such gladness is conditional, it can still be deep and heartfelt. Indeed, most instances of gladness implicitly have that structure. And dark surroundings often amplify, rather than dampen, the gladness we feel about glimmers of good. (Kahane 2022, p. 9)

184 THE PROBLEM OF EVIL FOR ATHEISTS

Kahane is correct in saying that gratitude is often expressed in a limited, personal sense. For instance, victims of an aeroplane crash may express gratitude for having survived the horrible accident. Here, by expressing gratitude, of course, they do not indicate that they are pleased on the whole about the accident, let alone about the whole environment in which they live. They merely indicate that, inasmuch as they *were* in a very dangerous situation, they are pleased that they did not die. This expression of limited or conditioned gratitude does not however entail that people do not also hold the existential gratitude thesis or, more generally, modest optimism in a broader sense. I submit, for example, that when rational and educated people procreate they have the underlying conscious or unconscious belief that, overall and fundamentally, the environment in which we exist is not bad. Procreation is the natural process of giving birth to offspring, who are expected to navigate diverse situations in various locations over the course of their lifetimes, enduring for an extended period. This perspective is indeed rooted in the belief that the environment we inhabit merits our appreciation and gratitude because it offers the opportunity or potential for offspring to flourish and lead meaningful lives. In this context, a parent's modest optimism is not limited to specific circumstances. Conversely, it seems irrational or even immoral for people to bring their offspring into existence if they reject modest optimism and believe that, overall and fundamentally, our environment *is* bad. In sum, while I agree with Kahane that people often express gratitude in a limited sense, I also believe that they often embrace gratitude in a broader sense as well.

8.4.7 Objection 7: My argument conflates whether or not our environment is overall good and whether or not our existence depends on suffering or injustice

In Chapter 7, I discussed Janna Thompson's apology paradox, which focuses on a causal link between our existence and historical injustices, such as slavery and war crimes (Thompson 2000). I claimed that the paradox is structurally in parallel with the problem of systemic evil, which focuses on a nomologically necessary link between our existence and the biological system including natural selection. Kahane argues, however, that by making this comparison I conflate two distinct items: the overall goodness of our environment and past evil (Kahane 2022, p. 10).

THE ADVANTAGES THAT TRADITIONAL THEISTS ENJOY   185

This objection is somewhat similar to Objection 3 above. I do agree with Kahane that the abovementioned two items are distinct. Whether or not our environment is overall good is not directly linked to whether or not our existence depends on past evil and suffering. For instance, there could be an environment which is overall very good even though human existence in it depends on horrific evil and suffering having occurred in the past. On the other hand, there could be an environment which is overall very bad even though human existence in it does not depend on evil and suffering having occurred in the past. The systemic part of systemic evil is still relevant to my argument, however, because whether or not our environment is fundamentally bad—in the sense that our existence depends nomologically on a system which *guarantees* the occurrence of a significant amount of pain and suffering—is an important factor in determining the cogency of modest optimism. Compare an overall bad environment in which our existence depends nomologically on such a system and an overall bad environment in which our existence does not depend on such a system. While the overall axiological value of these environments may be identical, it is more difficult to maintain modest optimism and the hope thesis (see Chapter 7 of the present book), which concern the fundamental aspects, in the former environment than in the latter. This is precisely because of the systemic and fundamental nature of evil in the first environment as opposed to the second environment.

8.4.8 Objection 8: The problem of systemic evil is not a problem for atheists per se

Critics might argue that it is misleading to say that the problem of systemic evil poses a challenge for atheists because it arises only for a specific subset of atheists: atheists *who endorse modest optimism.* (Here, we focus on atheism and set aside other versions of non-theism.) Atheism is merely a rejection of traditional theism, so it does not make any claim about the axiological value of our environment. This means, the critics might argue, that the problem of systemic evil is essentially a problem for modest optimists but not for atheists. If we aim to develop a problem of systemic evil specifically for atheists, the critics might continue, we would have to show that atheism itself, rather than modest optimism, entails an axiological expectation mismatch which constitutes the problem of systemic evil. This objection may be better illustrated through the following analogy.

186 THE PROBLEM OF EVIL FOR ATHEISTS

Suppose that a significant number of atheists are supporters of democracy. In such a context, it would be misleading to raise difficulties with democracy as a challenge for atheists.[4]

There are two responses to the above objection. First, the democracy example is not strictly analogous because while modest optimism is directly relevant to the existence of evil in relation to one's axiological assessment or worldview, democracy is not. Second, the objection correctly points out that the 'problem of systemic evil for atheists' raised here pertains specifically to *modest optimist* atheists, but this does not imply that atheism is irrelevant to the argument. Indeed, the atheist component of modest optimist atheism plays a crucial role in my argument because, as I have explained, the problem presents a more significant challenge for (modest optimist) atheists than for (modest optimist) traditional theists.

8.4.9 Objection 9: The problem of systemic evil does not arise for non-cognitivist atheists/non-theists

The problem of systemic evil is based on the proposition that the pain and suffering that arise for uncountably many sentient animals in the process of natural selection are bad. Critics might argue, however, that atheists/non-theists can avoid the problem by embracing non-cognitivism, which says that such a proposition lacks truth value entirely. This would mean, according to the critics, that my claim that atheists/non-theists are less advantaged than traditional theists when responding to the problem of systemic evil is incorrect.[5]

This objection is problematic in several respects. First, it is dialectically problematic because if non-cognitivism is true then the problem of systemic evil does not arise in the first place even for traditional theists. To formulate the problem, it has to be assumed that the proposition 'pain and suffering that arise for uncountably many sentient animals in the process of natural selection are bad' does have a truth value: true. If the proposition does not have any truth value, it cannot pose a challenge to anyone.

---

[4] Thanks to an anonymous referee for raising this objection.
[5] Thanks to Nick Trakakis, Jack Syme, and an anonymous referee for helpful comments on this objection.

THE ADVANTAGES THAT TRADITIONAL THEISTS ENJOY   187

At this point, critics might reformulate the objection in question as follows: the problem of systemic evil does not arise for atheists/non-theists, many of whom endorse non-cognitivism, while it does arise for traditional theists, many of whom reject non-cognitivism. Hence, the problem of systemic evil is a challenge primarily for traditional theists and not for atheists/non-theists. This is a better way of presenting the objection.[6] I submit, however, that it creates its own problem. Recall that the problem of systemic evil is a problem for traditional theists and atheists/non-theists who endorse modest optimism. As we have seen, modest optimists claim that, overall and fundamentally, the world in which we exist is not bad. This means that modest optimists, whether they are theists or atheists/non-theists, assign the value of true to the claim about the axiological status of our environment. In other words, in our context, modest optimists cannot maintain non-cognitivism. Hence, while non-cognitivism may allow atheists/non-theists to avoid the problem of systemic evil, it also precludes them from endorsing modest optimism. Therefore, the proposed approach does not help atheists/non-theists who wish to defend modest optimism.

It is also worth noting that the objection in question leads to a view that is more extreme than nihilism: the problem of systemic evil does not arise because, first, it is not the case that 'pain and suffering that arise for uncountably many sentient animals in the process of natural selection are bad' is true (not because the proposition is false, but because it does not have any truth value) and, second, it is not the case that 'overall and fundamentally, the environment in which we exist is not bad' is true (again, not because the proposition is false, but because it does not have any truth value). This means that, under the version of non-cognitivism that is relevant to this context, both the problem of systemic evil and modest optimism are non-starters.

8.4.10 Objection 10: Atheists/non-theists can simply embrace pessimism

Critics might claim that, contrary to what I have argued, atheists/non-theists enjoy a greater advantage than traditional theists when responding to the

---

[6] J. L. Mackie (1955) makes a similar point when he raises the logical problem of evil. See Chapter 1 of the present book.

188 THE PROBLEM OF EVIL FOR ATHEISTS

problem of systemic evil because they can avoid the problem simply by embracing pessimism.

Pessimism in our context says that, overall and fundamentally, the environment in which we exist is bad. It might in principle be possible for traditional theists to argue that the environment is bad because of, for instance, the human abuse of freedom. It seems impossible however for them to maintain that, *overall and fundamentally*, our environment is bad given their belief that the world was created by an omnipotent and wholly good God. On the other hand, atheists/non-theists can easily maintain that, overall and fundamentally, our environment is bad, because they do not have such a prior theistic commitment. Once they embrace pessimism, they do not face any mismatch between their expectation of how reality should be and their observation of how it actually is (unless their pessimistic expectation is so pessimistic that it does not match our not-so-pessimistic observation of reality). I acknowledge that pessimism is a coherent response to the problem of systemic evil which is probably available exclusively to atheists/non-theists. As we have seen in Chapter 6, however, there are philosophical and psychological reasons to believe that most atheists/non-theists are not pessimists; so the option to embrace pessimism in response to the problem of systemic evil is not attractive to most atheists/non-theists, as is also the case for traditional theists.

It is also important to highlight the point that the combination of pessimism and atheism/non-theism entails many unpleasant consequences. For instance, it would be difficult to expect ultimate justice or cosmic redemption if pessimism and atheism/non-theism are true. Also, it would be difficult to maintain a positive outlook for flourishing on a global scale under these assumptions. William Lane Craig, for instance, argues that life cannot be meaningful if traditional theism is false because without theism we cannot avoid pessimism, which implies that life is absurd (Craig 1994). Christophe de Ray, to take another example, argues that if naturalism is true there is no good reason to believe that life is worthwhile on the whole (de Ray 2023). One could construe the problem of systemic evil as a variation of this kind of idea. While atheists/non-theists *can* coherently respond to the problem by rejecting optimism and embracing pessimism, such a move would raise serious existential concerns as a consequence. This does not, of course, make pessimism false, but it carries significant existential implications which many would find

THE ADVANTAGES THAT TRADITIONAL THEISTS ENJOY   189

morally repugnant, especially in relation to topics like birth affirmation (Morioka 2021) and procreation (Benatar 2006).

8.4.11 Objection 11: Atheists/non-theists can respond successfully to the problem of systemic evil by appealing to a naturalist version of sceptical theism

In response to Objection 4, I discussed the possibility that atheists/non-theists can respond to the problem of systemic evil by developing a naturalist variation of the greater-good theodicy. Similarly, some atheists/non-theists may respond to the problem by trying to develop a naturalist variation of sceptical theism. As we saw in Chapter 2, sceptical theism says that even if God has good reason to allow (systemic) evil to occur, given our cognitive limitations it is reasonable to think that we may not have full epistemic access to God's justification for allowing evil. A naturalist variation of this response may say that even though there is good non-supernaturalist reason to think that the environment in which we exist is overall and fundamentally not bad, given our cognitive limitations it is reasonable to think that we do not have full epistemic access to it. This objection is introduced but ultimately rejected by Jonbäck (2021). I summarize Jonbäck's point below. It is worth discussing this objection despite its failure because, as he correctly points out, it underpins my point that traditional theists enjoy advantages over atheists/non-theists when responding to the problem of systemic evil.

The following list provided by Michael Bergmann includes four theses to which traditional theists often appeal when they develop sceptical theism (Bergmann 2012, pp. 11–12):

(ST1) We have no good reason for thinking that the possible goods we know of are representative of the possible goods there are.

(ST2) We have no good reason for thinking that the possible evils we know of are representative of the possible evils there are.

(ST3) We have no good reason for thinking that the entailment relations between the possible goods and the permission of the possible evils we know of are representative of all such entailments that there are.

190 THE PROBLEM OF EVIL FOR ATHEISTS

(ST4) We have no good reason for thinking that the total moral value or disvalue we perceive in certain complex states of affairs accurately reflects the total moral value or disvalue they really have.

It is interesting to note that theses (ST1)–(ST4) are compatible not only with traditional theism but also with atheism/non-theism because none of them mentions God. Assuming that these theses are correct we can undercut the problem of systemic evil by claiming the following. Despite the initial appearance we cannot conclude whether the pain and suffering of sentient animals that arise in the process of natural selection are good or bad or neither good nor bad. However, this is not necessarily good news for modest optimists because these theses also entail the following broader claim: despite the initial appearance we cannot conclude whether the environment in which we live is overall and fundamentally good or bad or neither good nor bad. This claim implies that we are cognitively excluded from determining the truth or falsity of modest optimism, which makes a bold claim about the axiological status of our environment. Inasmuch as my interest here is in the comparative advantages of traditional theism and atheism/ non-theism, it is important to examine how traditional theists and atheists/ non-theists can respond to this situation.

As Jonbäck correctly claims, traditional theists do not need to worry too much here because they can appeal to their theistic resources to maintain modest optimism despite our cognitive limitations. They can argue that given their belief in God it is reasonable to assume that the pain and suffering in question do not make our environment overall and fundamentally bad because an omnipotent and wholly good God would not allow gratuitous pain and suffering to occur. On the other hand, atheists/non-theists cannot borrow this response because they do not share theistic resources; in particular, they deny the existence of an omnipotent and wholly good God. As Jonbäck contends, all they can do then is *hope* that, overall and fundamentally, our environment is not bad. Hence, atheists/ non-theists cannot be as confident as traditional theists about the truth of modest optimism.

Moreover, if atheists/non-theists merely hope for the truth of modest optimism, they struggle to an even greater extent to maintain the existential gratitude thesis, according to which it is appropriate that we feel pleased about and grateful for our existence in the environment in which we live. Of course, whether (ST1)–(ST4) are true and whether sceptical theism is tenable are contentious issues. It seems safe however to conclude that if we try to respond to the problem of systemic evil by appealing to our ignorance, traditional theists, yet again, enjoy advantages over atheists/non-theists.

8.5 Conclusion

In Chapter 5, I introduced the problem of systemic evil as a new and substantial challenge for traditional theists who believe in the existence of an omnipotent and wholly good God. In Chapters 6 and 7 I tried to 'neutralize' the problem, arguing that there is a version of the problem which raises a challenge for both traditional theists and atheists/non-theists who endorse modest optimism. This, I believe, is an important finding because atheists/non-theists normally believe that they are immune to the problem of evil. In this chapter, I have taken a further step and argued that traditional theists enjoy advantages over atheists/non-theists when responding to the problem because they have enormous supernatural resources to which atheists/non-theists do not have access. This, I believe, is another substantial claim because the problem of evil is usually considered a reason to reject traditional theism and embrace atheism/non-theism. While I do not advocate that traditional theists can definitely succeed in responding to the problem, traditional theists remain in an advantageous position relative to atheists/non-theists because in any plausible situation, with respect to responding to the problem, traditional theists either win or draw while atheists/non-theists either lose or draw. There is no plausible situation in which atheists/non-theists win and traditional theists lose.

PART IV

THE PROBLEM OF EVIL FOR EASTERN ATHEISTS/NON-THEISTS

9

The Problem of Impermanence

9.1 Introduction

We have seen in Parts II and III of the present book that, contrary to a widely held assumption, the problem of evil does not apply uniquely and specifically to traditional theists who believe in the existence of an omnipotent and wholly good God; it raises a challenge for many atheists/non-theists as well. I have argued that by analysing the problem as a version of the problem of axiological expectation mismatch, we can see that it raises a broader challenge concerning one's expectation of how reality should be and one's observation of how it actually is. I believe, however, that our coverage so far has remained limited because we have confined our discussion to the Western philosophical and religious framework. Even though pantheists, axiarchists, atheists, and other non-theists whom we have addressed in previous chapters reject the existence of God according to traditional Western theism, their own views are still developed within the Western framework.

In this final part of the present book, my focus shifts to the Eastern tradition. Specifically, I explore the Japanese tradition, mainly in the Kamakura period (1185–1333), aiming to show that the problem of evil arises even for atheists/non-theists who live outside the Western philosophical and religious framework.[1] I identify what I call the 'problem of impermanence', which poses a challenge for those adhering to the philosophical and religious traditions of the East, and argue that this problem is a version of the problem of axiological expectation mismatch as well as a version of the problem of systemic evil. I discuss Japanese thinkers' attempts to respond to the problem and argue that the only response that is potentially successful requires supernaturalism.

---

[1] The categorization of the Japanese before this period as atheists or (non-atheistic) non-theists is a matter of definition. They could be viewed as atheists in the sense that they did not accept traditional theism (because they were unaware of it). Alternatively, they could be considered (non-atheistic) non-theists because they did not explicitly reject traditional theism (again because they were unaware of it).

The Problem of Evil for Atheists. Yujin Nagasawa, Oxford University Press. © Yujin Nagasawa 2024.
DOI: 10.1093/oso/9780198901884.003.0010

196 THE PROBLEM OF EVIL FOR ATHEISTS

My goal in the current part of the book is to strengthen my claim that the problem of evil raises a challenge for nearly everyone, including even people outside the West. More broadly speaking, though, I also wish to present this part of the book as a step towards realizing my aspiration to globalize the philosophy of religion. The contemporary philosophy of religion has been led mainly by Christian philosophers in English-speaking countries whose ultimate goal is to defend Christian theism through reason and argument. Even atheist and agnostic philosophers of religion have spent most of their time assessing arguments developed by Christian theists. Work produced by those philosophers has consistently been of high quality. Yet I believe that the field would benefit immensely from an expansion in both its scope and reach. It would be beneficial to share intellectual resources across distinct religious traditions to make progress in philosophical debates.[2] Also, if philosophers of religion do not address a variety of religious traditions, the field cannot be considered complete as a comprehensive philosophical study of religious concepts, beliefs, and practices.

This chapter has the following structure. In Section 9.2, I introduce Kamo no Chōmei's work *Hōjōki* (1212), which vividly describes a series of disasters that he witnessed in Kyoto. I explain how his writing invokes key concepts that are addressed in contemporary discussions of the problem of evil. In Section 9.3, I argue that, contrary to initial appearances, pain and suffering in the midst of disasters are not the main concerns of Chōmei or other Japanese thinkers. Their main concern is rather the impermanence or transience of our existence, which leads us to the problem of impermanence. In Section 9.4, I explain that the problem of impermanence can be considered a version of the problem of systemic evil, even though it does not address the system of natural selection or evolution. Section 9.5 concludes.

9.2 *Hōjōki* and the Problem of Evil

The most prominent work that is relevant to the problem of evil in medieval Japanese literature is undoubtedly *Hōjōki* (方丈記), which was written by Kamo no Chōmei (鴨 長明) in 1212. Chōmei was an author and poet who was born the second son of a Shinto priest but later in life lived in seclusion. *Hōjōki*, which records a series of disasters and catastrophes in Kyoto, is

---

[2] See Nagasawa (2018a) for my view of how the philosophy of religion can be globalized effectively.

THE PROBLEM OF IMPERMANENCE   197

recognized as one of the most important literary works of the Kamakura period.[3] In this section, I provide an overview of *Hōjōki* and explain how Chōmei's descriptions of the disasters and catastrophes are relevant to philosophical concepts concerning evil discussed by contemporary philosophers of religion in the West.

Chōmei reports a series of four disasters and catastrophes that people in Kyoto experienced within a nine-year period. The first disaster that he describes is a great fire in 1177. He explains how the fire started in a lodging house for dancers and spread very quickly on the fickle wind. He writes, 'For those caught up in the blaze, it must have seemed a nightmare. Some fell, choked with smoke; others were blinded by the flames and quickly perished. Where others managed to escape with their life, they left behind them all their worldly goods' (Meredith McKinney, Yoshida Kenkō, and Kamo no Chōmei 1212/1330–1332/2013, p. 6).

As I explained in Chapter 1 of the present book, in Western philosophy the term 'moral evil' is used to denote any negative states of affairs, such as wars or crimes, involving pain and suffering brought about by acts of or negligence on the part of morally significantly free agents. Natural evil involves any negative states of affairs, such as earthquakes or tornados, that cause pain and suffering through natural processes. Chōmei notes that an unpredictable wind contributed to the spread of the fire in the city. He implies, however, that this is not an instance of natural evil *alone* because humans are at least partly responsible for the disaster by having chosen to build houses in a crowded area. He writes, 'All human undertaking is folly, but it is most particularly futile to spend your wealth and trouble your peace of mind by building a house in the perilous capital'. We can hence conclude that the first disaster that Chōmei describes is a tragic combination of natural evil and moral evil.

The second disaster that Chōmei describes is a whirlwind in 1180. He describes how the swirling wind destroyed every single house, large or small, in its path and blew every last belonging inside the houses into the air, creating a horrible spiralling smoke of dust that blinded the eye. It was so horrific that he wonders if 'the karmic wind of hell itself would be such as this'. He also writes, 'Whirlwinds are quite common, but do they ever blow

---

[3] Tadamasa Isobe (1976), Junzō Karaki (1965), and Seiichi Takeuchi (2007) discuss many of the medieval Japanese texts that I address in this paper. It should be noted that these authors consider the texts in relation to the concept of impermanence in general rather than the problem of evil or the problem of impermanence specifically. I appreciate Takeuchi's careful, philosophical analysis of the texts, which has been particularly beneficial to my understanding.

198 THE PROBLEM OF EVIL FOR ATHEISTS

like this? This was no ordinary wind, and all wondered whether it was not some portent from on high' (McKinney, Kenkō, and Chōmei 1212/1330–1332/2013, pp. 6–7). It is notable that Chōmei speculates that the wind might have a supernatural cause. The 'karmic wind of hell' is a translation of '*jigoku no gō no kaze*' (地獄の業の風), which is an enormous storm that is believed to occur in hell in response to human wrongdoing, and the 'portent from on high' is a translation of '*mono no satoshi* (もののさとし)', which literally means the warning of spirits, where 'sprits' refer to gods or Buddhas. In his discussion of the free will defence, Alvin Plantinga discusses a similar idea raised by Augustine, according to which much of the evil we encounter is attributed to Satan and his cohorts. Plantinga writes:

> Satan, so the traditional doctrine goes, is a mighty nonhuman spirit who, along with many other angels, was created long before God created man. Unlike most of his colleagues, Satan rebelled against God and has since been wreaking whatever havoc he can. The result is natural evil. So the natural evil we find is due to free actions of nonhuman spirits. (Plantinga 1974a, p. 58)

Chōmei's speculation that the whirlwinds may have been caused by spirits is comparable to Augustine's idea.

The third disaster that Chōmei describes is a series of famines that took place over a two-year period in 1181–1182. He writes that the crops failed as a result of 'disaster followed on disaster' involving drought in the spring and summer and typhoons and floods in the autumn. Chōmei contends that this third disaster started with natural evil but resulted in moral evil. He reports that, because of poverty and hunger, some people went to old temples to steal the Buddhist images and dismantled and broke up woodwork in the worship hall to sell. He writes, 'Born into these vile latter days, it has been my lot to witness such heartbreaking things' (McKinney, Kenkō, and Chōmei 1212/1330–1332/2013, pp. 9–10). Chōmei also remarks that he observed not only immoral acts but also compassionate and altruistic acts in the midst of the disaster. He writes, 'Where a man could not bear to part from his wife, or a woman loved her husband dearly, it was always the one whose love was the deeper who died first—in their sympathy for the other they would put themselves second, and give their partner any rare morsel that came their way. So also, if parent and child lived together the parent was always the first to die; a baby would still lie suckling, unaware that its mother was dead' (McKinney, Kenkō, and Chōmei 1212/1330–1332/2013, p. 10).

THE PROBLEM OF IMPERMANENCE   199

These are examples of what Western philosophers consider greater goods realized through negative states of affairs.

The fourth and last disaster that Chōmei describes is a series of earthquakes that struck in 1185. He describes how mountainsides collapsed and tsunamis flooded the land. Not a single temple building or pagoda in the city remained intact and everyone who was indoors at the time was crushed. He remarks, 'Among all the terrors, I realized then, the most terrifying is an earthquake' (McKinney, Kenkō, and Chōmei 1212/1330–1332; 2013, pp. 10–11). Chōmei vividly describes a tragedy that he witnessed during this catastrophe. A small child, who was the only son of a samurai, was building a toy house under the roof of a mud wall when the earthquake struck. The wall collapsed and crushed the child's body so badly that people could not even recognize him. Chōmei writes, 'I saw with sympathy and sadness the parents who held the body of the child in their arms crying out loud. It was sad to see that the loss of a child was so unbearable that even a brave samurai could not hide his agony'.[4] This can be construed as an example of what contemporary Western philosophers call 'horrendous evil'. As I explained in Chapter 1 of the present book, Marilyn McCord Adams defines horrendous evil as a form of evil 'the participation in which (that is, the doing or suffering of which) constitutes prima facie reason to doubt whether the participant's life could (given their inclusion in it) be a great good to him/her on the whole' (Adams 1999, p. 26). While we might be comfortable believing that relatively minor mishaps are necessary for the realization of the greater good, it is significantly more difficult to believe that there is any point to the utterly awful pain and suffering of innocent victims like this.

We have seen Chōmei's descriptions of four terrible disasters, which seem to capture a variety of key philosophical concepts addressed in the contemporary debate in the West over the problem of evil. The first disaster, the great fire, is an outcome of a combination of moral evil and natural evil. It teaches us that moral evil can intensify the impact of natural evil, and vice versa. The second disaster, the whirlwind, seems to involve little human wrongdoing. Chōmei speculates that although the situation may seem like an instance of natural evil, it could actually have a supernatural cause intended to serve as a warning to people. The third disaster, consecutive famines, arose naturally but Chōmei describes how it led people to perform

---

[4] Puzzlingly enough, this important passage is omitted from both Michael Hoffmann's 1991 translation and Meredith McKinney's 2013 translation of *Hōjōki*.

200 THE PROBLEM OF EVIL FOR ATHEISTS

two contrasting types of acts: immoral acts and altruistic acts. The fourth disaster, a series of earthquakes, is comparable to the disaster of the whirlwind but Chōmei records an instance of horrendous evil that he witnessed as its tragic consequence.

9.3 The Problem of Impermanence

In the previous section, I introduced Chōmei's *Hōjōki* and explained how numerous key concepts concerning evil discussed in the West emerge in his report of disasters and catastrophes in Kyoto. If we were to place Chōmei's work in the Western framework, we would be able to use it as a vivid illustration of the problem of evil for traditional theists: how could an omnipotent and wholly good God allow these instances of moral and natural evil involving pain and suffering for many people in Kyoto in the Kamakura period? It is evident, however, that the problem that Chōmei raises is distinct from this particular problem because Chōmei and other medieval Japanese thinkers do not believe in the existence of an omnipotent and wholly good God; they are, in this sense, atheists or non-theists. Yet this is not the only reason that the problem that Chōmei raises is distinct from the problem of evil as conceived in the West. I argue that the other and more important reason is that Chōmei's problem focuses primarily on *impermanence* rather than pain and suffering. In what follows, I call the version of the problem of evil discussed mainly in the West today, which focuses on pain and suffering realized through moral or natural evil, the 'problem of pain and suffering'; and I call the version of the problem of evil discussed by Chōmei and other medieval Japanese thinkers, which focuses on the impermanence of reality highlighted by examples of moral or natural evil, the 'problem of impermanence'.

Chōmei considers the world and life to be transient, fragile, and impermanent. This is based on the Buddhist teaching that impermanence (無常; *mujō* in Japanese) is, along with suffering (苦; *ku* in Japanese) and non-self (無我; *muga* in Japanese), among the Three Marks of Existence (三相; *sansō* in Japanese). His worldview is summed up in the very first passage of *Hōjōki*:

> On flows the river ceaselessly, nor does its water ever stay the same. The bubbles that float upon its pools now disappear, now form anew, but never endure long. And so it is with people in this world, and with their dwellings. (McKinney, Kenkō, and Chōmei 1212/1330–1332/2013, p. 5)

THE PROBLEM OF IMPERMANENCE 201

Chōmei is making two claims here. The first is that the world is analogous to a ceaseless flow of water because it undergoes continuous change. This dynamic view of reality is often compared to Heraclitus's thesis that one cannot step into the same river twice. The second is that people and their dwellings are akin to floating bubbles in the water in the river because their existence is temporary, transient, and fragile. Chōmei continues:

> ...The places remain, as full of people as ever, but of those one saw there once now only one or two in twenty or thirty still survive. Death in the morning, at evening another birth—this is the way of things, no different from the bubbles on the stream.
>
> Where do they come from, these newborn? Where do the dead go? I do not know. Nor do I know why our hearts should fret over these brief dwellings, or our eyes find such delight in them. An owner and his home vie in their impermanence, as the vanishing dew upon the morning glory. The dew may disappear while the flower remains yet it lives on only to fade with the morning sun. Or perhaps the flower wilts while the dew still lies but though it stays, it too will be gone before the evening. (McKinney, Kenkō, and Chōmei 1212/1330–1332/2013, p. 5)

In the above quote, Chōmei says that we are all part of the perpetual, inescapable cycle of birth and death. He also wonders about the origins and ultimate destiny of our existence. This reflection suggests that Chōmei believes our existence transcends material reality, although he does not elaborate further on this point. He then considers the meaning of life. He wonders why our hearts should fret over our existence if its briefness is analogized to that of a vanishing dew drop on a flower. One might compare Chōmei's view to Seneca's well-known view of the shortness of life. Their views are, however, distinct. Seneca says that despite its short appearance life is actually long enough. He writes, 'Life is long enough, and a sufficiently generous amount has been given to us for the highest achievements if it were all well invested' (Seneca AD 49/2004, p. 1). Chōmei, on the other hand, says that life is indeed short.[5] It is worth emphasizing that Chōmei focuses

---

[5] Yoshida Kenkō, another author from the Kamakura period, makes a claim that may be more reminiscent of Seneca: 'Among all living creatures, it is man that lives longest. The brief dayfly dies before evening; summer's cicada knows neither spring nor autumn. What a glorious luxury it is to taste life to the full for even a single year. If you constantly regret life's passing, even a thousand long years will seem but the dream of a night' (McKinney, Kenkō, and Chōmei 1212/1330–1332/2013, pp. 23–24).

202 THE PROBLEM OF EVIL FOR ATHEISTS

mainly on impermanence, not pain and suffering, which are only reminders or highlighters of impermanence. This marks the difference between the problem of pain and suffering and the problem of impermanence.

Chōmei laments that while people recognize that pain and suffering experienced in disasters and catastrophes are good reminders of the impermanence of life, they tend to forget about it as time passes. After describing the earthquake disaster, Chōmei writes:

> At the time, all spoke of how futile everything was in the face of life's uncertainties, and their hearts seemed for a while a little less clouded by worldliness, but time passed, and now, years later, no one so much as mentions that time.
>
> (McKinney, Kenkō, and Chōmei 1212/1330–1332/2013, p. 11)

Interestingly enough, Chōmei's observation here is compatible with contemporary psychologists' studies of optimism bias. For example, as I noted in Chapter 6 of the present book, according to a study of the 1989 Northern California earthquake by Jerry M. Burger and Michele L. Palmer, the optimism bias that victims of the earthquake had previously espoused was suppressed immediately after the event, but it came back at a later time. (Burger and Palmer 1992).

The concept of impermanence is not unique to Chōmei's work. In fact, it is a theme that is widespread in Japanese literature and artwork, especially in the Kamakura period. For example, in his *Essays in Idleness* (徒然草; *Tsurezuregusa* in Japanese), the Buddhist monk Yoshida Kenkō presents a dynamic, impermanent worldview that is comparable to Chōmei's:

> This world is changeable as the deeps and shallows of Asuka River—time passes, what was here is gone, joy and grief visit by turns, once splendid places change to abandoned wastelands, and even the same house as of old is now home to different people. The peach and the plum tree utter nothing—with whom can we speak of past things? Still more moving in its transience is the ruin of some fine residence of former times, whose glory we never saw. (McKinney, Kenkō, and Chōmei 1212/1330–1332/2013, p. 33)

Like Chōmei, Kenkō compares the intransient nature of reality with a river and applies the metaphor to human life:

There is no choosing your moment, however, when it comes to illness, childbirth or death. You cannot call these things off because 'the time isn't right'. The truly momentous events of life—the changes from birth through life, transformation and death—are like the powerful current of a raging river. They surge ever forward without a moment's pause. Thus, when it comes to the essentials, both in religious and in worldly life, you should not wait for the right moment in what you wish to achieve, nor dawdle over preparations. Your feet must never pause.

... The seasons progress in a fixed order. Not so the time of death. We do not always see its approach; it can come upon us from behind. People know that they will die, but death will surprise them while they believe it is not yet close. (McKinney, Kenkō, and Chōmei 1212/1330–1332; 2013, p. 98)

Another well-known work from the Kamakura period that represents the concept of impermanence is *The Tale of the Heike* (平家物語; *Heike Monogatari* in Japanese), a war epic describing the rise and fall of the Taira clan over a twenty-year period. Starting with the victory of the clan in two civil wars against the Minamoto clan, Taira no Kiyomori from the Taira clan becomes the first courtier from a warrior family to rise in rank to chief minister of the government. At its peak, the Taira clan governed more than half of the country. Frustration among the oppressed public and their rivals, however, caused additional wars against the Taira clan, which ultimately ended with the defeat of the Taira clan by the Minamoto clan, led by Minamoto no Yoshitsune in the final battle of Dan-no-ura. Yet the epic does not end there. After a power struggle, even the war hero Yoshitsune is killed by his own brother, Minamoto no Yoritomo. The anonymous author of the tale presents the epic as a spectacular illustration of the impermanence of our existence and introduces the following passage:

The sound of the bell of Gionshoja echoes the impermanence of all things. The hue of the flowers of the teak tree declares that they who flourish must be brought low. Yea, the proud ones are but for a moment, like an evening dream in springtime. The mighty are destroyed at the last, they are but as the dust before the wind.

If thou ask concerning the rulers of other countries far off; Choko of Shin, Omo of Kan, Shui of Ryo, Rokuzan of To, all these, not following in the paths of the government of all the Kings and Emperors who went before them, sought pleasure only; not entering into council nor heeding the disorders of their country, having no knowledge of the affliction of

204   THE PROBLEM OF EVIL FOR ATHEISTS

their people, they did not endure, but perished utterly. (A. L. Sadler thirteenth century/1918, p. 1)

This passage is one of the most well-known expressions of *shogyō mujō* (諸行無常), the Buddhist thesis that everything in reality, in both appearances and essences, is impermanent. The assertion that 'they who flourish must be brought low' represents *jousha hissui no kotowari* (盛者必衰の理), which literally means the law or the principle (理; *ri* in Japanese) in accordance with which even the prosperous inevitably decay. It is notable that the author of the *Tale of the Heike* compares the rise and fall of those in power to 'an evening dream in springtime' because in Japanese culture a dream is a common metaphor for impermanence. As Seiichi Takeuchi notes, dreams share many characteristics or implications of impermanence, including transience, futility, perplexity, unpredictability, and incoherence (Takeuchi 2007, pp. 27–28). Dreams are considered 'unreal' because they are always elusive and ephemeral; yet these authors point out that life itself is also elusive and ephemeral.

The distinction between the problem of pain and suffering and the problem of impermanence can be marked by referencing the three types of suffering (三苦; *sanku* in Japanese) recognized in Buddhism, as follows:

- The suffering of suffering (苦苦; *kuku* in Japanese): the physical and mental sufferings that we experience when we face illness, death, or other difficulties in life.
- The suffering of change (壊苦; *eku* in Japanese): the sufferings that we experience when pleasurable things become unpleasurable because of the dynamic nature of reality. Since all is impermanent, even things that we find highly pleasurable will eventually become unpleasurable.
- The suffering of conditioned existence (行苦; *gyōku* in Japanese): the suffering that we experience due to our conditioned state and dissatisfaction with the impermanence of everything. Even if we are currently having pleasurable experiences, we can suffer existentially by recognizing that the pleasure does not last forever.

The problem of pain and suffering as it is discussed in the West focuses primarily on the 'suffering of suffering', which is realized through moral or natural evil. The problem of impermanence found in medieval Japanese literature, on the other hand, focuses primarily on the 'suffering of change'

THE PROBLEM OF IMPERMANENCE   205

and the 'suffering of existence', which arise from the impermanent nature of reality and our recognition of it.[6]

In Chapter 1 of the present book, I argued that the problem of evil comprises three variables: (i) God, (ii) evil, and (iii) the allegedly conflicting relationship between God and evil. Drawing on Buddhist terminology, we can say that the problem of impermanence assigns the suffering of change to variable (ii) while the problem of pain and suffering assigns the suffering of suffering to it. What about variable (i)? Unlike the problem of pain and suffering, which arises for traditional theists, the problem of impermanence does not assign an omnipotent and wholly good God to this variable because Buddhists do not believe in the existence of such a being. I argued in Part III of the present book that the problem of evil is more general than philosophers tend to think because the core of the problem is the alleged discrepancy between our optimistic expectation of our environment and our negative observation of it. In other words, variable (i) need not be specifically tied to belief in God; rather, it can be associated with our broader commitment to modest optimism. We can apply this reasoning to the problem of impermanence to show that it is also a version of the problem of axiological expectation mismatch.

Recall how the problem of pain and suffering for traditional theists can be presented as a version of the problem of axiological expectation mismatch. Traditional theism teaches us that the world was created by an omnipotent and wholly good God. Many traditional theists, therefore, naturally (and perhaps also naïvely) expect the world to be free from pain and suffering. Our observation shows, however, that the world *is* filled with pain and suffering. Hence, traditional theists face an axiological expectation mismatch: there is a gap between their optimistic expectation of how the world should be and their less positive observation of how the world actually is. As I explained in Chapter 2, the problem of divine hiddenness and the problem of no best world can also be construed as versions of the problem of axiological expectation mismatch as it arises for traditional theists.

How can we show that the problem of impermanence is also a version of the problem of axiological expectation mismatch even though it raises a

---

[6] The distinction between the three types of suffering is not always straightforward. For instance, Western philosophers sometimes discuss the problem of evil in connection with examples of pain and suffering experienced during the process of ageing or dying. These instances can be relevant not only to the suffering of suffering but also to the suffering of change and the suffering of conditioned existence. Thanks to an anonymous referee for raising this point.

206 THE PROBLEM OF EVIL FOR ATHEISTS

challenge for followers of Buddhist teaching? We often naïvely assume that everything, including our existence and dwellings, continues to exist indefinitely, or we suspend our belief regarding their impermanence for practical or psychological reasons. That is why, as the medieval Japanese authors point out, wealthy people pursue more wealth and powerful people pursue more power as if they could flourish indefinitely. According to Buddhism, however, everything is impermanent and transient. Even those who achieve significant wealth, power, or even happiness eventually age and die. This coincides with our less naïve and more careful observation of the world. Hence, followers of Buddhist teaching face an axiological expectation mismatch: there is a gap between our naïve, optimistic expectation of how the world should be and the less naïve, less optimistic observation of how the world actually is.

It is interesting to note a structural difference between the problem of pain and suffering and the problem of impermanence. On the one hand, the problem of pain and suffering derives an axiological expectation mismatch from an optimistic view of the world *based on religious belief* and a less optimistic view of the world *based on our observation*. On the other hand, the problem of impermanence derives an axiological expectation mismatch from an optimistic view of the world *based on our (naïve) observation* and a less optimistic view of the world *based on religious belief*. Hence, while religious belief underpins an optimistic view that is implicit in the problem of pain and suffering, it underpins a less optimistic view that is implicit in the problem of impermanence.

The crucial point in distinguishing the problem of impermanence from the problem of pain and suffering is the following: while pain and suffering can be used to illustrate the concept of impermanence, they are not intrinsic components of impermanence. In fact, the problem of impermanence can also be presented by referring to pleasure and joy instead of pain and suffering. Even if we have pleasure and joy we can still suffer from them because they do not last forever (the 'suffering of change') and we still remain conditioned and dissatisfied with our existence (the 'suffering of existence').

The above point concerning the suffering of change and existence is illustrated in Japanese literature. For instance, as we have seen, in *Essays in Idleness* Kenkō writes, 'time passes, what was here is gone, joy and grief visit by turns, once splendid places change to abandoned wastelands ... Still more moving in its transience is the ruin of some fine residence of former times, whose glory we never saw' (McKinney, Kenkō, and Chōmei

1212/1330–1332/2013, p. 33). Similarly, the author of the *Tale of the Heike* talks about people who once flourished but eventually 'perished utterly', describing their lives as 'an evening dream in springtime' (Sadler thirteenth century/1918, p. 3). Even if life is filled with success and glory, it is not everlasting and it always comes to an end. There are many more textual examples illustrating the idea that pleasure and joy, rather than pain and suffering, can occasion the problem of impermanence. The author, poet, and courtier in the Heian period (794–1185) Ki no Tomonori, for instance, writes in the *Kokin Wakashū*:

> When the everlasting
> Light shines gently
> From the sun in springtime,
> Why should, with unquiet hearts,
> The blossoms scatter?
>
> (Translation by Thomas McAuley[7])

Tomonori compares the joyful events in life to the magnificent cherry blossoms of a warm spring and ponders why such pleasurable things cannot endure, lasting only for short periods of time. Similarly, Ariwara no Narihira, another poet in the Heian period, writes:

> If, in this world of ours
> All the cherry blossom
> Disappeared
> The heart of spring
> Might find peace.
>
> (Translation by Thomas McAuley[8])

Like Tomonori, Narihira compares the pleasure of life to the beauty of cherry blossoms and asserts ironically that we would feel calm if life did not involve any pleasurable events, which never last forever. We often realize impermanence through the occurrence of negative events, such as sudden death and unexpected disasters, but we can also recognize it through positive

---

[7] Available on McAuley's Waka Poetry website, https://www.wakapoetry.net/kks-ii-84/ (accessed 11 November 2023).

[8] Available on McAuley's Waka Poetry website, https://www.wakapoetry.net/kks-i-53/ (accessed 11 November 2023).

208 THE PROBLEM OF EVIL FOR ATHEISTS

events that give us pleasure and joy. We could of course feel pain or suffering by observing the end of pleasure and joy but, again, pain and suffering are not essential to the problem of impermanence. Consider, for example, someone who experiences a great deal of pleasure and joy but suddenly falls into a deep coma and dies without waking up. Here, the problem of impermanence arises even though pain and suffering are not present.

In Section 9.2 above, we saw that Chōmei's descriptions of pain and suffering in the midst of disasters and catastrophes in Kyoto evoke important philosophical concepts concerning evil as Western philosophers discuss it. Yet I have argued in this section that the focus of Chōmei and other medieval Japanese authors is not on pain and suffering themselves. Their focus is rather on impermanence. For them, pain and suffering are only vivid reminders or highlighters of impermanence. Hence, these texts in medieval Japanese literature should be construed as works that are more relevant to the problem of impermanence than to the problem of pain and suffering.

9.4 The Problem of Impermanence as a Version of the Problem of Systemic Evil

In Part III of the present book, we discussed the problem of systemic evil. I used that term because it focuses our attention on the *system* of natural selection and evolution, which nomologically necessitates pain and suffering for uncountably many sentient animals. I argued that the problem of systemic evil is more persistent and fundamental than the standard problem of evil, which focuses on specific events or specific types of events involving pain and suffering.

I submit that the problem of impermanence can also be considered a version of the problem of systemic evil because Japanese thinkers who present the problem refer to impermanence as a systemic concern. Chōmei points out, for instance, that impermanence is one of the Three Marks of Existence, which are fundamental features of reality according to Buddhism. As noted above, he writes, 'Death in the morning, at evening another birth—this is *the way of things*, no different from the bubbles on the stream' (McKinney, Kenkō, and Chōmei 1212/1330–1332/2013, p. 5, emphasis added). 'The way of things' is an English translation of *narai* (ならひ), which is synonymous with *yonotsune* (世の常). '*Yono*' (世の) signifies 'the world's' and '*tsune*' (常) means the way or regularity. Chōmei hence contemplates that impermanence, which we observe in the cycle of birth and death, represents a fundamental systemic principle underlying reality. Like Chōmei, Kenkō also expresses a systemic concern when he contends that impermanence is beyond our control. 'There is no choosing your moment, however, when it comes to illness, childbirth or death. You cannot call these things off because "the time isn't right". The truly momentous events of life—the changes from birth through life, transformation and death—are like the powerful current of a raging river' (McKinney, Kenkō, and Chōmei 1212/1330–1332/2013, p. 98).

As is the case with a raging river, we cannot resist or avoid impermanence because, again, it is a fundamental feature of the system underlying our existence. Furthermore, as I mentioned above, the author of *The Tale of the Heike* describes impermanence in relation to *jousha hissui no kotowari* (盛者必衰の理). The concept of *kotowari* (理) originated in Chinese philosophy to denote the order or principle of nature. The author claims that the world is governed by this natural order, which guarantees that prosperity does not last forever. These observations suggest that when medieval Japanese thinkers present the problem of impermanence, they are not interested in specific examples of birth and death but in the more fundamental, systemic nature of impermanence that characterizes our existence. Like the problem of systemic evil which we discussed in Part III of the present book, the problem of impermanence cannot be undercut merely by explaining away specific types or instances of impermanence because it raises a more fundamental challenge concerning the system on which our existence is based.

9.5 Conclusion

Starting with Chōmei's *Hōjōki*, we have seen how medieval Japanese thinkers present the problem of impermanence. I have argued that Chōmei's descriptions of natural disasters illustrate many important concepts concerning evil that are discussed in the contemporary philosophical literature in the West. I have claimed, however, that the problem of impermanence, which Chōmei raises, is distinct from the problem of evil in the West because it focuses on the 'suffering of change' and the 'suffering of existence' rather than the 'suffering of suffering' to which the Western problem of evil appeals. The suffering of suffering can highlight impermanence, but it is not an essential ingredient of the problem of impermanence.

I have also argued that the problem of impermanence can be construed as a version of the problem of systemic evil because it focuses our attention on the regularity or order which necessitates impermanence. We cannot avoid impermanence because, like natural selection and evolution, it is a systemic matter underlying our existence.

10

Responses to the Problem
of Impermanence

10.1 Introduction

In the previous chapter, I argued that the problem of evil arises even outside of the Western philosophical and religious framework. Unlike the contemporary Western version of the problem of evil (that is, the problem of pain and suffering), which focuses on the 'suffering of suffering', the Eastern version of the problem of evil (that is, the problem of impermanence) focuses on the 'suffering of change' and the 'suffering of existence'. I tried to show that the problem of impermanence can be construed as a version of the problem of systemic evil because it regards impermanence as the fundamental order of the world that we cannot escape.

In this chapter, I critically discuss several responses to the problem of impermanence introduced by Japanese thinkers. Contemporary responses to the problem of pain and suffering in the West normally begin with theories explaining how God and evil can coexist. Responses to the problem of impermanence in the East are unique because they typically begin with practical advice, rather than abstract theories, concerning how we can react to or cope with impermanence.

In earlier chapters in which I discussed responses to the problem of pain and suffering in the West, I argued that traditional theists enjoy advantages over non-theists in responding to the problem. I make a similar claim in this chapter. I argue that a careful analysis shows that the only potentially satisfactory response to the problem of impermanence is a supernaturalist response and, hence, the problem poses a more significant challenge for naturalists than for supernaturalists. This is an important finding because atheism and non-theism, as we define them, are not compatible with supernaturalism.

This chapter has the following structure. In Section 10.2, I introduce and classify four distinct responses to the problem of impermanence found in the classical Japanese literature: hermitism, hedonism, indifferentism, and

The Problem of Evil for Atheists. Yujin Nagasawa, Oxford University Press. © Yujin Nagasawa 2024.
DOI: 10.1093/oso/9780198901884.003.0011

212 THE PROBLEM OF EVIL FOR ATHEISTS

transcendentalism. In Section 10.3, I offer a systematic analysis of the problem of impermanence and argue that, ultimately, only transcendentalism, which requires supernaturalism, has the potential to offer a satisfactory solution to the problem. The thesis that the problem of impermanence is, like other versions of the problem of evil, a form of the problem of axiological expectation mismatch plays a crucial role in my argument. Section 10.4 concludes.

10.2 Responses to the Problem of Impermanence

Western authors in the Judeo-Christian tradition respond to the problem of pain and suffering by trying to show how it is possible for God to allow pain and suffering despite His omnipotence and goodness. Japanese authors present radically distinct responses to the problem of impermanence. This is unsurprising because the problem of impermanence is not concerned with the existence of God; it is rather a problem concerning how we can understand, respond to, and cope with impermanence. It is difficult to locate clear statements made by Japanese authors in response to the problem of impermanence because they do not address the problem in a structured and systematic manner. We can nevertheless identify the following four distinct responses in their poetry and literary work: (1) hermitism, (2) hedonism, (3) indifferentism, and (4) transcendentalism.[1] Let me synopsize each of them here and assess them in detail in the next section.

10.2.1 Response 1: Hermitism

The first response to the problem of impermanence found in medieval Japanese literature is what I call 'hermitism'. According to hermits, the best response to the problem is to live a simple life as a hermit and minimize exposure to the disasters and catastrophes associated with living in civilization. Kamo no Chōmei claims that the key to enduring our impermanent and ephemeral existence is to place ourselves in the right environment in which we can stay calm and free ourselves from unnecessary concerns and worries. He writes:

---

[1] Some of the responses to the problem of impermanence and relevant texts are discussed in Seiichi Takeuchi's work (2007).

RESPONSES TO THE PROBLEM OF IMPERMANENCE   213

Yes, take it for all in all, this world is a hard place to live, and both we and our dwellings are fragile and impermanent, as these [horrific and disastrous] events reveal. And besides, there are the countless occasions when situation or circumstance cause us anguish...

If you live in a cramped city area, you cannot escape disaster when a fire springs up nearby. If you live in some remote place, commuting to and fro is filled with problems, and you are in constant danger from thieves. A powerful man will be beset by cravings, one without family ties will be scorned. Wealth brings great anxiety, while with poverty come fierce resentments. Dependence on others puts you in their power, while care for others will snare you in the worldly attachments of affection. Follow the social rules, and they hem you in; fail to do so, and you are thought as good as crazy. (McKinney, Kenkō, and Chōmei 1212/1330–1332/2013, p. 12)

Chōmei's hermitism is obviously influenced by the Buddhist teaching that advises us to relinquish all worldly attachments and pursue equanimity (捨; *sha* in Japanese). Equanimity is a mental state of perfect balance that leaves one free from emotional disturbances and should be cultivated to facilitate the pursuit of *nirvana* (涅槃; *nehan* in Japanese). It is important to note that Chōmei's response is not a mere theoretical solution to the problem of impermanence. It is indeed a lifestyle, one that Chōmei himself embraced. After turning thirty years old, Chōmei relocated to a small house, just one tenth the size of his previous dwelling, to lead a modest life. Eventually, at the age of fifty, he renounced the world to become a lay monk as well as a hermit. He writes, 'I had never had a wife and children, so there were no close ties that were difficult to break. I had no rank and salary to forgo. What was there to hold me to the world?' (McKinney, Kenkō, and Chōmei 1212/1330–1332/2013, p. 12).

Chōmei's last house, which he built at the age of sixty, was a mere ten feet square, and less than seven feet high. He continues:

... The hermit crab prefers a little shell for his home. He knows what the world holds. The osprey chooses the wild shoreline, and this is because he fears mankind. And I too am the same. Knowing what the world holds and its ways, I desire nothing from it, nor chase after its prizes. My one craving is to be at peace, my one pleasure to live free of troubles... (McKinney, Kenkō, and Chōmei 1212/1330–1332/2013, pp. 16–17)

214 THE PROBLEM OF EVIL FOR ATHEISTS

Yoshida Kenkō also describes, in his *Essays in Idleness*, his pursuit of hermitism as a response to the problem of impermanence. Like Chōmei, Kenkō emphasizes the importance of solitude in living in the impermanent world.

> What kind of man will feel depressed at being idle? There is nothing finer than to be alone with nothing to distract you.
>
> If you follow the ways of the world, your heart will be drawn to its sensual defilements and easily led astray; if you go among people, your words will be guided by others' responses rather than [coming] from the heart... Even if you do not yet understand the True Way, you can achieve what could be termed temporary happiness at least by removing yourself from outside influences, taking no part in the affairs of the world, calming yourself and stilling the mind. As *The Great Cessation and Insight* says, we must 'break all ties with everyday life, human affairs, the arts and scholarship'. (McKinney, Kenkō, and Chōmei 1212/1330–1332/2013, pp. 58–59)

The Great Cessation and Insight (摩訶止観; *Maka Shikan* in Japanese) is a Buddhist doctrinal treatise that originated in China in the sixth century. Notice that Kenkō suggests that, even if we do not succeed in attaining enlightenment, it is still practically valuable to detach ourselves from worldly affairs because we can still find temporary happiness.

Hermitism offers *practical* advice about how we should live in response to the problem of impermanence. This stands in clear contrast to common contemporary responses to the problem of pain and suffering in the West, which tend to be purely theoretical.

10.2.2 Response 2: Hedonism

The second response to the problem of impermanence is what I term 'hedonism'. Hedonism is akin to hermitism in that it too provides practical advice. However, its advice contrasts sharply with that of hermitism. As its name suggests, hedonists advise us to pursue physical and emotional pleasure by relishing our transient existence to the fullest, rather than withdrawing from the world and adopting a life of seclusion.

Ōtomo no Tabito, a court noble and poet whose life bridged the mid-Asuka (592–710) period through the early Nara period (710–794), presents his version of hedonism in the following poem:

RESPONSES TO THE PROBLEM OF IMPERMANENCE 215

Living people
Will eventually die.
Such are we, so
While in this world
Let's have fun!

(Translation by Thomas McAuley[2])

When referring to fun, Tabito means enjoying his time with the aid of alcoholic drink. In fact, the above is among his 'Thirteen Poems in Praise of Saké (rice wine)'. The use of alcohol is more explicit in another of his poems:

I'll not be a man
At all:
A wine jar
I'll become, maybe
And soak in wine.

(Translation by Thomas McAuley[3])

The use of alcohol, as opposed to other pastimes, is important in this context. Impermanence makes us feel that our existence is elusive and dream-like, but when we are drunk it feels even more elusive and dream-like. Seiichi Takeuchi therefore calls hermits' approach to impermanence 'going deeper into dreams' (Takeuchi 2007, p. 98).

In another poem in the same set, Tabito depicts hedonism as a form of anti-intellectualism:

Oh, how ugly!
People seeking wisdom and
Not drinking;
Look on them well
Don't they seem like monkeys?

(Translation by Thomas McAuley[4])

---

[2] Available on McAuley's Waka Poetry website, https://www.wakapoetry.net/mys-iii-349/ (accessed 11 November 2023).

[3] Available on McAuley's Waka Poetry website, https://www.wakapoetry.net/mys-iii-343/ (accessed 11 November 2023).

[4] Available on McAuley's Waka Poetry website, https://www.wakapoetry.net/mys-iii-344/ (accessed 11 November 2023).

216 THE PROBLEM OF EVIL FOR ATHEISTS

This poem represents Tabito's view that, unlike hermitism, which is often pursued by sophisticated intellectuals, hedonism is a down-to-earth response that is available to any ordinary person.

It is interesting to note that even though Tabito ridicules intellectuals who pursue hermitism, he also seems to acknowledge that the hedonist lifestyle is not commendable:

> In this world of ours
> If only I can have fun
> In the life to come
> An insect or a bird
> That's what I'll become!
>
> (Translation by Thomas McAuley[5])

Tabito accepts that his hedonism is not praiseworthy. That is why he thinks that its consequence may be that he will be reborn as an insect or a bird. Yet he says, or perhaps pretends, that he does not mind that prospect as long as he can enjoy his current moment in impermanent and ephemeral reality. Tabito also writes:

> Silently
> Seeking wisdom:
> Will never match
> Drinking wine and
> Drunken weeping.
>
> (Translation by Thomas McAuley[6])

The first line of the poem represents another example of Tabito's anti-intellectualism. Yet the phrase 'drunken weeping' also suggests that Tabito is not entirely content with hedonism. Hedonists cannot but weep because while they advocate drinking as the best response to the problem of impermanence, they still cannot overcome the sad reality that everything comes to an end. Perhaps, ironically, the more fun they have the more vividly they realize that their enjoyment will not last forever.

---

[5] Available on McAuley's Waka Poetry website, https://www.wakapoetry.net/mys-iii-348/ (accessed 11 November 2023).

[6] Available on McAuley's Waka Poetry website, https://www.wakapoetry.net/mys-iii-350/ (accessed 11 November 2023).

The *Kanginshū* is a collection of popular songs and ballads compiled by an unidentified Buddhist monk in the late Sengoku period (1336–1573). We can see a somewhat humorous defence of hedonism in one of its poems:

> Everything passes by at every moment—*chirori, chirori*
>
> Can't help it, can't help it, the world is like a leaf in stormy waves
>
> Can't help it, can't help it, since ancient times few people have lived to seventy
>
> Everything here and there is like a dream, like a bubble in water
> All things exist only in the brief moment that dew lingers on a leaf
> What an ephemeral world
>
> A dream? Damn it!
>
> Can't stand people who look serious
> In the world of dreams within dreams within dreams
> They pretend to understand
>
> How could it help to be serious?
> Life is a dream
> Just go mad
>
> (Translation by Yujin Nagasawa)

The phrase '*chirori*' (or '*chirari*' in modern Japanese) means a brief moment, which, in this context, refers to the short duration of our existence. Like Tabito's poem above, the song seems to contain a hint of pessimism. It compares the world to a small leaf in stormy waves lamenting the shortness and futility of life: 'All things exist only in the brief moment that dew lingers on a leaf'. Similar to Tabito's poem, this one also expresses a form of anti-intellectualism. It ridicules intellectuals who pretend to understand everything yet they themselves are no different from someone being carried on a small leaf in a storm. Hedonists discourage others from intellectualizing the impermanence of life and encourage them simply to accept it and go crazy while they are alive.

In sum: hedonism is comparable to hermitism in the sense that it offers a practical solution to the problem of impermanence. However, hedonists reject hermitism for its underlying intellectualism. According to hedonists, there is no sober, sophisticated intellectual answer to the problem of impermanence. All we can do is intoxicate ourselves to try to enjoy the present moment and forget about or go deeper into an elusive and ephemeral reality.

218 THE PROBLEM OF EVIL FOR ATHEISTS

10.2.3 Response 3: Indifferentism

The third response to the problem of impermanence is what I call 'indifferentism'. According to this response, we should simply accept the impermanence of reality because there is no point in trying to overcome it. We have no control over it, the view says, because we ourselves are fundamentally impermanent. This is a unique response because it does not offer any substantive 'solution' to the problem. In this sense, indifferentism is considered a 'no response' response.

We saw earlier that Kenkō pursues hermitism in response to the problem of impermanence. Yet he expresses self-criticism in the following passage:

> [Life] is like the game of *mamakodate*, played with *sugoroku* pieces, in which no one knows which in the line of pieces will be removed next—when the count is made and a piece is taken, the rest seem to have escaped, but the count goes on and more are picked off in turn, so that no piece is finally spared. Soldiers going into battle, aware of the closeness of death, forget their home and their own safety. And it is sheer folly for a man who lives secluded from the world in his lowly hut, spending his days in idle delight in his garden, to pass off such matters as irrelevant to himself. Do you imagine that the enemy Impermanence will not come forcing its way into your peaceful mountain retreat? The recluse faces death as surely as the soldier setting forth to battle. (McKinney, Kenkō, and Chōmei 1212/1330–1332/2013, p. 90)

Kenkō thinks that life is like a game which is guaranteed to end in loss (death) even though we do not know when that will happen. This view is consistent with the claim that I made in Chapter 9 of the present book: the problem of impermanence can be construed as a version of the problem of systemic evil because it is concerned with impermanence as the fundamental order of the world over which we have no control. In the above passage, Kenkō is critical of those like Chōmei and himself who intellectualize the problem of impermanence and willingly live as hermits hoping to escape it. Kenkō acknowledges that soldiers who forthrightly accept that their own deaths can happen at any moment know better than intellectual hermits because they face impermanence directly without pretending that it can be avoided. What soldiers embrace here is indifferentism.

Saigyō, a poet and Buddhist monk who lived in the late Heian period through the early Kamakura period, was another notable figure who

RESPONSES TO THE PROBLEM OF IMPERMANENCE   219

renounced the world to pursue hermitism. In his poetry, however, he also contemplates whether he is genuinely more successful in overcoming impermanence than ordinary people who seem to embrace impermanence as it is.

> Those who take vows
> May not truly
> Have renounced the world
> Those who don't take vows
> May better renounce the world
>
> (Translation by Yujin Nagasawa)

Saigyō chose to live in seclusion to free himself from his worldly desires. Yet he wonders if his very decision to make such a radical move indicates that he cares too much about the world. Perhaps ordinary people living ordinary lives are less concerned about worldly desires and, in this way, they react better to impermanence.

Kenkō goes further. He says not only that impermanence is inevitable but that it should be welcomed:

> If our life did not fade and vanish like the dews of Adashino's graves or the drifting smoke from Toribe's burning grounds, but lingered on for ever, how little the world would move us. It is the ephemeral nature of things that makes them wonderful.
>
> Among all living creatures, it is man that lives longest. The brief dayfly dies before evening; summer's cicada knows neither spring nor autumn. What a glorious luxury it is to taste life to the full for even a single year. If you constantly regret life's passing, even a thousand long years will seem but the dream of a night.
>
> (McKinney, Kenkō, and Chōmei 1212/1330–1332/2013, pp. 23–24)

Kenkō seems to be suggesting here that prolonging life does not make it worthwhile; life is worthwhile precisely because it ends at some point. Extending life much longer, he says, does not make it better.

In sum: indifferentists maintain that we should simply accept that life and the world are impermanent because that is beyond our control; hence, we should accept and live ordinary life as it is instead of attempting to resolve this unresolvable problem. We should even welcome impermanence because life could not be worthwhile if it was permanent.

10.2.4 Response 4: Transcendentalism

The fourth and final response to the problem of impermanence found in medieval Japanese literature is what I call 'transcendentalism'. According to this response, we can overcome impermanence by transcending our impermanent existence. Takeuchi uses the phrase 'going beyond dreams' to characterize this response and describes it as the belief that 'while the world is like a dream, there is an outer world that is more real which we can wake up into' (Takeuchi 2007, p. 27). Our goal is, according to this approach, to 'wake up' from an elusive, dream-like, impermanent reality into a new, transcendental reality.

Iroha is an old Japanese pangram poem comparable to an alphabet song, one that many people in Japan can recite even today. The earliest appearance of the song is found in *Readings of Golden Light Sutra* (金光明最勝王経音義; *Konkōmyōsaishōōkyō Ongi* in Japanese), which was written in the Heian period.

> The scent remains in the air,
>> but the flowers have scattered away
> Who in this world
>> stays ever the same?
> The deep mountains of transient existence
>> are to be crossed today
> No more shall we dream shallowly,
>> nor yield to intoxication
>>>> (Translation by Yujin Nagasawa)

The poem tells us to realize our impermanent existence in the constantly changing world by looking at blossoming flowers which, despite their beauty, will inevitably scatter in the end. It then encourages us to avoid allowing ourselves to be absorbed into the dream-like, elusive reality and instead overcome impermanence by crossing the deep mountains of karma. As Takeuchi contends, the Iroha song has two elements: first, the affirmation that reality is impermanent and, second, the determination to try to transcend that impermanence (Takeuchi 2007, p. 35). The first element corresponds to the problem of impermanence and the second element corresponds to transcendentalism as a response to the problem.

The following is a waka written by Ki no Tomonori in the *Kokin Wakashū*:

RESPONSES TO THE PROBLEM OF IMPERMANENCE   221

In my dreams, I see him
Awake, I see him still
Reflecting on all this
The world seems an empty cicada husk
Merely a fleeting dream

(Translation by Yujin Nagasawa)

Tomonori says that whether he is asleep or awake he can envision a deceased loved one. The deceased who left the impermanent realm for transcendental reality is, Tomonori says, comparable to a cicada that has shed its skin and flown away. Such a transcendental realm feels more real, and the fact that he was left alone in this world enhances his realization that our world is like an impermanent dream.

Saigyō, similarly, writes:

All I see in the world I realize is but a dream, and yet,
    and yet still so disheartening—
my still unawakened heart!

(Translation by Jack Stoneman)

Saigyō expresses his frustration that he still cannot wake up into a new reality despite his recognition that the world is as elusive as a dream. While he lived as a hermit, his poem above appears to imply a yearning for a transcendental reality beyond his reach.

We have seen four responses to the problem of impermanence. Hermitism suggests that we renounce civilization and avoid dangers and difficulties in our ephemeral and fragile existence. Hedonism suggests that we should enjoy ourselves with alcoholic drink so that we can forget about the impermanence of life. Indifferentism offers no solution to the problem but encourages us to live ordinary lives by accepting impermanence as unavoidable. Transcendentalism advises us to try to overcome impermanent reality by waking up into a new transcendental reality.

10.3 Assessing the Responses

I argued in Chapter 9 that the problem of impermanence is also a version of the problem of axiological expectation mismatch. Understanding the problem of impermanence in this way enables us to correctly assess the

222 THE PROBLEM OF EVIL FOR ATHEISTS

abovementioned four responses to it. In what follows, I argue that the only response that is potentially successful is transcendentalism, which requires supernaturalism, and that this finding suggests that the problem of impermanence poses a more significant challenge for naturalists than for supernaturalists. Conversely, I argue, the problem of impermanence can be taken as a motivation for embracing supernaturalism instead of naturalism.

10.3.1 Assessing Hermitism

The first response to the problem of impermanence to be assessed is hermitism. Considering the problem of impermanence as a version of the problem of axiological expectation mismatch, we can construe hermitism as an attempt to close the gap between our naïvely optimistic expectation of reality and the less optimistic view of reality according to Buddhism by minimizing negativity in reality. Hermits try to show that, despite impermanence, we can still be content with life if we avoid the negative consequences of human wrongdoings and natural disasters by living in isolation. This is a 'defensive' response to the problem of impermanence, a response that is designed to reduce the pain and suffering we experience.

I argue, however, that there are at least three reasons to conclude that hermitism cannot be the ultimate solution to the problem of impermanence. First, while hermits may successfully avoid certain types of pain and suffering associated with living in civilization, they may also inadvertently promote other types of pain and suffering that are unique to living in isolation. They may also inadvertently relinquish types of pleasure and joy that can be experienced only by living in civilization. Hence, it is not obvious that hermits can fill the gap between our naïvely optimistic expectation of reality and the less optimistic view of reality that Buddhism provides.

Second, hermits cannot escape negativity entirely by living in isolation because, according to Buddhism, pain and suffering arise from birth, ageing, illness, and dying, which are rooted in human nature. We cannot escape them because they represent the order or principle that underlies our existence. The gap between their expectation and reality will remain even if we adopt hermitism.

Third, and crucially, hermitism is at best a response to the problem of pain and suffering, not the problem of impermanence. If we succeed in avoiding pain and suffering, or the 'suffering of suffering', to use Buddhist terminology, by living as hermits, impermanence may become less visible because pain and suffering are highlighters of impermanence. Yet we still cannot escape the 'suffering of change' and the 'suffering of existence', which are directly related to the problem of impermanence. In this sense, hermits like Chōmei seem to conflate the highlighters of impermanence with impermanence itself. Hermits may be able to eliminate a certain amount of pain and suffering, but they cannot overcome impermanence itself.

One might argue at this point that my interpretation of hermitism is uncharitable. According to this criticism, hermits aim to minimize the 'suffering of change' by living in isolation, thereby avoiding the constant influence of the dynamic nature of human affairs and reality. Even if this interpretation is correct, though, the hermitic approach offers only limited value in addressing the problem of impermanence. Given the temporality of our existence, hermits remain susceptible to the 'suffering of change' and the 'suffering of existence'. As I discussed earlier, impermanence is a systemic issue, not confined to specific events or specific types of events. A critic might also attempt to challenge my interpretation of hermitism by arguing that hermits do not propose hermitism as the *ultimate* solution to the problem of impermanence; rather, it is seen as a transitional step towards transcendentalism, whose goal is to reach *nirvana*. This is not what Chōmei claims in *Hōjōki*, but Kenkō seems to be aware of this point in *Essays in Idleness* where he says, 'Even if you do not yet understand the True Way, you can achieve what could be termed *temporary happiness* at least by removing yourself from outside influences, taking no part in the affairs of the world, calming yourself and stilling the mind' (McKinney, Kenkō, and Chōmei 1212/1330–1332/2013, pp. 58–59, emphasis added). I do not reject Kenkō's claim here because it remains compatible with my thesis that transcendentalism is the only response with the potential to provide the ultimate solution to the problem of impermanence.

10.3.2 Assessing Hedonism

The second response to the problem of impermanence that we have seen is hedonism. Like hermitism, hedonism offers practical advice. However, hedonism provides us with an interesting contrast to hermitism because it is an 'offensive' rather than a 'defensive' response. Again, hermits claim that the best way to live out one's ephemeral existence is to eliminate unnecessary worries by living in isolation; their interest is not in maximizing pleasure but in minimizing worries. Hedonists maintain, on the other hand, that the best way to live out one's ephemeral existence is to try to enjoy oneself as much as

224 THE PROBLEM OF EVIL FOR ATHEISTS

possible, particularly with the help of alcoholic drink; their interest is not in minimizing worries but in maximizing pleasure. In other words, while hermits try to fill the gap in the axiological expectation mismatch by reducing negativity in reality, hedonists try to fill it by enhancing positivity in reality. This makes sense given that, as we have seen above, hedonism is often pursued in anti-intellectualist opposition to hermitism.

Hedonism also fails as the ultimate solution to the problem of impermanence. First, while hedonists may successfully promote hedonistic pleasure and joy, they may also inadvertently relinquish certain types of pleasure and joy that are unique to ordinary, non-hedonistic life. They may also inadvertently promote types of pain and suffering that arise only in hedonistic life. Hence, it is not obvious that hedonism can fill the gap between our naïvely optimistic expectation of reality and the less optimistic view of reality that Buddhism provides.

Second, if Buddhism is correct, hedonists cannot escape negativity entirely by living hedonistically because, again, pain and suffering arise from birth, ageing, illness, and dying. We cannot escape them because they represent the order of the system that underlies our existence.

Third, more importantly, hedonists' attempts to promote pleasure and joy can backfire because pleasure and joy, as much as pain and suffering, can highlight impermanence. As we have seen, medieval Japanese authors vividly illustrate impermanence by referring not only to pain and suffering but also to pleasure and joy. By enhancing pleasure and joy, therefore, hedonists may experience the 'suffering of change' and the 'suffering of existence' even more intensely than hermits.

Fourth, unlike hermitism, hedonism cannot be adopted even as a transitional step towards transcendentalism because, according to Buddhism, pursuing worldly desires like pleasure and joy will only divert us from pursuing *nirvana*. Tabito seems to recognize this problem when he expresses cynicism or guilt regarding his pursuit of hedonism in saying that he cannot but try to have fun even if he has to be reborn as a bird or a worm. I conclude, therefore, that hedonism cannot be the ultimate solution to the problem of impermanence.

10.3.3 Assessing Indifferentism

The third response to the problem of impermanence to assess is indifferentism. Unlike hermitism and hedonism, this response suggests that we should not do anything but simply live ordinary lives. Considering indifferentism as a response to axiological expectation mismatch, we can understand it as the view that we should accept reality as it is according to Buddhism; there is no need to attempt to reduce negativity or increase positivity in reality. Once we accept the dynamic Buddhist view of reality, our naïvely optimistic expectation should be corrected in a way that it is consistent with our expectation that life is impermanent and full of pain and suffering. Unlike hermitism and hedonism, indifferentism addresses the problem of impermanence directly. As I have argued, hermits and hedonists are misguided because they seek to eliminate or alleviate pain and suffering, which are only highlighters of impermanence rather than impermanence itself. Indifferentists, on the other hand, face the problem of impermanence directly and encourage us to accept our impermanent existence at face value and live ordinary lives accordingly. This is, again, a 'no response' response because it discourages us from changing our lifestyles. Hence, nearly everyone who is not aware of the problem of impermanence has in effect already adopted this response.

Indifferentism appears to face a paradox: there cannot be genuine indifferentism as a response to the problem of impermanence because, once we recognize impermanence as a problem, we can no longer live ordinary lives as ordinary people like soldiers, farmers, and merchants. Trying to live ordinary lives as reflective thinkers responding to the problem of impermanence is not the same as living ordinary lives as genuinely ordinary people. This point is compatible with Chōmei's claim that soldiers seem to accept impermanence better than intellectuals like himself and with Saigyō's claim that people who have never taken vows are better at renouncing the world than hermits like himself.

Setting aside the paradox of the impossibility of genuine indifferentism, I believe that indifferentism *is* a coherent response to the problem of impermanence. It accepts impermanence as it is and simply swallows it. It is comparable to pessimism about reality and life, which I also believe to be a coherent, if unattractive, view. Yet indifferentism is not a satisfying *solution* to the problem of impermanence because it merely accepts impermanence as an unsolvable problem. It would be preferable if a response existed that gives us an optimistic solution. I argue in what follows that transcendentalism can be the sole answer in providing such a solution.

226 THE PROBLEM OF EVIL FOR ATHEISTS

10.3.4 Assessing Transcendentalism

We have assessed three responses to the problem of impermanence: hermitism, hedonism, and indifferentism. These responses are compatible with naturalism because none of them requires any supernaturalist belief. The fourth and final response that we assess here is transcendentalism, which is the only response requiring supernaturalist belief. I argue that this is also the only response which has the potential to solve the problem of impermanence in a satisfactory manner. This means that the problem of impermanence may pose a more significant challenge for naturalists, particularly those who do not subscribe to indifferentism, than for supernaturalists.

As we have seen, transcendentalism suggests that we can overcome impermanence by waking up into a new reality. Yet in their writings the medieval Japanese thinkers that we have considered are not explicit about what such a new reality entails. I explore, therefore, two possible ways to formulate transcendentalism within the Eastern framework, corresponding to two distinct ways of understanding the new reality.

The first version of transcendentalism, which I call 'ineffable transcendentalism', is based on the Buddhist approach to impermanence. Given the influence of Buddhism in Japan, it is natural to guess that many medieval Japanese thinkers have this sort of view in mind when they write about the possibility of a new reality. Buddhism affirms impermanence through and through. It is not merely that our current realm or our bodily existence is impermanent; absolutely *everything* is impermanent. For instance, Pure Land Buddhism (浄土仏教; *jōdo bukkyō* in Japanese), which spread widely in Japan during the Kamakura period, encourages people to repeat a mantra to be reborn in the pure land. Yet even the pure land is not a permanent realm like heaven in the Christian tradition where God is believed to reign eternally. Anything that may exist, whether heaven, hell, gods, selves, or souls, is impermanent in Buddhist metaphysics.

How can we resolve the problem of impermanence if the possibility of permanence is precluded universally? More specifically, how can *we* overcome impermanence if there is no such thing as the permanent self? According to ineffable transcendentalism, we can respond to the problem of impermanence by transcending impermanence rather than by denying impermanence or stipulating permanence. Buddhism places us in *samsara* (輪廻; *rinne* in Japanese), the continuous cycle of death and rebirth, and

RESPONSES TO THE PROBLEM OF IMPERMANENCE 227

encourages us to escape from this cycle. There is no 'true self' or 'permanent soul' transmigrating in this metaphysical system. Our ultimate soteriological goal is *nirvana*, an ineffable and indescribable state of enlightenment, which represents an escape from the cycle.

Nirvana is analogized to 'blowing out' a flame, meaning it ends the cycle of rebirth and death, a long process which involves states of being that are conditioned, impermanent, and unsatisfactory. Liberation from impermanence and suffering is equivalent to realizing what Buddhism calls non-self (無我; *muga* in Japanese) or emptiness (空; *kū* in Japanese). That is, ineffable transcendentalism suggests that a solution to the problem of impermanence is not to try to find or realize the permanent self, which does not exist, but to achieve the state of non-self or the lack of any self, which constitutes a state of release from suffering and impermanence. *Nirvana* is not eternal in the conventional sense of enduring endlessly in time; rather, it is timeless in the sense of being beyond the confines of temporality. In other words, the state of *nirvana* is neither a form of 'super existence' nor one of mere 'extinction'; instead, it represents a state of liberation from suffering and impermanence (Collins 1992, p. 216). No language or concept can fully capture such a state because it is unthinkable or incomprehensible by logic or reason (不可思議; *fukashigi* in Japanese). Ineffable transcendentalism is a supernaturalist view because it requires *samsara*, the cycle of death and rebirth, which exceeds the limits of naturalist ontology, as well as *nirvana*, the soteriological goal that is beyond our present existence in the material universe.

The other version of transcendentalism that I wish to consider here within the Eastern framework is 'permanent transcendentalism'. This view is based on the Hindu rather than the Buddhist approach to impermanence. We saw above that, according to ineffable transcendentalism, the doctrine of impermanence applies to the entirety of reality. Permanent transcendentalism is, however, based on a more limited or nuanced interpretation of the doctrine of impermanence. This interpretation says that impermanence applies only to the reality in which we currently live and that there is another permanent reality beyond that. We exist in an impermanent realm of conditioned existence, but this realm does not exhaust all of reality.

In Hinduism, permanent transcendentalism is presented in terms of the *ātman*, the permanent, unchanging self that exists beyond phenomenality and external conditions. The Hindu belief in the *ātman* directly opposes the

228 THE PROBLEM OF EVIL FOR ATHEISTS

Buddhist doctrine of non-self, and this opposition demarcates, to a large extent, Hinduism from Buddhism. The *Chāndogya Upaniṣad*, one of the oldest Upaniṣads, says that the *ātman* 'is free from sin, free from old age, free from death, free from sorrow, and free from hunger and thirst' (Lokeswarananda 2017, verse 8.7.1) and also that it is 'immortal and fearless (Lokeswarananda 2017, verse 8.7.4). The *ātman* is an eternal, indestructible self that exists beyond the ego. It is unchanging and does not participate in the phenomenal world, but it can be 'realized' as one's true nature. The *jīva*, the individual self, which is bound to the fruits of the actions it has performed in each life, transmigrates into the body of another living being after death. We are part of *saṃsāra*, and when an individual dies the *jīva* is reborn and lives as another person or animal. Regarding the *dehī*, the embodied soul, the *Bhagavadgītā* remarks that, 'Just as a person discards his old garments and acquires new ones, the soul similarly gives up old bodies and accepts new ones' (Gosvami 2013, verse 2.22). This remark is reminiscent of Tomonori's analogy that a deceased soul who leaves the impermanent realm for transcendental reality is like a cicada that sheds its skin and flies away. This also reminds us of Takeuchi's characterization of transcendentalism, according to which, 'while the world is like a dream, there is an outer world that is more real which we can wake up into' (Takeuchi 2007, p. 27). Our current reality is a dream-like, ephemeral material existence, but another permanent reality exists beyond that.

If we take the right path towards liberation, we will eventually achieve *mokṣa* (解脱; *gedatsu* in Japanese), which is the blissful end of the cycle of death and rebirth where we are finally freed from suffering. The dualist tradition of Dvaita Vedānta asserts the distinction between the *jīva* and Brahman, the Ultimate Reality which permeates everything, whereas the non-dualist tradition of Advaita Vedānta asserts the non-difference between the *jīva* and *Brahman*.

Both versions of transcendentalism that I have discussed are rooted in metaphysical systems found in Eastern religions. Transcendentalism can also however be formulated within the Western framework. In this context, Western transcendentalism would not postulate rebirth or *nirvana/mokṣa*; instead, it would emphasize the notion of the eternal soul or God as an eternal, timeless, or necessarily existent being. It is crucial to examine distinct iterations of transcendentalism to determine which one provides the most compelling response to the problem of impermanence. For example, some versions rooted in Eastern monism may sidestep the issue of impermanence by positing something as permanent. Yet these perspectives might not be favourable if the form of permanence in question exists beyond our individual, personal existence.[7] Nonetheless, I lack the space to address evaluations of specific views. The crucial point is that any version of transcendentalism requires a supernaturalist ontology that allows us to affirm the existence of a reality that lies beyond impermanence. There is no hope of solving the problem of impermanence without a supernaturalist ontology because our current existence in the material universe is spatiotemporally finite.[8]

The thesis that a satisfactory solution to the problem of impermanence requires supernaturalism is significant because it entails the following two important points. First, the problem of impermanence poses a more significant challenge for naturalists, or at least for naturalists who reject indifferentism, than for supernaturalists. This is especially interesting given that impermanence is a close cousin of the problem of pain and suffering, which is commonly thought to pose a challenge only for supernaturalists, and more specifically for traditional theists. Second, and relatedly, the problem of impermanence can motivate the inclination to prefer supernaturalism over naturalism. If we believe that there is an ultimate and optimistic solution to the problem of impermanence, we have no choice but to accept supernaturalism. This is interesting too because the problem of pain and suffering is often used in part to motivate naturalism as opposed to supernaturalism.

10.4 Conclusion

I have examined in this chapter four responses to the problem of impermanence: hermitism, hedonism, indifferentism, and transcendentalism. I have argued that the first three, which are compatible with naturalism, are unsuccessful or unsatisfying; some may eliminate or alleviate pain and suffering but none resolves the problem of impermanence itself. I have then discussed two distinct versions of transcendentalism: ineffable transcendentalism, which is based on Buddhist metaphysics, and permanent

---

[7] Thanks to Josh Spears for raising this important point.

[8] One might argue that naturalism is compatible with impermanence because it seems compatible with Platonism about abstract objects, where these objects exist permanently. It is difficult to envision, however, how, within the naturalist framework, we can wake up into a permanent realm of abstract objects given that naturalists generally believe that physical death is the end of our existence. Conversely, if we could somehow wake up into a permanent realm of abstract objects then this would also exceed the limitations of naturalism; so we would need supernaturalism anyway. See Steinhart (2023) for relevant issues.

230 THE PROBLEM OF EVIL FOR ATHEISTS

transcendentalism, which is based on Hindu metaphysics. I have not discussed the tenability of either version. I have argued, however, that only transcendentalism, which requires supernaturalism, can constitute a potentially successful response to the problem of impermanence. I have also argued that if the only solution that is potentially successful requires supernaturalism, then the problem of impermanence raises a more significant challenge for naturalists than for supernaturalists. Finally, I have argued that this implies that the problem of impermanence can be construed as a reason to prefer supernaturalism over naturalism.

Conclusion

The main thesis for which I have argued throughout the present book holds that the problem of evil arises not only for traditional theists but also for atheists and other non-theists, including pantheists, axiarchists, and followers of Eastern religious traditions. I have also argued that traditional theists, who usually espouse supernaturalism, are in a better position than atheists and other non-theists, who usually espouse naturalism, to respond to the problem because any potentially successful response requires supernaturalist resources. Furthermore, I have argued that a supernaturalist ontology subsumes the naturalist ontology. This means that if atheists/non-theists can develop a successful response to the problem of evil, it is likely that traditional theists can adopt it as well. There is no response to the problem of evil to which atheists/non-theists can appeal but traditional theists cannot, even though there are many responses to which traditional theists can appeal but atheists/non-theists cannot. So, metaphorically speaking, with respect to grappling with the problem of evil, it seems that traditional theists can either win or draw while atheists/non-theists can at best draw but are more likely to lose.

Even if some of the specific claims I have made in the present book are not correct, I hope to have established over the course of our discussion that, contrary to the common belief, the problem of evil poses a profound challenge, which extends across a broad spectrum of atheists and other non-theists. The problem of evil should no longer be seen as a challenge only for traditional theists.

The Problem of Evil for Atheists. Yujin Nagasawa, Oxford University Press. © Yujin Nagasawa 2024.
DOI: 10.1093/oso/9780198901884.003.0012

References

Adams, Marilyn McCord (1989), 'Horrendous Evils and the Goodness of God', *Proceedings of the Aristotelian Society Supplementary Volume* 63, pp. 297–323.

Adams, Marilyn McCord (1999), *Horrendous Evil and the Goodness of God*. Ithaca, NY: Cornell University Press.

Adams, Marilyn McCord (2008), 'Plantinga on "Felix Culpa": Analysis and Critique', *Faith and Philosophy* 25, 123–140.

Adams, Robert Merrihew (1972), 'Must God Create the Best?', *Philosophical Review* 81, 317–332.

Adams, Robert Merrehew (1974), 'Theories of Actuality' *Noûs* 8, pp. 211–231.

Ai, Amy L., Christopher Peterson, and Bu Huang (2003), 'The Effect of Religious-Spiritual Coping on Positive Attitudes of Adult Muslim Refugees from Kosovo and Bosnia', *International Journal for the Psychology of Religion* 13, pp. 29–47.

Almeida, Michael (2011), 'Theistic Modal Realism', *Oxford Studies in Philosophy of Religion* 3, pp. 1–15.

Alvaro, Pascual-Leone, Gabriele Cattaneo, Macià Dídac, Javier Solana, José M. Tormos, and David Bartrés-Faz (2021), 'Beware of Optimism Bias in the Context of the COVID-19 Pandemic', *Annals of Neurology* 89, pp. 423–425.

Andrus, Paul F. (1975), *Why Me? Why Thine? Clear Thinking About Suffering*. Nashville, TN: Abingdon Press.

Anglin, William S. (1990), *Free Will and the Christian Faith*. Oxford: Clarendon Press.

Aranyosi, István (2013), *God, Mind, and Logical Space: A Revisionary Approach to Divinity*. Basingstoke, Hampshire: Palgrave Macmillan.

Arnett, Jeffrey Jensen (2000), 'Optimistic Bias in Adolescent and Adult Smokers and Nonsmokers', *Addictive Behaviors* 25, pp. 625–632.

Aronson, Roland (2006), 'Thanks Who Very Much?', *The Philosopher's Magazine* 34, pp. 33–36.

Attfield, Robin (2019), 'Panentheisms, Creation and Evil', *Open Theology* 5, pp. 166–181.

Avis, Nancy E., Kevin W. Smith, and John B. McKinlay (1989), 'Accuracy of Perceptions of Heart Attack Risk: What Influences Perceptions and Can They be Changed?', *American Journal of Public Health* 79, pp. 1608–1612.

Bar-Gill, Oren (2006), 'The Evolution and Persistence of Optimism in Litigation', *Journal of Law, Economics and Organization* 22, pp. 490–507.

Barrow, John D., and Frank J. Tipler (1986), *The Anthropic Cosmological Principle*. Oxford: Oxford University Press.

Basinger, David (1996), *The Case for Free Will Theism*. Downers Grove, IL: InterVarsity Press.

234 REFERENCES

Bayne, Tim, and Yujin Nagasawa (2006), 'The Grounds of Worship', *Religious Studies* 42, pp. 299–313.

Bayne, Tim, and Yujin Nagasawa (2007), 'Grounds of Worship Again: A Response to Crowe', *Religious Studies* 43, pp. 475–480.

Becker, Julia S., Douglas Paton, David M. Johnson, and Kevin R. Ronan (2013), *Risk Analysis* 33, pp. 1710–1727.

Benatar, David. 2006. *Better Never to Have Been: The Harm of Coming into Existence.* Oxford: Clarendon Press.

Bergmann, Michael (2001), 'Skeptical Theism and Rowe's New Evidential Argument from Evil', *Noûs* 35, pp. 278–296.

Bergmann, Michael (2012), 'Commonsense Skeptical Theism', in Clark, Kelly James, and Michael Rea (eds.) (2012), *Reason, Metaphysics and Mind: New Essays on the Philosophy of Alvin Plantinga.* Oxford: Oxford University Press, pp. 9–37.

Berkeley, George (1709–1712/1955), *The Works of George Berkeley Bishop of Cloyne*, Volume 7, edited by A. A. Luce and T. E. Jessop. London: Thomas Nelson and Sons.

Berkeley, George (1713/1979), *Three Dialogues between Hylas and Philonous.* Indianapolis, IN: Hackett.

Betenson, Toby (2014), 'Evaluative Claims within the Problem of Evil', *Religious Studies* 51, pp. 361–377.

Betenson, Toby (2021), 'The Problem of Evil Remains Logically Binding', *Religions* 12, pp. 1–11.

Bigelow, John and Pargetter, Robert (1987), 'Beyond the Blank Stare', *Theoria* 53, pp. 97–114.

Bishop, John (1993), 'Evil and the Concept of God', *Philosophical Papers* 22, pp. 1–15.

Bishop, John (1998), 'Can There be Alternative Concepts of God?', *Noûs* 2, pp. 174–188.

Bishop, John (2010), 'Secular Spirituality and the Logic of Giving Thanks', *Sophia* 49, pp. 523–534.

Bishop, John, and Ken Perszyk (2011), 'The Normatively Relativised Logical Argument from Evil', *International Journal for Philosophy of Religion* 70, pp. 109–126.

Bishop, John, and Ken Perszyk (2016), 'Concepts of God and Problems of Evil', in Buckareff, Andrei, and Yujin Nagasawa (2016), *Alternative Concepts of God: Essays on the Metaphysics of the Divine.* Oxford: Oxford University Press, pp. 106–127.

Bishop, John, and Ken Perszyk (2023), *God, Purpose, and Reality: A Euteleological Understanding of Theism.* Oxford: Oxford University Press.

Blackburn, Simon (1994), *The Oxford Dictionary of Philosophy.* Oxford: Oxford University Press.

Brown, Susan A., Viswanath Venkatesh, Jason Kuruzovich, and Anne P. Massey (2008), 'Expectation Confirmation: An Examination of Three Competing Models', *Organizational Behavior and Human Decision Processes* 105, pp. 52–66.

Buckareff, Andrei, and Yujin Nagasawa (2016), *Alternative Concepts of God: Essays on the Metaphysics of the Divine.* Oxford: Oxford University Press.

REFERENCES 235

Burger, Jerry M., and Michele L. Palmer (1992), 'Changes in and Generalization of Unrealistic Optimism Following Experiences with Stressful Events: Reactions to the 1989 California Earthquake', *Personality and Social Psychology Bulletin* 18, pp. 39–43.

Carr, Bernard (ed.) (2007), *Universe or Multiverse?*. Cambridge: Cambridge University Press.

Castel, Louis-Bertrand (1737), 'Essais de Théodicée', *Mémoires pour l'histoire des sciences & des beaux-arts* 37, pp. 5–36, pp. 197–241, and pp. 444–471.

Chalmers, David J. (2002), 'Does Conceivability Entail Possibility?', in Gendler, Tamar Szabó, and John Hawthorne, *Conceivability and Possibility*. Oxford: Clarendon Press, pp. 145–200.

Chang, Edward C. (1996a), 'Cultural Differences in Optimism, Pessimism, and Coping: Predictors of Subsequent Adjustment in Asian American and Caucasian American College Students', *Journal of Counselling Psychology* 43, pp. 113–123.

Chang, Edward C. (1996b). 'Evidence for the Cultural Specificity of Pessimism in Asians versus Caucasians: A Test of the General Negativity Hypothesis', *Personality and Individual Differences*, 21, pp. 819–822.

Chang Edward C., Lawrence J. Sanna, Jean M. Kim, and Kavita Srivastava (2010), 'Optimistic and Pessimistic Bias in European Americans and Asian Americans: A Preliminary Look at Distinguishing Between Predictions for Physical and Psychological Health Outcomes', *Journal of Cross-Cultural Psychology* 41, pp. 465–470.

Chapin, John (2000), 'Third-Person Perception and Optimistic Bias Among Urban Minority At-Risk Youth', *Communication Research* 27, pp. 51–81.

Chapin, John (2001a), 'It Won't Happen to Me: The Role of Optimistic Bias in African American Teens' Risky Sexual Practices', *Howard Journal of Communication* 12, pp. 49–59.

Chapin, John (2001b), 'Optimistic Bias Regarding Campus Violence', *Current Research in Social Psychology* 6.

Chapin, John, and Grace Coleman (2010), 'Optimistic Bias About Dating/Relationship Violence Among Teens', *Journal of Youth Studies* 15, pp. 645–655.

Chapin, John, Stacy de las Alas, and Grace Coleman (2005), 'Optimistic Bias Among Potential Perpetrators and Victims of Youth Violence', *Adolescence* 40, pp. 749–760.

Chapin, John, and Mari Pierce (2011), 'Optimistic Bias, Sexual Assault, and Fear', *Journal of General Psychology* 139, pp. 19–28.

Cho, Hichang, Jae-Shin Lee, and Seungjo Lee (2012), 'Optimistic Bias About H1N1 Flu: Testing the Links Between Risk Communication, Optimistic Bias, and Self-Protection Behavior', *Health Communication* 28, pp. 146–158.

Christina, Greta (2011), 'Intransitive Gratitude: Feeling Thankful in a Godless World', *The Orbit*, 28 November. Available at: http://freethoughtblogs.com/greta/2011/11/28/intransitive-gratitude-feeling-thankful-in-a-godless-world/ (accessed 11 January 2024).

Ciarrocchi, Joseph W., Gabriel S. Dy-Liacco, and Erin Deneke (2008), 'God or Rituals? Relational Faith, Spiritual Discontent, and Religious Practices as Predictors of Hope and Optimism', *Journal of Positive Psychology* 3, pp. 120–136.

236 REFERENCES

Cicero (originally 45 BC, 1972), *The Nature of Gods*, London: Penguin Books, translated by C. P. McGregor.

Clark, Kelly James, and Michael Rea (eds.) (2012), *Reason, Metaphysics and Mind: New Essays on the Philosophy of Alvin Plantinga*. Oxford: Oxford University Press.

Clarke, Valerie A., Tracy Williams, and Stephen Arthey (1997), 'Skin Type and Optimistic Bias in Relation to the Sun Protection and Suntanning Behaviors of Young Adults', *Journal of Behavioral Medicine* 20, pp. 207–222.

Clayton, Philip (2004), 'Panentheism Today: A Constructive Systematic Evaluation', in Clayton, Philip, and Arthur Peacock (eds.), *In Whom We Live and Move and Have Our Being: Panentheistic Reflections on God's Presence in a Scientific World*. Grand Rapids, MI: William B. Eerdmans, pp. 249–264.

Colledge, Richard J. (2013), 'Secular Spirituality and the Hermeneutics of Ontological Gratitude', *Sophia* 52, pp. 27–43.

Collins, Steven (1992), '*Nirvāṇa*, Time, and Narrative', *History of Religions* 31, pp. 215–246.

Cooper, Joel (2007), *Cognitive Dissonance: Fifty Years of a Classic Theory*. London: Sage Publications.

Corey, Michael A. (2000), *Evolution and the Problem of Natural Evil*. Lanham, MD: University Press of America.

Craig, William Lane (1994), 'The Absurdity of Life without God', in Craig, William Lane, *Reasonable Faith: Christian Truth and Apologies*. Wheaton, Ill: Good News Publishing/Crossway Books, pp. 57–75.

Cray, Wesley D. (2011), 'Omniscience and Worthiness of Worship', *International Journal for Philosophy of Religion* 70, pp. 147–153.

Crowe, Benjamin (2007), 'Reasons for Worship: A Response to Bayne and Nagasawa', *Religious Studies* 43, pp. 465–474.

Creegan, Nicola Hoggard (2013), *Animal Suffering and the Problem of Evil*. Oxford: Oxford University Press.

Cutello, Clara Alida, Clare Walsh, Yaniv Hanoch, and Elizabeth Hellier (2021), 'Reducing Optimism Bias in the Driver's Seat: Comparing Two Interventions', *Transportation Research Part F: Traffic Psychology and Behaviour* 78, pp. 207–217.

Da Cunha, Doigo Thimoteo, Anna Rafaela Cavalcante Braga, Estevão de Camargo Passos, Elke Stedefeldt, and Veridiana Verade Rosso (2015), 'The Existence of Optimistic Bias About Foodborne Disease by Food Handlers and its Association with Training Participation and Food Safety Performance', *Food Research International* 75, pp. 27–33.

Dalziel, James R., and R. F. Soames Job (1997), 'Motor Vehicle Accidents, Fatigue and Optimism Bias in Taxi Drivers', *Accident Analysis and Prevention* 29, pp. 489–494.

Danaher, John (2012), 'Stumbling on the Threshold: A Reply to Gwiazda on Threshold Obligations', *Religious Studies* 48, pp. 469–478.

Darwin, Francis (ed.) (1887) *The Life and Letters of Charles Darwin, Including an Autobiographical Chapter, Volume 2*. London: John Murray.

Davidson, Scott (2012), *On the Intrinsic Value of Everything*. London: Continuum.

Davies, Brian (1998), *Philosophy of Religion: A Guide to the Subject*. London: Cassell.

REFERENCES   237

Dawkins, Richard (2009), 'Atheism is the New Fundamentalism'. Debate sponsored by Intelligence Squared at Wellington College on November 29. Available at: https://www.youtube.com/watch?v=VVppTZxFn3Q&list=PLD085030118A3C9C4.

de Ray, Christophe (2023), 'Is the Desire for Life Rational?', *Religious Studies* 59, pp. 681–699.

Dealey, Justin J. (2021), *Why God Must Do What is Best: A Philosophical Investigation of Theistic Optimism*. London: Bloomsbury.

DeJoy, David M. (1987), 'The Optimism Bias and Traffic Safety', *Proceedings of the Human Factors Society Annual Meeting* 7, pp. 756–759.

Dember, William N. (2002), 'The Optimism-Pessimism Instrument: Personal and Social Correlates', in Chang, Edward C. (ed.), *Optimism and Pessimism: Implications for Theory, Research and Practice*. Washington D.C.: American Psychological Association, pp. 281–299.

Diller, Kevin (2008), 'Are Sin and Evil Necessary for a Really Good World?: Questions for Alvin Plantinga's Felix Culpa Theodicy', *Faith and Philosophy* 25, pp. 87–101.

Dougherty, Trent (2014a), *The Problem of Animal Pain: A Theodicy For All Creatures Great and Small*. Basingstoke, Hampshire: Palgrave Macmillan.

Dougherty (2014b), 'Skeptical Theism', *The Stanford Encyclopedia of Philosophy* (Winter 2016 Edition), edited by Edward N. Zalta, https://plato.stanford.edu/archives/win2016/entries/skeptical-theism/.

Dougherty, Trent, and Justin P. McBrayer (2014), *Skeptical Theism: New Essays*. Oxford: Oxford University Press.

Draper, Paul (1989), 'Pain and Pleasure: An Evidential Problem for Theists', *Noûs* 3, pp. 331–350.

Draper, Paul (1992), 'Probabilistic Arguments from Evil', *Religious Studies* 28, pp. 303–317.

Draper, Paul (2009), 'The Problem of Evil', in Flint, Thomas P., and Michael Rea, *The Oxford Handbook to Philosophical Theology*. Oxford: Oxford University Press, pp. 332–351.

Draper, Paul (2012), 'Darwin's Argument from Evil', in Nagasawa, Yujin (ed.), *Scientific Approaches to the Philosophy of Religion*. Houndmills, Basingstoke: Palgrave Macmillan, pp. 49–70.

Draper, Paul (2014), 'Confirmation Theory and the Core of CORNEA', in Dougherty, Trent, and Justin P. McBrayer, *Skeptical Theism: New Essays*. Oxford: Oxford University Press, pp. 132–141.

Draper, Paul (forthcoming), *Atheism and The Problem of Evil*. Oxford: Oxford University Press.

Druică, Elena, Fabio Musso, and Rodica Ianole-Călin (2020), 'Optimism Bias During the Covid-19 Pandemic: Empirical Evidence from Romania and Italy', *Games* 11.

Ekstrom, Laura W. (2021), *God, Suffering, and the Value of Evil*. Oxford: Oxford University Press.

Evans, Dyan, Annerieke Heuvelink, and Daniel Nettle (2003), 'The Evolution of Optimism: A Multi-Agent Based Model of Adaptive Bias in Human Judgement', *Proceedings of the AISB* 3, pp. 20–25.

238 REFERENCES

Fontaine, Kevin R., and Sylvia Smith (1995), 'Optimistic Bias in Cancer Risk Perception: A Cross-National Study', *Psychological Reports* 77, pp. 143–146.

Forrest, Peter (1997), 'Pantheism and Science', *The Monist* 80, pp. 307–319.

Ganeri, Jonardon, and Itay Shani (2022), 'What is Cosmopsychism?', *The Monist* 105, pp. 1–5.

Gasser, Georg (2019), 'God's Omnipresence in the World: On Possible Meanings of 'en' in Panentheism', *International Journal for Philosophy of Religion* 85, pp. 43–62.

Geach, Peter (1977), *Providence and Evil*. Cambridge: Cambridge University Press.

Gendler, Tamar Szabó, and John Hawthorne (2002), *Conceivability and Possibility*. Oxford: Clarendon Press.

Gervais, Will M., Dimitris Xygalatas, Ryan T. McKay, Michiel van Elk, Emma E. Buchtel, Mark Aveyard, Sarah R. Schiavone, Ilan Dar-Nimrod, Annika M. Svedholm-Hakkinen, Tapani Riekki, Eva Kundtová Klocová, Jonathan E. Ramsay, and Joseph Bulbulia (2017), 'Global Evidence of Extreme Intuitive Moral Prejudice Against Atheists', *Nature Human Behaviour*, 1(8), pp. 1–15.

Gillham, Jane E., Andrew J. Shatté, Karen J. Reivich, and Martin E. P. Seligman (2002), 'Optimism, Pessimism, and Explanatory Style', in Chang, Edward C. (ed.), *Optimism and Pessimism: Implications for Theory, Research, and Practice*. Washington D.C.: American Psychological Association, pp. 53–75.

Gierlach, Elaine, Bradley Belsher, Larry Beutler (2010), 'Cross-Cultural Differences in Risk Perceptions of Disasters', *Risk Analysis* 30, 1539–1549.

Gifford, Robert, Leila Scannell, Christine Kormos, Lidia Smolova, Anders Biel, Stefan Boncu, Victor Corral, Hartmut Güntherf, Kazunori Hanyu, Donald Hine, Florian G. Kaiser, Kalevi Korpela, Luisa Marie Lima, Angela G. Mertig, Ricardo Garcia Mira, Gabriel Moser, Paola Passafaro, José Q. Pinheiro, Sunil Saini, Toshihiko Sako, Elena Sautkina, Yannick Savina, Peter Schmuck, Wesley Schultz, Karin Sobeck, Eva-Lotta Sundblad, and David Uzzellv (2009), 'Temporal Pessimism and Spatial Optimism in Environmental Assessments: An 18-Nation Study', *Journal of Environmental Psychology* 29, pp. 1–12.

Göcke, Benedikt Paul (2013), 'Panentheism and Classical Theism', *Sophia* 51, pp. 61–75

Göcke, Benedikt Paul (2015), 'There is no Panentheistic Paradigm', *The Heythrop Journal* 56, pp. 1–8.

Göcke, Benedikt Paul (2019), 'Panentheism, Transhumanism, and the Problem of Evil – From Metaphysics to Ethics', *European Journal for Philosophy of Religion* 11, pp. 65–89.

Gosvami, Narayana (2013), *Shrimad Bhagavad-gita*. Vrindavan: Gaudiya Vedanta Publications. Available at: https://www.wisdomlib.org/hinduism/book/shrimad-bhagavad-gita.

Gouveia, Susana O., and Valerie Clarke (2001), 'Optimistic Bias for Negative and Positive Events', *Health Education* 101, pp. 228–234.

Green, Adam, and Eleonore Stump (2016), *Hidden Divinity and Religious Belief: New Perspectives*. Cambridge: Cambridge University Press.

Green, Morgan, and Marta Elliott (2010), 'Religion, Health, and Psychological Well-Being', *Journal of Religion and Health* 49, pp. 149–163.

REFERENCES 239

Grove, Richard C., Ayla Rubenstein, and Heather K. Terrell (2019), 'Distrust Persists After Subverting Atheist Stereotypes', *Group Processes and Intergroup Relations* 23, pp. 1103–1124.

Guleserian, Theodore (1983), 'God and Possible Worlds: The Modal Problem of Evil', *Noûs* 17, pp. 221–238.

Gwiazda, Jeremy (2011), 'Worship and Threshold Obligations', *Religious Studies* 47, pp. 521–525.

Harmon-Jones, Eddie (2019), *Cognitive Dissonance: Reexamining a Pivotal Theory in Psychology*. Washington D.C.: American Psychological Association.

Harmon-Jones, Eddie, and Judson Mills (1999), *Cognitive Dissonance: Progress on a Pivotal Theory in Social Psychology*. Washington, D.C.: American Psychological Association.

Harper, Leland Royce (2020), *Multiverse Deism: Shifting Perspectives of God and the World*. Lanham, MD: Lexington Books.

Harper, Marcel (2007), 'The Stereotyping of Nonreligious People by Religious Students: Contents and Subtypes', *Journal for the Scientific Study of Religion* 46, pp. 539–552.

Harris, Joshua Lee, Kirk Lougheed, and Neal DeRoo (2023), *Philosophical Perspectives on Existential Gratitude: Analytic, Continental, and Religious*. London: Bloomsbury.

Hasker, William (1992), 'The Necessity of Gratuitous Evil', *Faith and Philosophy* 9, pp. 23–44.

Hatfield, Julie, and R. F. Soames Job (2001), 'Optimism Bias About Environmental Degradation: The Role of the Range of Impact of Precautions', *Journal of Environmental Psychology* 21, pp. 17–30.

Hayward, R. David, Neal Krause, Gail Ironson, Peter C. Hill, and Robert Emmons (2016), 'Health and Well-Being Among the Non-Religious Atheists, Agnostics, and No Preference Compared with Religious Group Members', *Journal of Religion and Heath* 55, pp. 1024–1037.

Hecht, David (2013), 'The Neutral Basis of Optimism and Pessimism', *Experimental Neurobiology* 22, pp. 173–199.

Heine, Steven J., and Darrin R. Lehman (1995), 'Cultural Variation in Unrealistic Optimism: Does the West Feel More Vulnerable than the East?', *Journal of Personality and Social Psychology* 68, pp. 595–607.

Heller, Mark (2003), 'The Immorality of Modal Realism, or: How I Learned to Stop Worrying and Let the Children Drawn', *Philosophical Studies* 14, pp. 1–22.

Helweg-Larsen, Marie (1999), '(The Lack of) Optimistic Biases in Response to the 1994 Northridge Earthquake: The Role of Personal Experience', *Basic and Applied Social Psychology* 2, pp. 119–129.

Helweg-Larsen, Marie, and James A. Shepperd (2001), 'Do Moderators of the Optimistic Bias Affect Personal or Target Risk Estimates? A Review of the Literature', *Personality and Social Psychology Review* 5, pp. 74–95.

Hewitt, Harold (1991), *Problems in the Philosophy of Religion: Critical Studies of the Work of John Hick*. London: Macmillan.

Hick, John (1966), *Evil and the God of Love*. London: Macmillan.

240 REFERENCES

Hick, John (1976), *Death and the Eternal Life*. London: Collins.

Hill, Scott (2014), 'Giving Up Omnipotence', *Canadian Journal of Philosophy* 44, pp. 97–117.

Hoffmann, Michael, and Kamo no Chōmei (1212/1991), *Hōjōki: Visions of a Torn World*. Berkley, CA: Stone Bridge Press.

Holt, Jim (2012), *Why Does the World Exist?* London: Profile Books.

Homaei, Rezvan, Zahra Dasht Bozorgi, Maryam Sadat Mirbabaei Ghahfarokhi, and Shima Hosseinpour (2016), 'Relationship between Optimism, Religiosity and Self-Esteem with Marital Satisfaction and Life Satisfaction', *International Education Studies* 9, pp. 53–61.

Hoorens, Vera, and Bram P. Buunk (1993), 'Social Comparison of Health Risks: Locus of Control, the Person-Positivity Bias, and Unrealistic Optimism', *Journal of Applied Social Psychology* 23, pp. 291–302.

Hossain, Mohammad Alamgir, and Mohammed Quaddus (2011), 'Expectation–Confirmation Theory in Information System Research: A Review and Analysis', in Dwivedi, Yogesh K., Michael R. Wade, and Scott L. Schneberger (eds.), *Information Systems Theory: Explaining and Predicting Our Digital Society*, Volume 1. New York: Springer, pp. 441–469.

Howard-Snyder, Daniel, and Paul K. Moser (eds.) (2002), *Divine Hiddenness: New Essays*. Cambridge: Cambridge University Press.

Hunt, William (2021), *Evil and May Worlds: A Free-Will Theodicy*. Lanham, MD: Lexington Books.

Isobe, Tadamasa (1976), *'Mujō' No Kouzou* (「無常」の構造; *The Structure of 'Impermanence'*). Tokyo: Kodansha.

Ji, Li-Jun, Zhiyong Zhang, Esther Usborne, and Yanjun Guan (2004), 'Optimism Across Cultures: In Response to the Severe Acute Respiratory Syndrome Outbreak', *Asian Journal of Social Psychology* 7, pp. 25–34.

Johnson, Dominic D. P., and James H. Fowler (2011), 'The Evolution of Overconfidence', *Nature* 477, pp. 317–20.

Jonbäck, Francis (2021), 'The Sceptical Response to the Existential Problem of Systemic Suffering', *Open Theology* 7, pp. 102–110.

Joshi, Mary Sissons, and Wakefield Carter (2013), 'Unrealistic Optimism: East and West?', *Frontiers in Psychology* 4, pp. 1–15.

Kahane, Guy (2011), 'Should We Want God to Exist?', *Philosophy and Phenomenological Research* 82, pp. 674–696.

Kahane, Guy (2021), 'Is Anti-Theism Incoherent?', *American Philosophical Quarterly* 58, pp. 373–386.

Kahane, Guy (2022), 'Optimism without Theism? Nagasawa on Atheism, Evolution, and Evil', *Religious Studies* 58, 345–58.

Karaki, Junzō (1965), *Mujō* (無常; *Impermanence*). Tokyo: Chikuma Shobō.

Keltz, B. Kyle (2020), *Thomism and the Problem of Animal Suffering*. Eugene, OR: Wipf and Stock.

Kirk, Robert (2005), *Zombies and Consciousness*. Oxford: Oxford University Press.

Kivy, Peter (1979), 'Voltaire, Hume and the Problem of Evil', *Philosophy and Literature* 3, pp. 211–224.

REFERENCES   241

Klein, Cynthia T. F., and Marie Helweg-Larsen (2002), 'Perceived Control and the Optimistic Bias: A Meta-Analytic Review', *Psychology and Health* 17, pp. 437–446.

Kollmann, Josianne, Yael Benyamini, Nadine C. Lages, and Britta Renner (2022), 'The Role of Personal Risk Experience: An Investigation of Health and Terrorism Risk Perception in Germany and Israel', *Risk Analysis* 42, pp. 818–829.

Kraay, Klaas (2008), 'Creation, World-Actualization, and God's Choice Among Possible Worlds', *Philosophy Compass* 3, pp. 854–872.

Kraay, Klaas J. (2010), 'Theism, Possible Worlds, and the Multiverse', *Philosophical Studies* 147, pp. 355–368.

Kraay, Klaas (2011), 'Theism and Modal Collapse', *American Philosophical Quarterly* 48, pp. 361–372.

Kraay, Klaas J. (2018), *Does God Matter? Essays on the Axiological Consequences of Theism*. London: Routledge.

Krray, Klaas J. (2021), *The Axiology of Theism*. Cambridge: Cambridge University Press.

Krause, Neal, and R. David Hayward (2014), 'God-Mediated Control and Optimism: Exploring Variations by Denominational Affiliation', *Review of Religious Research* 56, pp. 275–290.

Kuper-Smith, Benjamin J., Lisa M. Doppelhofer, Yulia Oganian, Gabriela Rosenblau, and Christoph W. Korn (2021), 'Risk Perception and Optimism During the Early Stages of the COVID-19 Pandemic', *Royal Society Open Science* 8, pp. 1–21.

Lacewing, Michael (2016), 'Can Non-Theists Appropriately Feel Existential Gratitude?', *Religious Studies* 52, pp. 145–165.

Langtry, Bruce (1998), 'Structures of Greater Good Theodicies: The Objection from Alternative Goods', *Sophia* 37, pp. 1–17.

Langtry, Bruce (2008), *God, the Best, and Evil*. Oxford: Oxford University Press.

Lataster, Raphael, and Purushottama Bilimoria (2018), 'Pantheism(s): What Is It and Is Not', *Journal of World Philosophies* 3, pp. 49–64.

Leftow, Brian (2016), 'Naturalistic Pantheism', in Buckareff, Andrei, and Yujin Nagasawa, *Alternative Concepts of God: Essays on the Metaphysics of the Divine*. Oxford: Oxford University Press, pp. 64–90.

Leibniz, G. W. (1710/1985), *Theodicy: Essays on the Goodness of God, the Freedom of Man and the Origin of Evil*, translated by E. M. Huggard. La Salle, IL: Open Court.

Leslie, John (1989), *Universes*. Oxford: Routledge.

Leslie, John (2001), *Infinite Minds: A Philosophical Cosmology*. Oxford: Oxford University Press.

Leslie, John (2016), 'A Way of Picturing God', in Buckareff, Andrei, and Yujin Nagasawa, *Alternative Concepts of God: Essays on the Metaphysics of the Divine*. Oxford: Oxford University Press, pp. 50–63.

Leslie, John (2019), 'What God Might Be', *International Journal for Philosophy of Religion* 85, pp. 63–75.

Levine, Michael P. (1994a), *Pantheism: A Non-Theistic Concept of Deity*. London: Routledge.

Levine, Michael P. (1994b), 'Pantheism, Theism and the Problem of Evil', *International Journal for Philosophy of Religion* 35, pp. 129–151.

242 REFERENCES

Lewis, David (1986), *On the Plurality of Worlds*. Oxford: Blackwell.

Lin, Chieh-Peng, Yuan Hui Tsai, and Chou-Kang Chiu (2009), 'Modeling Customer Loyalty from an Integrative Perspective of Self-Determination Theory and Expectation-Confirmation Theory', *Journal of Business and Psychology* 24, pp. 315–326.

Lokeswarananda, Swami (2017), *Chandogya Upanisad: Translated with Notes Based on Sankara's Commentary*. Kolkata: Ramakrishna Mission Institute of Culture, https://www.exoticindiaart.com/book/details/IDH291/aff11436/.

Lougheed, Kirk (2020), *The Axiological Status of Theism and Other Worldviews*. Basingstoke, Hampshire: Palgrave Macmillan

MacIntyre, Alasdair (1967), 'Pantheism', in Edwards, Paul (ed.) (1967), *Encyclopedia of Philosophy*, Volume 5. New York: Macmillan and Free Press, pp. 31–35.

Mackie, J. L. (1955), 'Evil and Omnipotence', *Mind* 64, pp. 200–212.

Mackie, J. L. (1982), *The Miracles of Theism: Arguments for and against the Existence of God*. Oxford: Clarendon Press.

Maitzen, Stephen (2006), 'Divine Hiddenness and the Demographics of Theism', *Religious Studies* 42, pp. 177–191.

Mander, William (2020), 'Pantheism', *Stanford Encyclopedia of Philosophy* (Spring 2020 Edition), edited by Edward N. Zalta, https://plato.stanford.edu/archives/spr2020/entries/pantheism/.

Martin, Michal (1974), 'A Disproof of the God of the Common Man', *Question* 7, pp. 115–124, reprinted in Martin, Michael, and Ricki Monnier (eds.) (2003), *The Impossibility of God*. Amherst New York: Prometheus Books, pp. 232–241.

Masiero, Marianna, Silvia Riva, Serena Oliveri, Chiara Fioretti, and Gabriella Pravettoni (2018), 'Optimistic Bias in Young Adults for Cancer, Cardiovascular and Respiratory Diseases: A Pilot Study on Smokers and Drinkers', *Journal of Health Psychology* 23, pp. 645–656.

Mawson, T. J. (2002), 'Omnipotence and Necessary Moral Perfection are Compatible: A Reply to Morriston', *Religious Studies* 38, pp. 215–223.

McBrayer, Justin P. (2010), 'Skeptical Theism', *Philosophy Compass* 4, pp. 1–13.

McClure, John, Liv Henrich, David Johnston, and Emma E. H. Doyle (2016), 'Are Two Earthquakes Better than One? How Earthquakes in Two Different Regions Affect Risk Judgments and Preparation in Three Locations', *International Journal of Disaster Risk Reduction* 16, pp. 192–199.

McClure, John, Celine Wills, David Johnston, and Claudia Recker (2011), 'How the 2010 Canterbury (Darfield) Earthquake Affected Earthquake Risk Perception: Comparing Citizens Inside and Outside the Earthquake Region', *Australasian Journal of Disaster and Trauma Studies* 2, pp. 3–10.

McKinney, Meredith, Yoshida Kenkō, and Kamo no Chōmei (1212/1330–1332/2013), *Essays in Idleness and Hōjōki*. London: Penguin Books.

Meister, Chad (2017), 'Ancient and Contemporary Expressions of Panentheism', *Philosophy Compass* 12.

Mesle, Robert C. (1991), *John Hick's Theodicy: A Process Humanist Critique*. New York: St. Martin's Press.

Miele, Frank (1995), 'Darwin's Dangerous Disciple: An Interview with Richard Dawkins', *Skeptic* 3 (4), pp. 80–85.

REFERENCES 243

Mizrahi, Moti (2014), 'The Problem of Natural Inequality: A New Problem of Evil', *Philosophia* 42, pp. 127–136.

Moon, Jordan W., Jaimie Arona Krems, and Adam B. Cohen (2021), 'Is There Anything Good About Atheists? Exploring Positive and Negative Stereotypes of the Religious and Nonreligious', *Social Psychological and Personality Science* 12, pp. 1505–1516.

Moreland, J. P., and William Lane Craig (2003), *Philosophical Foundations for a Christian Worldview*. Downers Grove, IL: InterVarsity Press.

Morioka, Masahiro (2021), 'What is Birth Affirmation?: The Meaning of Saying "Yes" to Having Been Born', *Journal of Philosophy of Life* 11, pp. 43–59.

Morris, Thomas V. (1984), 'Duty and Divine Goodness', *American Philosophical Quarterly* 21, pp. 261–268.

Morris, Thomas V. (1985), 'The Necessity of God's Goodness', *New Scholasticism* 59, pp. 418–448, reprinted in Morris, Thomas V. (1987), *Anselmian Explorations: Essays in Philosophical Theology*. Notre Dame, IN: University of Notre Dame Press, pp. 42–69 (pages in reference to reprinting).

Morris, Thomas V. (1991), *Our Idea of God: An Introduction to Philosophical Theology*. Downers Grove, IL: InterVarsity Press.

Morriston, Wes (2001a), 'Omnipotence and Necessary Moral Perfection: Are They Compatible?', *Religious Studies* 37, pp. 143–160.

Morriston, Wes (2001b), 'Omnipotence and the Anselmian God', *Philo* 4, pp. 7–20.

Morriston, Wes (2002), 'Omnipotence and the Power to Choose: A Reply to Wielenberg', *Faith and Philosophy* 19, pp. 358–367.

Morriston, Wes (2003), 'Are Omnipotence and Necessary Moral Perfection Compatible?: Reply to Mawson', *Religious Studies* 39, pp. 441–449.

Mulgan, Tim (2015), *Purpose in the Universe: The Moral and Metaphysical Case of Ananthropocentric Purposivism*. Oxford: Oxford University Press.

Mulgan, Tim (2017), 'Beyond Theism and Atheism: Axiarchism and Ananthropocentric Purposivism', *Philosophy Compass* 12, pp. 1–11.

Mullins, R. T. (2016), 'The Difficulty with Demarcating Panentheism', *Sophia* 55, pp. 325–346.

Murphy, Mark C. (2017), *God's Own Ethics: Norms of Divine Agency and the Argument from Evil*. Oxford: Oxford University Press.

Murray, Michael J. (2008), *Nature Red in Tooth and Claw: Theism and the Problem of Animal Suffering*. Oxford: Oxford University Press.

Nagasawa, Yujin (2008a), *God and Phenomenal Consciousness: A Novel Approach to Knowledge Arguments*. Cambridge: Cambridge University Press.

Nagasawa, Yujin (2008b), 'A New Defence of Anselmian Theism', *Philosophical Quarterly* 58, pp. 577–596.

Nagasawa, Yujin (2016), 'Hiddenness, Silence and Shusaku Endo', in Green, A., and E. Stump (eds.), *Hidden Divinity and Religious Belief: New Perspectives*. Cambridge: Cambridge University Press, pp. 246–259.

Nagasawa, Yujin (2017), *Maximal God: A New Defence of Perfect Being Theism*. Oxford; Oxford University Press.

244 REFERENCES

Nagasawa, Yujin (2018a), 'Global Philosophy of Religion and its Challenges', in Draper, Paul, and J. L. Schellenberg (eds.), *Renewing Philosophy of Religion: Beyond the Faith-Based Model*. Oxford: Oxford University Press, pp. 33–47.

Nagasawa, Yujin (2018b), 'The Problem of Evil for Atheists' and 'Reply to Critics', in Trakakis, N. N. (ed.), *The Problem of Evil: Eight Views in Dialogue*. Oxford University Press, pp. 151–163.

Nagasawa, Yujin, and Khai Wager (2017), 'Panpsychism and Priority Cosmopsychism', in Brüntrup, Godehard, and Ludwig Jaskolla (eds.), *Panpsychism: Contemporary Perspectives*. Oxford University Press, pp. 113–129.

Nagasawa, Yujin, and Mohammad Saleh Zarepour (forthcoming), *Global Dialogue in the Philosophy of Religion*. Oxford: Oxford University Press.

Nes, Lise Solberg, and Suzanne C. Segerstrom (2006), 'Dispositional Optimism and Coping: A Meta-Analytic Review', *Personality and Social Psychology Review* 10, pp. 235–251.

Nietzsche, Friedrich (1966), *Beyond Good and Evil*, translated by Walter Kaufmann. New York: Random House.

Oppy, Graham (1997), 'Pantheism, Quantification and Mereology', *The Monist* 80, pp. 320–336.

Osborn, Ronald E. (2014), *Death Before the Fall: Biblical Literalism and the Problem of Animal Suffering*. Downers Grove, IL: InterVarsity Press.

Otto, Rudolf (1917/1950), *The Idea of the Holy*, translated by John W. Harvey. Oxford: Oxford University Press.

Owen, H. P. (1971), *Concepts of Deity*. London: Macmillan.

Parfit, Derek (1992), 'Why Does the Universe Exist?', *Times Literary Supplement*, 3 July, pp. 3–5.

Parfit, Derek (1998), 'Why Anything? Why This?', *London Review of Books*, 22 January, pp. 24–27.

Parry, Sharon M., Susan Miles, Ascanio Tridente, and Stephen R. Palmer (2004), 'Differences in Perception of Risk Between People Who Have and Have Not Experienced Salmonella Food Poisoning', *Risk Analysis* 24, pp. 289–300.

Pascal, Blaise (1670/1958), *Pensées*, translated by W. F. Trotter. New York: E. P. Dutton.

Paley, William (1802/2006), *Natural Theology*. Oxford: Oxford University Press.

Peterson, Gregory R. (2004), 'Whither Panentheism?', *Zygon* 36, pp. 395–405.

Pike, Nelson (1969), 'Omnipotence and God's Ability to Sin', *American Philosophical Quarterly* 6, pp. 208–216.

Plantinga, Alvin (1967), *God and Other Minds: A Study of the Rational Justification of Belief in God*. Ithaca, NY: Cornell University Press.

Plantinga, Alvin (1974a), *God, Freedom and Evil*. London: George Allen and Unwin.

Plantinga, Alvin (1974b), *The Nature of Necessity*. New York: Oxford University Press.

Plantinga, Alvin (2004), 'Supralapsarianism, or "O Felix Culpa"', in van Inwagen, Peter, *Christian Faith and the Problem of Evil*. Grand Rapids, MI: William B. Eerdmans, pp. 1–25.

Poston, Ted (2014), 'Social Evil', *Oxford Studies in Philosophy of Religion* 5, pp. 208–233.

Prescott, Paul (2021), 'The Secular Problem of Evil: An Essay in Analytic Existentialism', *Religious Studies* 57, pp. 101–119.

REFERENCES 245

Pruss, Alexander R., and Joshua L. Rasmussen (2018), *Necessary Existence*. Oxford: Oxford University Press.

Radcliffe, Nathan M., and William M. P. Klein (2002), 'Dispositional, Unrealistic, and Comparative Optimism: Differential Relations with the Knowledge and Processing of Risk Information and Beliefs about Personal Risk', *Personality and Social Psychology Bulletin* 28, pp. 836–846.

Rae, Michael C. (2018), *The Hiddenness of God*. Oxford: Oxford University Press.

Rescher, Nicholas (1984), *The Riddle of Existence: An Essay on Idealistic Metaphysics*. Washington D.C.: University Press of America.

Rescher, Nicholas (2010), *Axiogenesis: An Essay in Metaphysical Optimalism*. Lanham, MY: Lexington Books.

Ritter, Ryan S., Jesse Lee Preston, and Ivan Hernandez (2014), 'Happy Tweets: Christians Are Happier, More Socially Connected, and Analytical Than Atheists on Twitter', *Social Psychological and Personality Science* 5, pp. 243–249.

Rodrigues, Kelly Lameiro, Anita Eves, Caroline Pereira das Neves, Baruna Kerstner Souto, and Sara Joana Gadotti dos Anjos (2020), 'The Role of Optimistic Bias in Safe Food Handling Behaviours in the Food Service Sector', *Food Research International* 130, pp. 1–10.

Rolston, Holmes, III (1994), 'Does Nature Need to be Redeemed?', *Zygon* 29, pp. 205–229.

Rossi, Maria de Sousa Carvalho, Elke Stedefeldt, Doigo Thimoteo da Cunha, and Veridiana Vera Rosso (2017), 'Food Safety Knowledge, Optimistic Bias and Risk Perception Among Food Handlers in Institutional Food Services', *Food Control* 73, pp. 681–688.

Rowe, William L. (1979), 'The Problem of Evil and Some Varieties of Atheism', *American Philosophical Quarterly* 16, pp. 335–341.

Rowe, William L. (1988), 'Evil and Theodicy', *Philosophical Topics* 16, pp. 119–132.

Rowe, William L. (1991), 'Ruminations About Evil', *Philosophical Perspectives* 5, pp. 69–88.

Rowe, William L. (1994), 'The Problem of No Best World', *Faith and Philosophy* 11, pp. 269–271.

Rowe, William L. (1996), 'The Evidential Argument from Evil: A Second Look', in Howard-Snyder, Daniel (ed.), *The Evidential Argument from Evil*. Bloomington and Indianapolis: Indiana University Press, pp. 262–285.

Rowe, William L. (2004), *Can God Be Free?* Oxford: Oxford University Press.

Rundle, Bede (2004), *Why There is Something Rather Than Nothing*. Oxford: Oxford University Press.

Sadler, A. L. (thirteenth century/1918), *The Heike Monogatari*, *Transactions of the Asiatic Society of Japan* 46(2). Tokyo: The Asiatic Society of Japan.

Salmon, Charles T., Hyun Soon Park, and Brenda J. Wrigley (2003), 'Optimistic Bias and Perceptions of Bioterrorism in Michigan Corporate Spokespersons, Fall 2001', *Journal of Health Communication* 8, pp. 130–143.

Schellenberg, J. L. (1993), *Divine Hiddenness and Human Reason*. Ithaca, NY: Cornell University Press.

Schellenberg, J. L. (2009), *The Wisdom to Doubt: A Justification of Religious Skepticism*. Ithaca, NY: Cornell University Press.

246 REFERENCES

Schellenberg, J. L. (2010), 'The Hiddenness Problem and the Problem of Evil', *Faith and Philosophy* 27, pp. 45–60.

Schellenberg, J. L. (2013), 'A New Logical Problem of Evil', in McBrayer, Justin P., and Daniel Howard-Snyder (eds.), *The Blackwell Companion to the Problem of Evil*. Oxford: Blackwell, pp. 34–48.

Schellenberg, J. L. (2015), *The Hiddenness Argument: Philosophy's New Challenge to Belief in God*. Oxford: Oxford University Press.

Schellenberg, J. L. (2017a), 'Divine Hiddenness: Part 1 Recent Work on the Hiddenness Argument', *Philosophy Compass* 12, https://onlinelibrary.wiley.com/doi/abs/10.1111/phc3.12355.

Schellenberg, J. L. (2017b), 'Divine Hiddenness: Part 2 Recent Enlargements of the Discussion', *Philosophy Compass* 12, https://onlinelibrary.wiley.com/doi/abs/10.1111/phc3.12413.

Schipper, Burkhard C. (2021), 'The Evolutionary Stability of Optimism, Pessimism, and Complete Ignorance', *Theory and Decision* 90, pp. 417–454.

Schneider, John R. (2020), *Animal Suffering and the Darwinian Problem of Evil*. Cambridge: Cambridge University Press.

Schopenhauer, Arthur (1844/1909), *The World As Will and Idea*, Volume I, translated by Richard Burdon Haldane and John Kemp. London: Kagan Paul, Trench, Trübner & Co.

Schopenhauer (1851/1913), 'On the Sufferings of the World', in Saunders, Thomas Bailey (ed. and trans.), *Studies in Pessimism: A Series of Essays by Arthur Schopenhauer*. London: George Allen and Company, pp. 9–30.

Schultz, P. Wesley, Taciano L. Milfont, Randie C. Chance, Giuseppe Tronu, Silvia Luis, Kaori Ando, Faiz Rasool, Pamela Linera Roose, Charles Adedayo Ogunbode, Juana Castro, and Valdiney V. Gouveia (2014), 'Cross-Cultural Evidence for Spatial Bias in Beliefs About the Severity of Environmental Problems', *Environment and Behavior* 46, pp. 267–302.

Scott, Mark S. M. (2010), 'Suffering and Soul-Making: Rethinking John Hick's Theodicy', *Journal of Religion* 90, pp. 313–334.

Segev, Mor (2022), *The Value of the World and of Oneself: Philosophical Optimism and Pessimism from Aristotle to Modernity*. Oxford: Oxford University Press.

Seneca, Lucius Annaeus (49 AD/2004), *On the Shortness of Life*, translated by C. D. N. Costa. London: Penguin.

Sharot, Tali (2011), 'The Optimistic Bias', *Current Biology* 21, pp. 941–945.

Shaw, W. Douglass, and Justin Baker (2010), 'Model of Location Choice and Willingness to Pay to Avoid Hurricane Risks for Hurricane Katrina Evacuees', *International Journal of Mass Emergencies and Disasters* 28, pp.87–114.

Sherman-Morris, Kathleen, and Idamis Del Valle-Martinez (2017), 'Optimistic Bias and the Consistency of Hurricane Track Forecast', *Natural Hazards* 88, pp. 1523–1543.

Smith, Quentin (1991), 'An Atheological Argument from Evil Natural Laws', *International Journal for Philosophy of Religion* 29, pp. 159–174.

Smuts, Aaron (2012), 'The Power to Make Others Worship', *Religious Studies* 48, pp. 221–237.

Southgate, Christopher (2008), *The Groaning of Creation: God, Evolution and the Problem of Evil*. Louisville: Westminster John Knox Press.

Spittal, Matthew J., John McClure, Richard J. Siegert, and Frank H. Walkey (2005), 'Optimistic Bias in Relation to Preparedness for Earthquakes', *Australasian Journal of Disaster and Trauma Studies* 1, pp. 1–10.

Steinhart, Eric (2004), 'Pantheism and Current Ontology', *Religious Studies* 40, pp. 63–80.

Steinhart, Eric (2023), *Atheistic Platonism: A Manifesto*. Hampshire: Palgrave Macmillan.

Stenmark, Mikael (2018), 'Panentheism and its Neighbors', *International Journal for Philosophy of Religion* 85, pp. 23–41.

Sterba, James P. (2019), *Is a Good God Logically Possible?* Basingstoke, Hampshire: Palgrave Macmillan.

Stewart, Melville Y. (1993), *The Greater-Good Defence: An Essay on the Rationality of Faith*. Basingstoke, Hampshire: Palgrave Macmillan.

Strickland, Lloyd (2010), 'False Optimism? Leibniz, Evil, and the Best of All Possible Worlds', *Forum Philosophicum* 15, pp. 17–35.

Strickland, Lloyd (2019), 'Staying Optimistic: The Trials and Tribulations of Leibniziean Optimism', *Journal of Modern Philosophy* 1, pp. 1–21.

Strickland, Lloyd (2021), 'Do We Need a Plant Theodicy?', *Scientia et Fides* 9, pp. 221–246.

Suls, Jerry, Jason P. Rose, Paul D. Windsschitl, and Andrew R. Smith (2013), 'Optimism Following a Tornado Disaster', *Personality and Social Psychology Bulletin* 39, pp. 691–702.

Swinburne, Richard (1973), *An Introduction to Confirmation Theory*. London: Methuen & Co.

Swinburne, Richard (1981), *Faith and Reason*. Oxford: Clarendon Press.

Takeuchi, Seiichi (2007), *'Hakanasa' To Nihonjin: 'Mujō' No Nihon Seishinshi* (「はかなさ」と日本人「無常」の日本精神史; *'Impermanence' and the Japanese: Japanese Spiritual History of 'Mujō'*). Tokyo: Heibonsha.

Thomas, Emily (2016), 'Samuel Alexander's Space-Time God: A Naturalist Rival to Current Emergentist Theologies', in Buckareff, Andrei, and Yujin Nagasawa, *Alternative Concepts of God: Essays on the Metaphysics of the Divine*. Oxford: Oxford University Press, pp. 255–273.

Thompson, Janna (2000), 'The Apology Paradox', *Philosophical Quarterly* 50, pp. 470–475.

Tooley, Michael (2019a), *The Problem of Evil*. Cambridge: Cambridge University Press.

Tooley, Michael (2019b), 'The Problem of Evil', *The Stanford Encyclopedia of Philosophy* (Spring 2019 Edition), edited by Edward N. Zalta, https://plato.stanford.edu/archives/spr2019/entries/evil/.

Trakakis, Nick (1997), 'The Absolute Theory of Omnipotence', *Sophia* 36, pp. 55–78.

Trumbo, Craig, Michelle Lueck, Holly Marlatt, and Lori Peek (2011), 'The Effect of Proximity to Hurricanes Katrina and Rita on Subsequent Hurricane Outlook and Optimistic Bias', *Risk Analysis* 31, pp. 1907–1918.

248 REFERENCES

Trumbo, Craig, Michelle A. Meyer, Holly Marlatt, Lori Peek, and Bridget Morrissey (2014), 'An Assessment of Change in Risk Perception and Optimistic Bias for Hurricanes Among Gulf Coast Residents', *Risk Analysis* 34, pp. 1013–1024.

Trumbo, Craig W., Lori Peek, Michelle A. Meyer, Holly L. Marlett, Eve Grutfest, Brian D. McNoldy, and Wayne H. Schubert (2016), 'A Cognitive-Affective Scale for Hurricane Risk Perception', *Risk Analysis* 36, pp. 2233–2246.

Untied, Amy Saling, and Cynthia L. Dulaney (2015), 'College Students' Perceived Risk of Sexual Victimization and the Role of Optimistic Bias', *Journal of Interpersonal Violence* 30, pp. 1417–1431.

van Inwagen, Peter (2002), 'What is the Problem of the Hiddenness of God?', in Howard-Snyder, D., and Moser, P. K. (eds.), *Divine Hiddenness: New Essays*. Cambridge: Cambridge University Press, pp. 24–32.

Vitorino, Luciano Magalhães, Mariana Fernandes Cazerta, Natália Roriz Corrêa, Emanuelle Dos Passos Foresto, Marcia Ap F de Oliveira, and Giancarlo Lucchetti (2022), 'The Influence of Religiosity and Spirituality on the Happiness, Optimism, and Pessimism of Brazilian Medical Students', *Health Education and Behavior* 49, pp. 884–893.

Voltaire (1759/1947), *Candide*, translated by John Butt. Harmondsworth, Middlesex: Penguin Books.

Weidner, Veronika (2021), *Divine Hiddenness*. Cambridge: Cambridge University Press.

Weinstein, Neil D. (1980), 'Unrealistic Optimism about Future Life Events', *Journal of Personality and Social Psychology* 39, pp. 806–820.

Weinstein, Neil D. (1983), 'Reducing Unrealistic Optimism About Illness Susceptibility', *Health Psychology* 2, pp. 11–20.

Weinstein, Neil D., Judith E. Lyon, Alexander J. Rothman, and Cara L. Cuite (2000), 'Changes in Perceived Vulnerability Following Natural Disaster', *Journal of Social and Clinical Psychology* 19, pp. 372–395.

White, Melanie J., Lauren C. Cunningham, and Kirsteen Titchener (2011), 'Young Drivers' Optimism Bias for Accident Risk and Driving Skill: Accountability and Insight Experience Manipulations', *Accident Analysis and Prevention* 43, pp. 1309–1315.

Whitney, Barry L. (1993), *Theodicy: An Annotated Bibliography on the Problem of Evil, 1960–1990*. New York: Garland Publishing.

Williams, Tracy, and Valerie A. Clarke (1997), 'Optimistic Bias in Beliefs about Smoking', *Australian Journal of Psychology* 49, pp. 106–112.

Wykstra, Stephen (1984), 'The Humean Obstacle to Evidential Arguments from Suffering: On Avoiding the Evils of "Appearance"', *International Journal for Philosophy of Religion* 16, pp. 73–93.

Index

For the benefit of digital users, indexed terms that span two pages (e.g., 52–53) may, on occasion, appear on only one of those pages.

acosmism 59
Adams, Marilyn McCord 28, 88, 171–2, 199
Adams, Robert Merrihew 104–5
all-inclusive unity 55–6, 62–73, 75–8, 82–4
Almeida, Michael 82, 100–1
ananthropocentric purposivism 110–11, 146n.9
Anselmian being 38
anti-theism 182–3
apology paradox 154, 164–8, 184
Aristotelians 145–6
Armstrong, David 1
Aronson, Roland 161
atheism 40, 52, 55–6, 58–62, 68–70, 72, 75, 77–8, 89–91, 128–9, 145–6, 153, 170, 173, 175–8, 182–3, 185–6, 188–91, 211
ātman 227–8
Augustine 197–8
axiarchism 40, 45–6, 58–62, 88–99, 101–13
axiarchist 2, 91–8, 100–11, 113, 117, 133, 145–6, 153, 195, 231

Balbus 71–2, 85–6
Bayes's Theorem 16, 45
Bayle, Pierre 120, 147
Benatar, David 144
Bergmann, Michael 189
Berkeley, George 1–3, 52
birth affirmation 162, 188–9
Bishop, John 37n.3
Buddhism 27–8, 204–6, 208–9, 222, 224–8
Buddhist 198–200, 202, 204–6, 213–14, 217–19, 222–30
Burger, Jerry M. 150–1, 202

Chōmei, Kamo no 196–203, 206–10, 212–14, 218–19, 222–3, 225
Christina, Greta 161–2
Cicero 71–2, 85
Clayton, Philip 60–1

cognitive dissonance 163–4, 183
confirmation theory 45, 163–4
Craig, William Lane 1, 188–9
creatively effective ethical requirement 58, 91–2, 95–8, 101–9, 111, 117, 141, 145–6

Darwin, Charles 118–20, 164
Davies, Brian 37–8
Dawkins, Richard 68–70, 119–20, 161–2
divine simplicity 39
divinity thesis 62, 64, 71, 75
Draper, Paul 16–17, 57–8, 121

Epicureans 145–6
equanimity 213
evil
    actual 31–3, 93, 126
    appalling 92–3, 95–6, 98–102, 106–7
    axiological 20–1, 123, 134–5
    collective moral 19, 24–5, 33, 124, 127
    deontological 20–1, 25, 123, 134–5
    extensity of 19, 29–34, 123, 125–7
    gratuitous 19, 22, 26–7, 121, 123–5, 127
    horrendous 28–9, 88, 125, 127, 171–2, 199–200
    individual moral 19, 24–5, 33, 124, 127
    intensity of 19, 28–9, 34, 123, 125–7
    moral 19, 22–6, 62, 81, 123–4, 149–50, 152–3, 197–200
    natural 19, 22–6, 44, 81, 123–4, 127, 149, 152–3, 197–200, 204–5
    non-actual 31–3, 93, 126
    non-gratuitous 19, 26–7, 33, 123–5, 127
    specific 19, 122–4
    unspecific 19, 21–2, 122–4
evolutionary process 57–8, 69, 121, 125–6, 161–3, 180
existential gratitude thesis 160–3, 166–7, 183–4, 190–1

250 INDEX

fine-tuning problem 45–6, 83
free will defence 12–15, 23n.5, 48, 197–8

Geach, Peter 36–7
God
    omnipotent and wholly good 1–2, 9–14,
        20–2, 30–1, 33–5, 41–3, 45–51, 92–3,
        95, 118, 121–3, 129–30, 133–5, 141,
        145–6, 156, 158, 171–2, 188, 190–1,
        200, 205
    panentheistic 8–9, 57n.3, 79n.14
    pantheistic 8–9, 63, 65, 78–80, 85–6,
        88–90
    greater good 22, 26–7, 124–5, 136–7,
        198–9
Guleserian, Theodore 31n.10, 92–3, 93n.2

Hawking, Steven 44–5
hedonism 146, 211–12, 214–17, 221, 223–6,
        229–30
Heian period 206–7, 218–20
Heraclitus 201
hermitism 211–14, 216–19, 221–6,
        229–30
Hick, John 49
Hill, Scott 37
Hindu 227–30
Hōjōki 196–7, 200, 209–10, 223

idealism 1–2, 52
indifferentism 211–12, 218, 221, 224–6,
        229–30
ineffable transcendentalism 226–7, 229–30

Jonbäck, Francis 170, 175, 189–90
Judeo-Christian 8, 23–4, 212

Kahane, Guy 170, 175–85
Kamakura period 195–7, 200, 201n.5, 202–3,
        218–19, 226
Kenkō, Yoshida 197–201, 201n.5, 202–3,
        206–9, 213–14, 218–19, 223
Kivy, Peter 129–30
Kraay, Klaas J. 88–9, 106–8

Leibniz, Gottfried Wilhelm 97–8, 120, 129,
        134–7, 147–8
Leibnizian hierarchy 98, 107–8
Leslie, John 93–4, 106

Levine, Michael 36, 55–6, 62–7, 71, 73, 77–8,
        85–6, 89–90
Lewis, David 76–7, 82, 100
libertarianism 48

MacIntyre, Alasdair 62
Mackie, J. L. 8–14, 16, 18–19, 27, 34, 36–8,
        40, 48, 51, 63–4, 95, 124–5, 187n.6
Malthus, Thomas 119
Mander, William 69–70
merotheism 57–9
modal actualism 96–7, 101–2, 106, 108–9
modal collapse
    anti-total 99, 101–2, 107–9
    partial 102, 109
    total 96–102, 106–7, 109
modal intuition 93, 101, 103
modal realism 76–7, 81–2, 86–7, 99–101, 107–9
    positive 107–9
mokṣa 228–9
monism 228–9
Moreland, J. P. 1
Morioka, Masahiro 162
Morris, Thomas V. 102, 160–1
Morriston, Wes 37
Mulgan, Tim 93–4, 93n.5, 110–11, 146n.9
Mullins, R. T. 61
Murphy, Mark 38

Nara period 214
Narihira, Ariwara no 207–8
natural selection 118–21, 124–7, 155–8, 165,
        167–9, 171, 179–80, 184, 186–7, 190, 196
    and evolution 118, 121, 124–7, 131, 133,
        155–9, 168–9, 208–10
naturalism 44–5, 174, 188–9, 221–2, 226,
        229–31
naturalist atheists 2–3
naturalists 59–62, 211, 221–2, 226, 229–30,
        229n.8
Nietzsche, Friedrich 145–6
nirvana 213, 223–4, 226–9
non-religious people 148–9, 153
non-theists 2–3, 8

optimal multiverse 106–9
optimism
    anti-Leibnizian 99, 101–2, 107–9
    bias 149–53, 156–8, 202

INDEX   251

Leibnizian 96–103, 106, 109–10, 135–6, 138–41, 143, 145–7
    unrealistic 151–2
Otto, Rudolf 65, 67, 85
Owen, H. P. 62

Paley, William 158
Palmer, Michele L. 150–1, 202
panentheism 40, 55–8, 57n.3, 59–62, 89–90
panentheists 8, 60–2
pantheism 36, 40, 45–6, 55–7, 59–66, 68–71, 73–5, 77–9, 79n.14, 84–6, 89–92, 117
    multiverse 55–6, 75–6, 78–87, 90–1
    naturalistic 57, 62, 68
pantheists 2, 8, 55–6, 62–75, 77–8, 81–6, 89–91, 117, 133, 142n.5, 145–6, 153, 195, 231
    multiverse 55–6, 75–89, 91
Parfit, Derek 93–4
Pascal, Blaise 70
permanent transcendentalism 227–30
philosophy of religion 2–3, 43, 46, 62, 83, 134, 196
physicalism 8–9, 42n.6, 52
physicalists 8–9, 52
Plantinga, Alvin 12–13, 23n.5, 50, 128, 197–8
Plato 93–4, 103–4
Platonism 105–7, 156–8, 229n.8
Platonists 145–6, 153, 142n.5
problem of axiological expectation
    mismatch 34–6, 41–52, 55–6, 64–6, 68, 75, 81–3, 89, 95–6, 133, 139, 148, 155–9, 163–4, 169, 185–6, 195, 205–6, 211–12, 221–5
problem of divine hiddenness 42–4, 46, 83, 205
problem of evil
    abductive version of evidential evil 15–18, 34, 128
    actual evil 31–4, 92–6, 102, 109–11, 113
    axiological evil 20–1, 33
    collective moral evil 24, 124
    deductive 13–14, 16, 18
    deductive version of evidential evil 15–18, 34
    deontological evil 20–1, 134–5
    divinity 55–6, 64–70, 73–5, 77–8, 81–90
    evidential 14–18, 34, 128
    gratuitous evil 26–7, 33
    horrendous evil 28–9, 34, 88

individual moral evil 24, 124
inductive version of evidential evil 15–18, 34, 128
inequality of evil 30–1, 33–4
logical 10–16, 18–19, 34, 38, 48, 128, 187n.6
moral evil 22–6, 124
natural evil 22–6, 33, 124
non-actual evil 31–3, 31n.10, 32n.12, 34, 46, 92–3, 93n.4, 94–6, 98–9, 101–2, 106–7, 109–11, 113, 126
non-gratuitous evil 26–7, 33
specific evil 21–2, 24, 29, 123–4
systemic evil 117–18, 121–9, 131–3, 154–60, 163–79, 181–91, 195–6, 208–11, 218
unspecific evil 21–2, 24, 29, 123–4
problem of impermanence 195–6, 197n.3, 200–2, 204–14, 216–18, 220–30
problem of no best world 43–4, 46, 83, 103–4, 205
Pure Land Buddhism 226

Quasi-logical rules 13–14, 40

Rescher, Nicholas 93–4, 97–8, 138
response
    amended divine attribute 47–8
    experiential 55–6, 68–72, 80–1
    non-experiential 55–6, 70–3, 75, 77–8, 80–1
Rolston III, Holmes 119–20
Rowe, William L. 12–13, 15–16, 26–7, 121, 128–9

Saigyō 218–19, 221, 225
samsara 226–7
sceptical theism 49–51, 74, 171–2, 189–91
Schopenhauer, Arthur 130–1, 142–4, 156–7
Sengoku period 217
Sentient animal 25–6, 118–19, 121–2, 124, 127, 131, 133, 155, 163, 165, 168–9, 178–81, 183, 186–7, 190, 208
shogyō mujō 204
Smith, Quentin 121
Stoljar, Daniel 1
suffering
    of change 27–8, 204–7, 209–11, 222–4
    of existence 204–6, 209–11, 222–4
    of suffering 27–8, 204–5, 209–11, 222–3
    three types of 204, 205n.6

252 INDEX

supernaturalism 8, 59–62, 89–90, 174, 195, 211–12, 221–2, 229–30, 229n.8, 231
supernaturalist 61–2, 171–2, 189, 211, 221–2, 226–7, 229–30
  ontology 173–4, 228–9, 231
  resource 2, 61–2, 170, 174, 178–9, 181, 191, 231
Swinburne, Richard 160–1

Tabito, Ōtomo no 214–16, 224
Takeuchi, Seiichi 204, 215, 220, 227–8
theists
  supernaturalist 2–3
  traditional 1–3, 7–12, 20–2, 28, 31–42, 46–8, 51–2, 55–6, 60, 63–7, 71, 73–5, 80–1, 83–4, 88–96, 98, 101–5, 108–10, 112–13, 117–18, 121–9, 131–6, 138–9, 145, 153–7, 160–1, 169–75, 177–9, 181–3, 186–91, 195, 200, 205, 211, 229, 231

theodicy
  Felix Culpa 50–1
  free will 48–9
  greater Good 51
  soul-making 49, 51, 74, 171–2
theory of evolution 118–20
Thompson, Janna 154, 164–7, 184
Three Marks of Existence 200, 208–9
Tomonori, Ki no 206–8, 220–1, 227–8
Tooley, Michael 15, 20–1
Trakakis, Nick 100
transcendentalism 211–12, 220–30

unity thesis 62, 71, 75

Voltaire 118, 129–31, 134
  Candide 129–30, 134, 136
  Pangloss 129–30, 134

Whitney, Barry L. 1